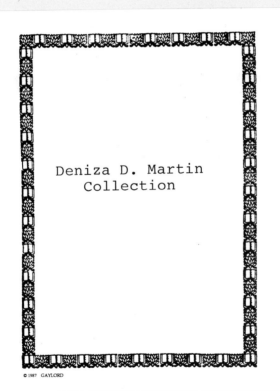

Deniza D. Martin
Collection

© 1987 GAYLORD

CAMBRIDGE STUDIES
IN ENGLISH LEGAL HISTORY

Edited by
H. A. HOLLOND
Fellow of Trinity College, Cambridge
and sometime Rouse Ball Professor of English Law

THE
MEDIEVAL CORONER

BY

R. F. HUNNISETT

An Assistant Keeper of the Public Records,
Lecturer of New College, Oxford

CAMBRIDGE
AT THE UNIVERSITY PRESS
1961

#5736898

PUBLISHED BY
THE SYNDICS OF THE CAMBRIDGE UNIVERSITY PRESS

Bentley House, 200 Euston Road, London, N.W.1
American Branch: 32 East 57th Street, New York 22, N.Y.
West African Office: P.O. Box 33, Ibadan, Nigeria

©

CAMBRIDGE UNIVERSITY PRESS
1961

Printed by The Broadwater Press Limited
Welwyn Garden City, Hertfordshire

CONTENTS

GENERAL EDITOR'S PREFACE

MR HUNNISETT's book strengthens the association of this series
with his college, New College, which began with Mr Ogg's *Ad
Fletam Dissertatio* in 1925, and was carried on by Mr Bell's *The
Court of Wards and Liveries* in 1953. Indeed it was the latter, so the
present author tells us, who first inspired his interest in medieval
problems. Mr Hunnisett has already established himself as the
leading living authority on the medieval coroner by his paper on
'The Origins of the Office of Coroner' in the *Transactions of the
Royal Historical Society* (5th ser. VIII, 85–104), and other articles.[1]

Not many offices surviving at the present day in any country have
travelled as long or as far as those of the sheriff and the coroner. For
the latter had its beginning nearly eight hundred years ago, and the
former in the Anglo-Saxon age. And both flourish as transplanta-
tions across the Atlantic. These facts enhance their interest for the
non-specialist.

A reader trying to visualise medieval life in the light of the
coroner's activities will be puzzled by the extent to which the king
was able to get the tasks of government performed by men who, in
theory at any rate, were unpaid. The duties of the unpaid coroner
of the thirteenth century were onerous, though, as it now appears,
somewhat fewer than contemporary law books such as those of
Bracton and Britton suggest. For instance, though there are some
cases, early in the century, of coroners dealing with wreck and
treasure trove, they did not in general concern themselves with such
matters. But they had to hold inquests on all dead bodies found
within a wide area, and unexplained dead bodies were common.
The enforcement of the rule that a thing which caused the death of
a person, either by human contrivance or by accident, had to be
surrendered to the crown as a deodand often gave the coroner much

---

[1] Mr Hunnisett's other articles are: 'Pleas of the Crown and the Coroner',
Bulletin of the Institute of Historical Research, vol. XXXII; 'An Early Coroner's
Roll', *B.I.H.R.* vol. XXX; 'The Medieval Coroners' Rolls', *The American Journal
of Legal History*, vol. III; 'Sussex Coroners in the Middle Ages', *Sussex Archaeo-
logical Collections*, vols. XCV, XCVI and XCVIII. He is also editing for the Bedfordshire Historical Record Society all the surviving Bedfordshire coroners' rolls in
a volume which will appear in the current year.

trouble. And, besides, he had to receive abjurations of the realm
made by felons in sanctuary, to hear confessions of felons and
appeals (in the medieval sense) of 'approvers', to attend and sometimes organise exactions and outlawries promulgated in the county
court. The men performing all those duties must have been constantly on horseback. And yet they had to be men of substance,
knights for preference, who must have found the work a great inter-
ference with their normal lives, and a source of expense unless they
recouped themselves unlawfully, for we do not know of claims for
out-of-pocket expenses.

Against these drawbacks must be set the sense of power and self-
importance which the office doubtless conferred. The less scru-
pulous had opportunities for making money. For, although no fees
were sanctioned until the reign of Henry VII, a 'regular, if moderate' extortion was practised by many. The author points out that
this abuse may well have contributed to efficiency. 'The virtual
certainty of being able to extort with impunity meant that coroners
continued to hold a large number of inquests when they were no
longer regularly supervised, and that they wasted little time going
to hold them.'

Whether the office was more often shunned because of its irk-
someness than it was sought because of its advantages it is impossible to determine. Many writs survive for the replacement of coroners, and many different reasons are alleged for such replacements,
the most usual of them being insufficient qualification. It is rarely
possible to establish the reasons behind such incidents. Were the
coroners concerned 'continually elected against their will, with the
result that their lives were a constant struggle to free themselves
from office, or did they like the office and make efforts to get themselves re-elected each time their opponents removed them? . . . It is
usually impossible to tell whether the coroner was escaping from an
unwanted office or being forced from one he liked.'

It seems to have been intended originally that every coroner
should attend every inquest and abjuration within his county, but it
soon became obvious that this was impossible, and thus there grew
up in all counties an unofficial division into coroners' districts. At
the end of Edward I's reign the thirty-nine English counties had
approximately one hundred and fifteen coroners between them;
most counties retained throughout the Middle Ages the number
which they then had. In addition to the county coroners there were

borough coroners, approximately one hundred in fifty-seven towns in the year 1300, and franchisal coroners, the number of which can less easily be estimated, but exceeded fifty at that date. Theoretically it was necessary that the privilege of having its own coroner should be granted by the king to a borough or to a franchise, but in practice if there had been long, continuous and proper exercise of the privilege confirmation of it could easily be obtained. Certain hundreds which were parts of the ancient demesne of the crown had coroners of their own. Another privileged area was the verge—the area which extended twelve miles round the king's court wherever it might be situated during his progresses through the country. Jurisdiction in this area was exercised by the coroner of the king's household, also called coroner of the Marshalsea or coroner of the verge. This official not only had the duties of a normal coroner within the verge but also acted as king's attorney in cases heard in the Marshalsea court.

It will appear from these few words what a variety of topics is illuminated by Mr Hunnisett's examination of the original sources. His readers will discover with what human interest he has clothed the dry bones of writs, rolls and charters. Those who follow him through his researches will be glad that he has expressed his intention to turn now to the later history of the coroner's office.

H. A. H.

TRINITY COLLEGE, CAMBRIDGE
April 1961

PREFACE

It is now over sixty years since Charles Gross produced his
scholarly edition of *Select Cases from the Coroners' Rolls, 1265–1413*
(Selden Soc. vol. 9). In the present work I have been forced to criti-
cise some of his ideas. It is therefore the more essential that I should
recognise here my great indebtedness to this invaluable pioneering
work, a model of record scholarship, which paved the way for all
subsequent historians of the coroner. When one considers how important the medieval coroner was in local justice and administration,
that the office has had a continuous existence of nearly eight hundred years and that it has been successfully exported to many lands
overseas, including the United States, it is surprising that no full-
scale study has previously been attempted.

My task has been considerably eased by the almost embarrassing
generosity of many friends. My interest in the Middle Ages was first
aroused and has ever since been encouraged by Mr H. E. Bell. To
Mr L. F. Salzman I am indebted for the suggestion that I should
work upon the coroner and for his continued interest, particularly
in sections relating to our common county of Sussex. Professor V.
H. Galbraith supervised my researches in their early stages; I owe
much to his kindly help and never-failing enthusiasm both at that
time and since. I am grateful to Dr H. M. Cam for her scholarly
criticisms and for generously assisting me from her vast knowledge
of local administration. It was a piece of great good fortune that I
met Dr J. D. J. Havard before this book went to press. His suggestions, particularly on medico-legal points, have been invaluable and
I also profited much from his courtesy in allowing me to read the
typescript of his book, *The Detection of Secret Homicide* (Cambridge
Studies in Criminology, xi, 1960).

My colleagues at the Public Record Office have always been most
co-operative, particularly Mr H. C. Johnson with his patient and
kindly interest, Mr C. A. F. Meekings with his wide knowledge of
medieval law and archival history, and Dr R. L. Storey, who voluntarily undertook the burden of reading the proofs. As general editor
of the series, Professor H. A. Hollond has greatly assisted the
publication of this book and has also made suggestions which have
much improved it, and I am grateful to the Syndics of the

Cambridge University Press for generously voting a grant in aid of publication. To all those on whom I have inflicted the coroner over the last few years I can but apologize. I am especially appreciative of the manner in which my wife and her mother have accepted him as a constant companion and of their help and encouragement at all times. May they bear with me when I turn, as I hope to soon, to the later history of the office.

R. F. H.

BROMLEY, KENT
November 1961

LIST OF ABBREVIATIONS

C.47	Chancery, Miscellanea
C.60	Chancery, Fine Rolls
C.144	Chancery, Criminal Inquisitions
C.145	Chancery, Miscellaneous Inquisitions
C.202	Chancery, Files
Chester 17	Palatinate of Chester, Eyre Rolls
Chester 18	Palatinate of Chester, Coroners' Inquisitions
E.13	Exchequer, Exchequer of Pleas, Plea Rolls
E.37	Exchequer, Treasury of the Receipt, Marshalsea Court Rolls
E.101	Exchequer, King's Remembrancer, Accounts Various
E.137	Exchequer, King's Remembrancer, Estreats
E.153	Exchequer, King's Remembrancer, Escheators' Files
E.159	Exchequer, King's Remembrancer, Memoranda Rolls
E.163	Exchequer, King's Remembrancer, Miscellanea
E.368	Exchequer, Lord Treasurer's Remembrancer, Memoranda Rolls
J.I.1	Justices Itinerant, Assize Rolls
J.I.2	Justices Itinerant, Coroners' Rolls
J.I.3	Justices Itinerant, Gaol Delivery Rolls
K.B.9	King's Bench, Ancient Indictments
K.B.26	King's Bench, Curia Regis Rolls
K.B.27	King's Bench, Coram Rege Rolls
K.B.29	King's Bench, Controlment Rolls
S.C.1	Special Collections, Ancient Correspondence

The records listed above are all preserved in the Public Record Office.

CHAPTER I

THE EARLY YEARS

THE office of coroner was established in September 1194, when the justices in eyre were required to see that three knights and one clerk were elected in every county as 'keepers of the pleas of the crown'.[1] These were the first county coroners. The first borough coroners were authorised by royal charters in 1200[2] and franchisal coroners began to appear a little later.[3] Throughout the Middle Ages the coroner could be ordered to perform almost any duty of an administrative or inquisitorial nature within his bailiwick, either alone or with the sheriff, but there were other duties which belonged more specifically to his office and which he performed without being ordered. These consisted of holding inquests upon dead bodies, receiving abjurations of the realm made by felons in sanctuary, hearing appeals, confessions of felons and appeals of approvers, and attending and sometimes organising exactions and outlawries promulgated in the county court. These were the 'crown pleas' which the coroner had to 'keep', and he kept them in four ways: by taking the actions just mentioned, attaching or arresting witnesses, suspects and others, appraising and safeguarding any lands and goods which might later be forfeited, and by recording all the details.

These duties were not new in 1194.[4] They, or many of them, had previously been performed by other local officials, notably by the county justiciar and by the serjeant or bailiff of the hundred. Under Henry I and Stephen every county had its justiciar, who had some of the duties which later belonged to the coroner, especially those concerning forfeitures to the crown. The county justiciar, however, was

---

[1] *Praeterea in quolibet comitatu eligantur tres milites et unus clericus custodes placitorum coronae: Select Charters*, ed. W. Stubbs, 9th ed. (Oxford, 1913), p. 254. The formal title of *custos* (or occasionally *conservator*) *placitorum corone* continued to be used throughout the Middle Ages, but the more convenient shorter forms *coronarius*, which was confined to a short period around 1200, and *coronator* rapidly gained greater currency. The English form was 'coroner' or 'crowner'.

[2] *Rotuli Chartarum*, ed. T. D. Hardy (Rec. Comm. 1837), pp. 46, 56, 57, 65.

[3] See below, p. 138.

[4] For further details on the points summarised in the next two paragraphs see my paper on 'The Origins of the Office of Coroner', *Trans. R. Hist. Soc.* 5th ser. VIII, 85–104.

far more important than the coroner, since he not only 'kept' crown pleas but he could also determine them. He naturally tended to grow over-powerful and Henry II therefore discontinued the office early in his reign. Thereafter the hundred and wapentake serjeants held inquests upon dead bodies and heard appeals in their early stages and confessions, and almost certainly received abjurations of the realm and heard appeals of approvers as well—duties which they may well have performed under the county justiciars earlier. But whereas the coroner was less eminent than the county justiciar, he was far more important than the hundred serjeant had ever been. The county coroner's sphere of activity was the whole county, while the serjeant was confined to his hundred. The coroner had to be a knight or a considerable landowner, while most serjeants were lesser men. The serjeant was appointed by and responsible to the sheriff, of whom the coroner, an elected official, was much more independent. Finally, the hundred serjeant not only had many petty duties under the sheriff, which he retained throughout the Middle Ages, but he had never exercised some of the more important of the coroner's functions. Because he was merely a shrieval official, he had no duties in connection with appeals and exactions and outlawries in the county court, at which his master presided, and his written records could not compare in authority with the coroner's rolls.

The introduction of coroners in 1194 therefore brought about a considerable change in the machinery of local administration. There were several reasons why such a change should have been made at that time. Because of his perennial continental wars and the need to pay his ransom, Richard I was desperate for money. He could not afford to lose any of the financial issues of crown pleas. This meant that a full-time local official was needed to minister to the recently organised general eyre: it was essential to ensure that all crown pleas were presented to the justices, however long before the eyre they had arisen and although they might result in financial loss to the presenting jurors. Neither the sheriff nor his subordinates could adequately accomplish this task. The sheriff was already overburdened and his tendency to become over-powerful and corrupt, always strong, had undoubtedly been fostered by John's recent rising, while his subordinates could naturally not act as an adequate check upon him. In the closely integrated interests of good order, justice and royal revenue a new local official was urgently needed. Administrative efficiency would be served by relieving the sheriff of some of

his burdens; and judicial efficiency and royal revenue would benefit
from having an official who could concentrate mainly upon pre-
serving full details of crown pleas between eyres and who, being
elected and of some social eminence locally, could be expected to reduce if not prevent peculation by the sheriff, at least in crown pleas.
The office of coroner was one of Hubert Walter's remedies for the
difficult situation of 1194.

The only instruction issued in 1194 seems to have been that the
coroners should keep the pleas of the crown. Similarly, the charters
by which John granted certain boroughs the right to have their own
coroners merely stated that they were to keep pleas and other matters pertaining to the crown and to see that the reeves dealt justly
with both rich and poor. Not until Bracton wrote, when the office of
coroner was over fifty years old, was any attempt made to give a comprehensive account of its obligations. The earlier absence of any
authoritative definition of the term 'pleas of the crown', coupled
with the rapid development of crown pleas during the thirteenth
century, had several important results.

Firstly, the transfer from hundred serjeant to coroner of the custody of those pleas which the serjeant had previously kept was so
leisurely that it was not complete until 1225 at the earliest. The eyre
rolls of the previous thirty years prove that serjeants' inquests on
dead bodies were just as valid as coroners' inquests, if less frequent
towards the end;[1] the only difference was that the serjeant could not
attach suspects and others who lived outside his hundred, but had to
secure their attachment by the sheriff and coroners.[2] In this period
the serjeant occasionally received abjurations and also heard confessions, which the felons were no more able to repudiate than if
they had been made before the coroner.[3] After 1225, however, although, as will be seen later, the hundred serjeant had duties at
coroners' inquests and abjurations of the realm, at both of which he
had to attend upon the coroner, it was a punishable offence for him
to assume the coroner's functions.[4] Only then was the demand of the

---

[1] *Trans. R. Hist. Soc.* 5th ser. VIII, 93. If, therefore, the *Annales Londonienses*
is right and in 1208, as one of the counter-measures taken against the Interdict,
John forbade coroners to hold inquests upon the bodies of slain clerks (*Chronicles
of the reigns of Edward I and Edward II*, ed. W. Stubbs (Rolls Series, 1882–3), I,
8), this need not have caused undue discomfort even if it had been strictly
obeyed.

[2] E.g. *The Earliest Lincolnshire Assize Rolls, 1202–1209*, ed. D. M. Stenton
(Linc. Rec. Soc. XXII), no. 701.

[3] *Trans. R. Hist. Soc.* 5th ser. VIII, 94–5.   [4] *Ibid.* p. 93, n. 2.

barons of 1215, 'that no sheriff concern himself with pleas of the crown without the coroners',[1] fully realised; there would have been no point in excluding the sheriff if his minions had been, in many cases, the coroners' peers.

A much more important result of the failure to define the coroner's duties in or shortly after 1194 was that an immense gap soon appeared between the theoretical implications of his formal title, 'keeper of the pleas of the crown', and the few pleas with which he came to be concerned by virtue of his office.[2] Not only was the coroner never concerned *ex officio* with crown pleas other than felonies and unnatural deaths, but homicide and suicide were the only felonies with which he was invariably concerned. Other felonies only entered his orbit when they resulted in homicides, abjurations, appeals, confessions or exactions, or if he were specially commissioned to inquire about them. This development cannot have been intended in 1194, when, as his formal title shows, he was expected to keep all pleas of the crown. But he was also closely linked with the general eyre, and in the probable absence of any authoritative list of crown pleas, his guide must have been the presentments made to the eyre articles. In the early years of the thirteenth century, felonies provided the vast majority of such presentments and practically every felony resulted in an appeal. The coroner therefore concentrated on appeals and upon those crown pleas previously kept by hundred serjeants, and ultimately became associated with these alone. When, during the thirteenth century, the number of appeals greatly declined and the number and variety of crown pleas equally increased, his duties were not extended. Whereas the office of coroner was established in order that the hundred jurors' presentments might be checked and no crown plea concealed from the justices in eyre, by Edward I's reign all the coroners' cases were presented in answer to one article (the second) of the eyre.

The limits of his jurisdiction, which were established so early in the coroner's life, were to be preserved intact throughout the Middle Ages despite the thirteenth-century law-books and statutes. They assigned to him duties, usually including the holding of an inquest, in connection with other felonies, notably wounding, rape, house-

---

[1] Articles of the Barons, c. 14 (*Select Charters*, p. 287).
[2] For further details on the points summarised in the next six paragraphs see my 'Pleas of the Crown and the Coroner', *Bull. Inst. Hist. Research*, XXXII, 117–37.

breaking and breaking prison. These statements are inaccurate and many of them stem from Bracton, who implied that the coroner had to hold inquests into wounding and house-breaking. Bracton, however, based his treatise *De Legibus et Consuetudinibus Angliae* on cases collected from early thirteenth-century plea rolls, in which most cases of wounding and house-breaking were prosecuted by appeals and were therefore attested in court by coroners. Bracton's work had great authority, and the section concerning the coroner, because it was the first description of the office, was extracted and, under the title *Officium Coronatoris*, came to be regarded as a statute. *Britton* specifically stated that coroners should hold inquests into wounding, rape and prison-breach. There can be little doubt that it confused the view of wounds and rape, which the coroner was supposed to make in the early stages of an appeal, with an inquest; and that it was misled by the fact that many abjurations of the realm received by coroners were made by felons who had just escaped from prison. To study the medieval coroner solely from the law-books and statutes is thus to gain a completely erroneous picture. Far from dealing with nearly all felonies *ex officio*, he was necessarily concerned only with homicide and suicide.

This limitation of his activities was seriously threatened by the law-books and statutes of the late thirteenth century. Their effect was probably delayed by the fact that they did not agree on exactly what extra duties the coroner was supposed to have and by the coroner's natural disinclination to take on any more. Nevertheless, there are slight signs that the coroner was weakening under Edward II, when a few are known to have exceeded their normal bounds. A gradual transference of all presentments of felonies from the sheriff's tourn to coroners' inquests might well have occurred but for the rise of the keepers of the peace, who soon became justices of the peace and who took indictments of all felonies from the early fourteenth century. So it was that the coroner's inquest became and remained confined to cases of death, although in a few exceptional areas coroners had dealings with other felonies. In Northumberland and Newcastle-upon-Tyne coroners' inquests took the place of the sheriff's tourn for felonies; in Chester and Flintshire the coroners sometimes took indictments of burglary and theft; and many borough coroners, in obedience to the charge that they should see that the reeves dealt justly with both rich and poor, sat in the local court with the bailiff or mayor whatever the type of case.

An inevitable consequence of the previous misconception was the assumption that the coroner had the duty of appraising the chattels of felons of all kinds. The Statute of Exeter, for example, assumed that he normally appraised by inquest the chattels of all who had fled on suspicion of robbery or of receiving felons, enrolled them and committed them to safe-custody. In fact, with very few exceptions, unless he was specially ordered by a royal writ to make such an appraisal, the coroner only concerned himself with the chattels of homicides and suicides, abjurors of the realm, appellees, confessed felons and outlaws. Moreover, the exceptions derive entirely from the early thirteenth century before the coroner's duties had firmly crystallised, from the early fourteenth century when the coroner weakened slightly at the height of the impact of the law-books and statutes concerning his office, and from boroughs whose coroners often had more general duties than their county counterparts.

It is often said that the medieval coroner could pass judgment on felons who were caught in the act. There is no evidence to support this view, which derives from *Britton* and is probably a misconception of or development from the statement, frequently made in the thirteenth century, that he had to attend local courts whenever they exercised the liberty of *infangenetheof* in the absence of a royal justice. But when he attended such judgments of death, he did not pass the judgment himself; he merely recorded it. And once again, despite the law-books and justices' dicta, the only known instances of coroners attending judgments of death come from the early thirteenth century, when it is probable that they also attended some ordeals until their abolition in 1215, and from boroughs, where they normally sat in the borough court for all pleas with the other local officials. The hundred serjeant attended both ordeals and judgments of death before 1194. After some initial uncertainty, the county coroner failed to take his place.

The hundred serjeant also held preliminary inquiries concerning treasure trove and wreck of the sea before 1194, and the law-books again assumed that the coroner had taken over this duty. Some of them describe the coroner's obligations in considerable detail: he was supposed to hold a full inquiry, attach anybody suspected of making away with any part of the treasure or wreck (which included royal fish) and to appraise the remainder and secure its safe custody for the king. Once again the treatises are misleading. The coroner only dealt with wreck and treasure trove *ex officio* in the early thirteenth century, and later in just a few special areas—both wreck and treasure trove in Northumberland, and wreck alone in Cornwall and Devon. Otherwise there is only one known case of a coroner holding an inquest into wreck unordered, significantly in Edward II's reign, and none of his inquiring about treasure trove. There are several reasons to account for the fact that the coroner was able to ignore with impunity what learned and influential contemporaries thought to be his lawful duties. The regalian right of *wreccum maris* was early granted to or usurped by local lords around much of the coast and the justices were not likely to insist that the coroner should concern himself with wrecks which could bring the king no profit. When wrecks occurred on parts of the coast where the right was retained by the king or was temporarily in his hand, either the sheriff or the hundred bailiff acted, as authorised by the first Statute of Westminster, or a special commission was appointed to deal with it. The right to retain treasure trove was also granted out, although less frequently. When an appreciable find was made, special commissioners were appointed to deal with it. Otherwise the hundred bailiff or sheriff held the preliminary inquiry and the matter was also presented at the tourn. The sheriff and his underlings thus retained their duties in connection with both treasure trove and wreck of the sea during the thirteenth century. The authority of the law-books might thereafter have proved irresistible but for the rise of the escheator, who came to hold inquisitions by virtue of his office into all occurrences of wreck and treasure trove in the later Middle Ages.

Bracton thought that the sheriff and county coroners together attached persons who broke the assizes of bread and ale and measures.[1] They may have done so occasionally, but certainly not as a general rule. In 1197 six special *custodientes* were appointed in each county and town, who have been called 'coroners over one class of offences, the use of false weights and measures'[2] and who were quite distinct from the normal coroners. Three things possibly helped to mislead Bracton. Firstly, the hundred serjeant was often in charge of wine sold contrary to the assize in the early thirteenth century.[3] Secondly, the clerk or keeper of the market, who had charge of measures within the verge, was usually the same man as the coroner of

[1] *De Legibus et Consuetudinibus Angliae*, ed. G. E. Woodbine (New Haven, 1915–42), II, 437.
[2] W. S. McKechnie, *Magna Carta*, 2nd ed. (Glasgow, 1914), p. 316, n. 2.
[3] Linc. Rec. Soc. XXII, xlvi.

the verge.[1] Thirdly, in 1221, when two men became coroners of Worcester during the eyre, they were given the custody of both crown pleas and the assize of wine; if anyone sold wine at a higher price than was allowed, they had to take the wine into the king's hand, sell it and safeguard the money realized for the king.[2]

Enrolment was the indispensable basis of the coroner's custody of crown pleas. Only by keeping a written record could he act as a check upon the hundred jurors' presentments. The negative evidence of the coroners' rolls must therefore be preferred even to the contemporary law-books and statutes. They prove beyond question that the medieval coroner had fewer duties, and was to that extent less important, than has usually been thought. Nevertheless, those which he exercised were considerable and in the thirteenth century made him second in importance to the sheriff alone in the local governmental hierarchy, while he also received innumerable writs requiring him to perform others for which he has never received adequate credit.

[1] *Britton*, i.1.6 (ed. F. M. Nichols (Oxford, 1865), i, 4).

[2] *Rolls of the Justices in Eyre for Lincolnshire, 1218–9, and Worcestershire, 1221*, ed. D. M. Stenton (Selden Soc. vol. 53), no. 1270. The statement that one of the two Chichester city coroners had charge of the assize of bread and ale (*Victoria County History: Sussex*, iii, 93) is completely without foundation. For details see my 'Sussex Coroners in the Middle Ages', *Sx. Arch. Colls.* XCVIII, 46.

CHAPTER II

THE CORONER'S INQUEST

HOLDING inquests upon dead bodies was the duty which exercised
the medieval coroner most frequently, as the surviving coroners'
rolls show. Indeed, in times of plague or famine its burden could become insupportable. During the famine of 1257–8, for example, so
many people died of hunger in the eastern counties that the coroners
were unable to view them all; permission was therefore granted for
the bodies to be viewed and buried by the men of the neighbourhood without the coroner, unless a wound was found or there was
any suspicion of homicide.[1] Normally, however, the coroner had to
view and hold an inquest upon the bodies of all those who died unnaturally, suddenly or in prison, or about whose death there might
or was said to have been any suspicious circumstances.[2]

The coroner could only hold an inquest concerning a death if
there was a body, unless he had a special warrant; and indictments
of homicide could only be made before him upon view of the body.[3]
If a homicide was committed or suspected but no body was found,
the matter had to be presented at the sheriff's tourn or, later, before
the J.P.'s. The term 'body', however, was not interpreted narrowly.
Although the flesh was in the last stages of putrefaction or the bones
alone remained, the coroner could hold his view and inquest. Sometimes bones were found with no flesh upon them and so decayed that
they could not be identified and the cause of death could not be discovered, but inquests were nevertheless held.[4]

When a dead body had been found after a sudden or unnatural

---

[1] *Close Rolls, 1256–1259*, p. 212. For an example see *The Assizes held at Cambridge, 1260*, ed. W. M. Palmer (Linton, 1930), pp. xix, 23. I am indebted to
Dr J. D. J. Havard for the last reference.

[2] The statement in *The Mirror of Justices*, i. 13 (ed. W. J. Whittaker (Selden
Soc. vol. 7), pp. 31–2), that coroners did not need to hold inquests into deaths
occurring in 'tournaments, combats, jousts and medleys', if no felony were suspected, may be true, but it cannot have been ordained by Henry II and this
treatise is often wildly inaccurate in matters concerning the coroner (e.g.
Trans. R. Hist. Soc. 5th ser. VIII, 85).

[3] *The Eyre of Kent 6 & 7 Edward II*, I, ed. F. W. Maitland, L. W. V. Harcourt and W. C. Bolland (Selden Soc. vol. 24), p. 141; *Year Books 9–10 Henry V
(1421–2)*, ed. R. V. Rogers (Privately printed, 1948), p. 20.

[4] J.I.2/120, m. 17; 32, m. 2. See also J.I.2/211, m. 1 (a body so mauled by
pigs, crows and other creatures as to be unidentifiable).

death, the coroner had to be summoned—by the neighbours according to *Fleta*, by the bailiff or the lawful men of the neighbourhood according to Bracton and the *Officium Coronatoris*.[1] Practice varied from county to county, but not radically. Everywhere it was the duty of the 'first finder' to raise the hue and cry. In Essex in the mid-fourteenth century he normally informed the four nearest neighbours, who informed the bailiff of the hundred, who, in turn, informed the coroner.[2] In Bristol, where the coroner can never have been far away, the 'first finder' had to notify him and the bailiff personally.[3] It was the township in which the fatality occurred which most frequently suffered amercement when the coroner was not summoned,[4] but at the 1221 Warwickshire eyre both the township in which a misadventure occurred and one to which the body had been removed were amerced.[5] By the fourteenth century it is occasionally possible to discover who within the townships had this responsibility. In Derbyshire twelve men of the township informed the king's serjeant and the coroner of fatalities,[6] and one Lincolnshire coroner's roll states that the coroner held his inquest on the body of a man who died a natural death because the constable, undoubtedly acting on behalf of the township, asked him to.[7] In most counties the process of summoning the coroner thus began with the raising of the hue and cry by the 'first finder' and ended with the hundred bailiff or some other local official summoning the coroner. When a death was witnessed, the witnesses naturally had the duties of the 'first finder'.[8]

Some bodies were found extremely quickly. A Nottinghamshire man, 'hearing a tumult' in a well, found that a man had fallen in and been drowned.[9] But there is much evidence to show that the duties of the 'first finder' and his consequent chances of punishment for defaults tended to postpone the official 'finding' and that the 'first finder' in law, the man who ultimately raised the hue and cry, might often have been more correctly termed the 'last finder', many having previously noticed the body in silence and hurried by. In 1383, for

---

[1] *Fleta*, i. 25 (ed. H. G. Richardson and G. O. Sayles, II (Selden Soc. vol. 72), 64); Bracton, II, 342; *Statutes of the Realm*, I, 40.

[2] E.g. J.I.2/35, mm. 11–14.   [3] E.g. J.I.2/34, m. 1.

[4] E.g. *Pleas of the Crown for the County of Gloucester, 1221*, ed. F. W. Maitland (1884), no. 83.

[5] *Rolls of the Justices in Eyre for Gloucestershire, Warwickshire and Shropshire, 1221–1222*, ed. D. M. Stenton (Selden Soc. vol. 59), no. 762.

[6] E.g. J.I.2/25, m. 3.   [7] J.I.2/221, m. 4.

[8] E.g. *Select Coroners' Rolls*, p. 8.   [9] J.I.2/120, m. 11d.

example, a Carmelite friar was drowned while bathing in the Cherwell. Some clerks took his body from the water, but another man was the 'first finder'.[1] Early fourteenth-century Oxford provides two examples of the same man being the 'first finder' in two separate cases. It has been suggested that someone who was sure to be in the town for several years, possibly an under-bailiff, was selected as 'first finder' in these cases,[2] and in Oxford, with its constantly fluctuating population, this is possible. But it is unlikely that an official would have been so burdened by his colleagues. The answer more probably is that a man who had become a 'first finder' in one case felt that he had little to lose by 'finding' other bodies; his amercement, if he failed to attend the eyre, would be little if at all increased.

It was the responsibility of the townships to guard dead bodies from their discovery until the coroner's arrival.[3] When one Devon coroner delayed holding his inquest for eight days, a hedge was constructed around the body to guard it.[4] Nevertheless, the coroner was frequently impeded by the burial of the body before his arrival, when he had to cause it to be disinterred and to record the names of the buriers.[5] Such burials were a punishable offence. According to Bracton the township would be amerced[6] and it was the township or tithing which most frequently suffered,[7] but so might four townships,[8] the whole hundred,[9] or any combination of townships and individuals;[10] in short, whoever buried the body or authorised or connived at its burial was amerced. Any number of people or groups

[1] *Records of Mediaeval Oxford: Coroners' Inquests, the Walls of Oxford, Etc.*, ed. H. E. Salter (Oxford, 1912), p. 43. Cf. *ibid.* p. 13.

[2] *Ibid.* p. 15.

[3] For amercements of townships for failing to do this see J.I.2/111, m. 12d. In 1288 the whole hundred of Staple in Sussex was amerced because, on account of the default 'of the country', a corpse lay in a hedge for three weeks before the coroner viewed it, by which time it had been completely torn to pieces so that only the bones remained (J.I.1/926, m. 4d). It is uncertain whether the default lay in not guarding the body, not summoning the coroner, or both. In any event, this case is interesting as showing one of the very small Sussex hundreds having duties normally performed by one or a few townships in most counties.

[4] J.I.1/194, m. 1.

[5] *Britton*, i.2.3; *The Mirror of Justices*, i. 13 (Selden Soc. vol. 7, p. 29).

[6] II, 344.   [7] E.g. J.I.1/909A, m. 23; 921, m. 18d.

[8] E.g. J.I.1/912A, m. 43.   [9] E.g. J.I.1/921, m. 3.

[10] E.g. J.I.1/912A, m. 35d (one man and four townships); 921, m. 22d (twelve men and three townships); 946A, m. 7 (a son and another man); *Calendar of the Roll of the Justices on Eyre, 1247*, ed. G. H. Fowler (Beds. Hist. Rec. Soc. XXI), no. 633 (a serjeant and four townships). In 1248 the arrest of an outlaw's wife, a chaplain and another man and his wife was ordered at the Sussex eyre because they had buried the outlaw without a coroner's view (J.I.1/909A, m. 26d). This

of people might feel that their interests would be served by burying the body without the coroner's knowledge. The comfort and health of the neighbours were the least of the motives. The fact that sudden and unnatural deaths, when presented at the eyre, almost invariably resulted in financial loss to the township or hundred or both was far greater, while the felons obviously had the greatest incentive to bury the body.[1] An alternative to burial was to remove the body from the scene of the crime. Once again the local inhabitants often did this in order to escape amercements,[2] while the felons sometimes did so in order to avert suspicion from the neighbourhood in which they lived.[3] Such removals were also an offence which the coroner had to enrol.[4] There can be little doubt that the unlawful removals and burials of bodies of which the coroners came to hear and which therefore appear on their rolls and on the eyre rolls were only a small proportion of the total, the majority having been successfully hidden from them, since the convenience of the whole hundred was served if as many sudden and unnatural deaths as possible escaped official notice.[5] Although the medieval coroners held many inquests,

proves that coroners were expected to hold inquests into outlaws' deaths. During the 1279 Northumberland eyre judgment was passed against the coroners, mayor and bailiffs and the town of Newcastle-upon-Tyne and its liberties were taken into the king's hands, because a slain man had been buried with the knowledge of the whole town without the coroner's view (*Three Early Assize Rolls for the County of Northumberland*, ed. W. Page (Surtees Soc. LXXXVIII), p. 367).

[1] E.g. J.I.1/1317, m. 2 (alleged burial in sands of several slain men). Other felons threw their victims into ponds or down wells (e.g. J.I.1/921, m. 19; 930, m. 18).

[2] E.g. J.I.1/926, m. 17: the body had been moved from the tithing in which it had been found into another and from there into a half-tithing in a different hundred, which threw it into the sea.

[3] E.g. J.I.1/926, m. 23 (slain man removed in a cart to a wood).

[4] They must have been an offence before the coroner existed, since in 1201 two Cornishmen were amerced for moving a body without the permission of the sheriff and his bailiff (*Pleas Before the King or his Justices, 1198–1202*, ed. D. M. Stenton, II (Selden Soc. vol. 68), no. 245).

[5] Between 1241 and 1248 twenty-five cases came to light of burial before the Sussex coroners' views, but only six between 1255 and 1262 and five between 1279 and 1288 (J.I.1/909A; 912A; 930). This radical decrease can only represent a greater appreciation of the need for complete secrecy. At the 1248 eyre the township of Peasmarsh was amerced for burying a body found in a field without the coroner's view. The 'first finders' seem to have raised the hue and cry, but Goldspur hundred had suppressed it and was amerced for not presenting the death at the hundred court, while the two bailiffs of the hundred, who had been bribed with 40s. to conceal it, were arrested. Finally, the hundred incurred the *murdrum* fine, because no Englishry had been presented (J.I.1/909A, m. 26). It would have been surprising if this hundred had not been encouraged to greater secrecy in future.

it is therefore impossible to assess the incidence of sudden and un-natural deaths in any county during any period from the surviving coroners' rolls.

When informed of such a death, the coroner had to go immedi-ately to the body.[1] In Nottinghamshire in 1330 the interval between death and inquest rarely exceeded three days,[2] and the same is true of most other counties in normal circumstances.[3] In towns which had their own coroners there was naturally even less delay. The Ox-ford coroners usually viewed the body on the day on which it was found, although the inquest was sometimes deferred.[4] Speed was essential to enhance the slight chance of capturing any suspects, to ensure the preservation of all financial issues due to the crown and to prevent the burial, removal or corruption of the body.

Before setting out to view the body the coroner had to order the sheriff or hundred bailiff to summon a jury for a certain day;[5] in practice the order was almost always given to the hundred bailiff.[6] According to Bracton and the *Officium Coronatoris* the order should have been given after the coroner's arrival at the body,[7] and this may well have been the early practice, later modified in the interests of efficiency. In boroughs, whose compact size made the task of as-sembling the jury much easier, the order may usually have been given on the coroner's arrival at the body. This would account for the fact that the Oxford coroners usually viewed the body alone and held the inquest later, occasionally days later.[8]

The thirteenth-century law-books agreed that the coroner's in-quest jury had to consist of four or more neighbouring townships.[9] Originally every male over twelve years of age was required to at-tend from each, but the Provisions of Westminster of 1259 decreed

[1] Bracton, II, 342.
[2] H. M. Cam in *The English Government at Work, 1327–1336*, III, ed. J. F. Willard, W. A. Morris and W. H. Dunham (Cambridge, Mass. 1950), pp. 159–60.
[3] For Sussex see *Sx. Arch. Colls.* XCV, 44.
[4] *Records of Mediaeval Oxford*, pp. 3–51; *Oxford City Documents, 1268–1665*, ed. J. E. Thorold Rogers (Oxon. Hist. Soc. XVIII), pp. 150–74.
[5] *Britton*, i.2.2; *Fleta*, i. 25 (Selden Soc. vol. 72, p. 64); 12 Edw. I (Statute of Wales), c. 5.
[6] E.g. *Select Coroners' Rolls*, pp. 42–3.
[7] Bracton, II, 342; *Statutes of the Realm*, I, 40.
[8] E.g. *Records of Mediaeval Oxford*, p. 14.
[9] Four, five or six according to Bracton (II, 342) and the *Officium Coronatoris* (*Statutes of the Realm*, I, 40), four or more according to *Fleta* (i. 25: Selden Soc. vol. 72, p. 64) and four with others if necessary according to *Britton* (i.2.2).

that in future, provided that sufficient attended, the presence of everyone was not necessary,[1] and the county of Oxford was wise enough to remind the eyre justices of this at the opening of the next general eyre there.[2] In 1267, however, the Statute of Marlborough again required that all over twelve should attend unless they had reasonable cause for absence,[3] and this requirement was repeated in 1284 for Wales.[4] In most cases after 1300, however, from twelve to sixteen men represented the four townships at the inquest,[5] although sometimes each township attended by its reeve or bailiff and four men,[6] its tithingman and tithing,[7] or by its constable and other representatives,[8] while in one exceptional Derbyshire case seventeen men represented nine townships.[9]

The eyre and coroners' rolls provide examples of a large number of different kinds of inquest juries and show that there was considerable variation both from county to county and at different times within the same county. Nevertheless, for inquests held in the body of counties before county coroners and outside those townships and tithings which claimed the privilege of attending by themselves,[10] the coroner's jury seems to have undergone the same general evolution in most counties. There were three main phases, although they did not coincide exactly in time from county to county and within any particular county one phase gave way only gradually and hesitantly to the next. During most of the thirteenth century, as the law-books would lead one to expect, the juries generally consisted of four or more townships; in the last quarter of the century they were reinforced by twelve freemen of the hundred; and during the next century these freemen became the essential part of the jury and the townships gradually ceased to return a verdict, although their other functions in connection with the inquest remained and they still had to present the fatality at the next county court.[11] It is significant that the statute of 1360, which ordered that juries at coroners' and other

---

[1] C.24 (*Statutes of the Realm*, I, 11).   [2] J.I.1/701, m. 19.

[3] 52 Hen. III, c. 24. This statute is ignored in the discussion of the coroner's jury in 'The Veredictum of Chippenham Hundred, 1281', ed. R. E. Latham and C. A. F. Meekings, *Collectanea* (Wilts. Arch. and Nat. Hist. Soc., Rec. Branch, XII), p. 67.

[4] 12 Edw. I, c. 5 (everyone of twelve and over from the township in which the death occurred and four neighbouring townships).

[5] E.g. J.I.2/67, m. 7.   [6] E.g. *Select Coroners' Rolls*, p. 42; J.I.2/138, m. 1.

[7] E.g. J.I.2/201.   [8] E.g. J.I.2/228, mm. 1–3.

[9] J.I.2/31, m. 1.   [10] For these see below, pp. 145–6.

[11] E.g. J.I.2/220.

local inquests should be recruited from the immediate neighbourhood, was promulgated when the four neighbouring townships
were becoming less important in coroners' inquests.[1] Some hundreds were large and there was a danger that the jurors might all live
at a distance from the place where the death occurred. Partly as a
result of this statute and partly because the thirteenth-century statutes and precepts remained in force, the coroners' inquest juries
came in the late fourteenth and fifteenth centuries to consist of from
twelve to twenty-four men, who were sometimes described as men
of the four neighbouring townships.[2]

It is interesting to compare the development of the coroner's jury
with that of the petty jury. After the abolition of ordeals it became
common for justices in eyre to associate the four neighbouring
townships with the presenting jury, which consisted of twelve freemen of the hundred, to try felonies, but in the later thirteenth century petty juries consisted of twelve men only.[3] Thus while the
coroner's juries may have provided both the idea and part of the
personnel for the early petty juries,[4] they seem to have evolved later
in emulation of them.

When both the townships and the men of the hundred attended
inquests, there is rarely any indication as to whether they sat apart
and delivered separate verdicts, but this does seem to have happened occasionally. The inquest held by the freemen of the hundred
seems to have been more highly regarded, possibly on account of the
greater social eminence of the jurors. In Northamptonshire, for example, the twelve seem to have returned the detailed verdict, the
four townships merely agreeing;[5] and in other counties, while the
inquest seems to have been held by the twelve freemen, there is
merely a cursory note on the coroners' rolls that the four townships
attended.[6] The author of *The Mirror of Justices* may not have been
strictly correct when writing that the jurors should be separated into

---

[1] 34 Edw. III, c. 4.

[2] For an analysis of the development of the coroner's jury in Sussex see
Sx. Arch. Colls. xcv, 43–4. Because the Sussex hundreds were so small, territorial tithings or 'borghs' often undertook the duties performed by townships
elsewhere (*The Three Earliest Subsidies for the County of Sussex*, ed. W. Hudson
(Sx. Rec. Soc. x), pp. xviii–xxvi). In Derbyshire townships and sokes sometimes
jointly formed the inquest jury (e.g. J.I.2/25).

[3] T. F. T. Plucknett, *A Concise History of the Common Law*, 4th ed. (1948),
pp. 116–17, 122.

[4] As suggested by Gross, *Select Coroners' Rolls*, pp. xxxii–xxxiv.

[5] E.g. J.I.2/111, m. 12.   [6] E.g. J.I.2/96.

dozens, no dozen being allowed to speak to another, but each answering for itself;[1] but the practice of holding separate inquests may have been more widespread than the legal records suggest. There is even some evidence that in early times each of the four townships sometimes made separate statements.[2]

In towns the same general development as in counties is apparent, with parishes and wards taking the place of townships. During the thirteenth and fourteenth centuries, most towns seem to have developed a jury of twelve freemen, which became rather more than twelve in the fifteenth century, out of one of four neighbouring parishes or wards, with an intermediate stage when both elements sat together.[3] Doubtless for most of the thirteenth century every male over twelve was expected to come from each parish,[4] but later twelve men from all four sufficed,[5] while the alderman and four men often represented each ward.[6] London was exceptional in that the average number of jurors there in the fourteenth century was thirty; there might be as few as twelve from one ward only or as many as fifty from four or more.[7] The development of the Oxford jury is interesting. In and shortly after the 1290's the town coroners operated in both the town itself and in Northgate hundred, the juries consisting of four parishes or the equivalent number of parishes, hamlets, tithings and townships. Each was represented by from four to fifteen men, between twenty and thirty thus constituting the average jury.[8] By the 1340's, however, and for the rest of the century at least, the Oxford coroner's jury invariably consisted of twelve men, who were still derived from the four neighbouring parishes, tithings,

[1] i. 13 (Selden Soc. vol. 7, p. 33). Elsewhere (*ibid.* p. 30) he wrote that 'it is the coroner's duty to make panels of the better folk by themselves, the mean folk by themselves, and the small folk by themselves'. Here he was probably only exaggerating the tendency towards separate inquests by the twelve freemen and the representatives of the townships. That the latter were of lower status can be deduced from the fact that they are never, while the twelve of the hundred are often, called 'freemen'.

[2] E.g. *Select Coroners' Rolls*, pp. 2, 8, 25, 58–9, 60, 63. Separate verdicts were often returned by the component parts of petty juries (Plucknett, *op. cit.* pp. 116–17).

[3] E.g. *Records of Mediaeval Oxford*, pp. 3–8 (four parishes); J.I.2/196, mm. 3–5 (twelve freemen and four wards); J.I.2/85, m. 1 (twelve men and four parishes); *Sx. Arch. Colls.* xcv, 45, 47–8, 53, 55 (twelve or more men).

[4] From the whole city in Chichester (J.I.1/921, m. 26; 926, m. 28).

[5] E.g. J.I.2/76.   [6] E.g. J.I.2/199.

[7] *Calendar of Coroners Rolls of the City of London, 1300–1378*, ed. R. R. Sharpe (1913), p. xiv.

[8] Oxon. Hist. Soc. XVIII, 150–68; *Records of Mediaeval Oxford*, pp. 13–20.

townships and hamlets in most cases. Sometimes the coroners recorded that one of these districts failed to attend, but the remaining three still invariably provided twelve jurors.[1] This suggests that, as in earlier years, a large number, if not all, of the men of the four districts were summoned, but whereas earlier all who came sat on the jury, from the 1340's onwards twelve were selected from them.

In both county and borough it was the coroner himself who had the final choice of jurors, since interested parties had no right to challenge any of them.[2] The Articles of Lincoln assumed that the coroner directed the bailiff as to the type of person he was to summon,[3] but his choice was severely limited by two factors. Firstly, many people were exempt. On the one hand, there were those who were wealthy and influential enough to be able to buy exemptions from assizes, juries and recognitions,[4] and, on the other, men who were regarded as untrustworthy and unfit to serve on them after being found guilty of conspiracies against justice on coroners' and other inquests.[5] Secondly, the coroner's difficulty usually lay less in deciding who to choose than in getting a sufficient number to attend.

This difficulty is best illustrated by a Cambridgeshire case of 1338. John FitzJon, a county coroner, ordered the hundred bailiff to summon all the freeholders of the hundred and the reeve and four men from each of four townships. On the day arranged for the inquest the bailiff returned the names of twenty freeholders, but neither they nor the representatives of the townships arrived. They were therefore declared 'in mercy' and the coroner ordered the bailiff to distrain them by all their lands and chattels to attend on the next day. On this day the townships came, but only six of the freeholders. The bailiff accounted for the issues of the absentees' lands and was ordered to distrain them to appear on the following day, to which the inquest was again postponed. This time the townships attended with eight freeholders, who did not include any of the first six. The bailiff accounted for the issues of the lands of the missing twelve, who, like the previous fourteen, were declared 'in mercy', and was again required to distrain them to attend three days later. At last they all appeared and the inquest proceeded with a jury of

---

[1] *Records of Mediaeval Oxford*, pp. 23–47.

[2] *Britton*, i.2.11; *The Mirror of Justices*, i. 13 (Selden Soc. vol. 7, p. 30).

[3] C.9 ('Original Documents illustrative of the Administration of the Criminal Law in the time of Edward I', ed. F. M. Nichols, *Archaeologia*, XL, 103).

[4] E.g. *Cal. Pat. Rolls, 1266–1272*, pp. 94–5.

[5] E.g. J.I.1/934, m. 1d.

C

four townships and twelve of the freeholders.[1] William de Whatele and Richard de Eynesham, Oxford town coroners, were also unfortunate; once in 1342 and again in 1343 they could only hold inquests at the third attempt, since the twelve jurors from four parishes ignored the first two summonses.[2] These cases were exceptional. Despite frequent defaults, coroners very rarely had to postpone inquests for lack of jurors, but it is understandable that Thomas Houkyn, coroner of Northgate hundred near Oxford, should have found it convenient to use almost identical juries for two completely unconnected inquests held on 23 July 1394.[3] Similarly, one can sympathise with Robert Stoket, the bailiff of Chippenham hundred, who was accused in 1281 of summoning all the freemen and every township within his bailiwick whenever he was ordered to summon twelve freemen and four townships.[4] There is thus every reason to believe the complaint voiced in the Articles of Lincoln that whereas the poor either did not know or dared not speak the truth at coroners' inquests, the 'better people' despised the coroners and refused to obey them.[5]

The coroner had no authority to amerce those who refused or omitted to attend his inquest when summoned, but had to enrol their names.[6] This he regularly did in the thirteenth century, and the defaulters were amerced during the eyre.[7] With the suspension of general eyres soon after 1300, few coroners continued to note

[1] *Select Coroners' Rolls*, pp. 42–5.
[2] *Records of Mediaeval Oxford*, pp. 25–6, 29.   [3] *Ibid.* p. 47.
[4] Wilts. Arch. and Nat. Hist. Soc., Rec. Branch, XII, 95, 126.
[5] C.9 (*Archaeologia*, XL, 103).
[6] *Britton*, i.2.4; *The Mirror of Justices*, i. 13 (Selden Soc. vol. 7, p. 30). The roll of John Tuwe, a Northamptonshire coroner of the 1330's, is exceptional in that it contains many inquests which end with a statement of the amercement of one or more townships for not coming or not coming fully or for not guarding the body before the coroner's arrival, and even a few amercements of hundred bailiffs for not performing their duties at inquests; some even give the amount of the amercement (J.I.2/111, mm. 12, 12d). These entries show no signs of crowding or of any late additions, but were written in their entirety at one time. This coroner must therefore have exceeded his powers and taken amercements. He must have acted in ignorance or he would not have recorded the amercements, which were normally treated as an offence when imposed by the coroner (e.g. *Somersetshire Pleas*, ed. C. E. H. Chadwyck Healey (Somerset Rec. Soc. XI), nos. 973, 1037. Cf. *Rotuli Hundredorum*, ed. W. Illingworth (Rec. Comm. 1812–18), II, 308).
[7] Between 1271 and 1279 one or more townships failed to attend or to attend fully at over sixty Sussex inquests and there were similar defaults at over eighty between 1279 and 1288 (J.I.1/921; 930). These represent almost half the inquests presented at the eyres.

defaults unless they necessitated postponing the inquest, although many of the inquests on the roll of William Sanford, a Berkshire coroner of the late fourteenth century, which were usually attended by a jury of four townships and twelve men, end with a note that 'all over the age of twelve did not come'[1]—a requirement which was never enforced at that period elsewhere.

When the jurors had assembled, the coroner swore them in; they had to swear on the Gospels that they would speak the truth on any points on which he might question them.[2] Both coroner and jurors had then to view the body, unless, in the event of homicide, the slain man had received the last rites of the church,[3] when he could have been expected to have been able to explain exactly how he had been wounded. In Oxford the coroner often viewed the body before the jurors' arrival and recorded only his view.[4] This indicates that in Oxford at least it was the coroner's view which was the really important one, although there is no reason to suppose that the jurors did not also view the body later, as *Britton* said was required.[5] The view was not just a formality. In Essex the 'first finder' showed the coroner the body and the coroner both viewed and felt it.[6] It had to be naked and the coroner had to look particularly for wounds, bruises and signs of strangulation.[7] The view was of the utmost importance in cases of death from natural causes occurring shortly after an accident or wound. Thus in 1343 the Oxford coroners viewed a body because there was a rumour that a man had hit the deceased over the heart with his fist; the coroners found the body uninjured and their jury returned a verdict of natural death.[8] In 1342 the same coroners held an inquest upon the body of a woman who had died of old age and diseases; 'and because there was much talk that her husband beat her unduly, therefore the body was rolled over and over before the eyes of the coroners'. She also was found to be uninjured.[9] If this appears to have been a rather rough-and-ready post-mortem examination, it was nevertheless probably adequate,

[1] E.g. J.I.2/10, m. 5.

[2] Bracton, II, 342; *Britton*, i.2.2; *The Mirror of Justices*, i. 13 (Selden Soc. vol. 7, p. 30); *Officium Coronatoris* (*Statutes of the Realm*, 1, 40); 12 Edw. I, c. 5.

[3] Selden Soc. vol. 24, p. 112. Also the Cinque Ports had their own rule that bodies need not be viewed if the cause of death was well known to be an accident (*Borough Customs*, ed. M. Bateson, I (Selden Soc. vol. 18), p. 17, n. 4).

[4] See above, p. 13.   [5] i.2.3.   [6] E.g. J.I.2/35, m. 11.

[7] Bracton, II, 344; *Officium Coronatoris* (*Statutes of the Realm*, I, 41); *Fleta*, i. 25 (Selden Soc. vol. 72, p. 65).

[8] *Records of Mediaeval Oxford*, p. 28.   [9] *Ibid.* p. 24.

for a glance through any roll of crown pleas shows that there was nothing subtle or sophisticated about medieval homicides.[1] In the thirteenth century the length, breadth and depth of all wounds had to be carefully measured and recorded. Thereafter the exact measurements were rarely recorded, although the practice never completely died out in the Middle Ages.[2] Finally, if the deceased had several wounds produced by different weapons, any one of which would by itself have proved fatal, the coroner was always careful to record this in order that all the weapons might be forfeited.[3]

Strictly, the body should not have been buried until the inquest had ended,[4] and it is possible that the early practice may have been for the inquest to be held around the body wherever it had been found, but experience would soon have shown that when the body had been viewed the rest of the proceedings might equally well take place in greater comfort indoors. The next development was for the body to be buried as soon as it had been viewed, and this practice must have been fairly general by the late thirteenth century when it came to be recognized as not only lawful but the rule.[5] Throughout the fourteenth century, however, some coroners paid at least lip-service to the earlier custom and noted the burial of the body at the end of the record of their inquests.[6] Before retiring indoors the coroner and jurors had two more duties: to receive presentments of Englishry,[7] and to decide whether the deceased had died or been slain where he was found or elsewhere. If they found that death had occurred elsewhere, they had to do their utmost, [by tracing any signs of blood, footsteps or tracks of a horse or cart, to discover how, by whom and whence he had been carried.[8] This was important less for facilitating the discovery and arrest of any felons than for the allocation of any subsequent *murdrum* fine or amercements.

During the inquest, the jurors had to answer on oath a series of questions put to them by the coroner. The first point to be determined was whether death had been caused feloniously, by misad-

---

[1] By contrast, autopsies were practised in Italy during the fourteenth century (Havard, *The Detection of Secret Homicide*, p. 1).

[2] For an example from 1451 see *Sx. Arch. Colls.* XCV, 55.

[3] E.g. *ibid.* pp. 56, 58.

[4] Bracton, II, 344; *Officium Coronatoris* (*Statutes of the Realm*, I, 41); *Fleta*, i. 25 (Selden Soc. vol. 72, p. 65).

[5] *Britton*, i.2.3; *The Mirror of Justices*, i. 13 (Selden Soc. vol. 7, p. 30).

[6] E.g. J.I.2/67, m. I.   [7] For this see below, pp. 27-9.

[8] Bracton, II, 343; *Officium Coronatoris* (*Statutes of the Realm*, I, 40); *Fleta*, i. 25 (Selden Soc. vol. 72, p. 64).

venture or naturally; and if feloniously, whether by homicide or suicide.[1] Suicide was comparatively rare in the Middle Ages, although some verdicts of misadventure, especially by drowning, may conceal suicides.[2] There were five main circumstances which necessitated inquests into natural deaths: if they were sudden or unexpected; when the body was found in the open and the cause of death was unknown; if there was any suspicion or possibility of felony; if the hue and cry was raised maliciously; and in the event of death in prison, which will be considered separately at the end of this chapter. The great majority of coroners' inquests, however, were into homicides and deaths by misadventure. All homicides, whether felonious, accidental or in self-defence, and all misadventures had to be investigated.

The coroner's questions aimed at discovering all the circumstances and details of the death, which the jurors, as men of the neighbourhood, usually knew a lot about. If the coroner suspected that the jury had concealed the truth or for any reason thought that further inquiry was necessary, he might hold one or more subsequent inquests with other jurors provided that he enrolled all the verdicts.[3] Very few medieval examples of more than one inquest being held on the same body are known, and two are from fourteenth-century London. In one case the first inquest was held where the dead man was found and a second, for further information, six days later at the place where he had been wounded.[4] The other case concerned a man who was slain in a fight between men of the mystery of skinners and the mystery of fishmongers. After a normal inquest had been held, juries of each of the mysteries were summoned in turn to hold two more.[5] In yet another London case the jury asked for more time to make further inquiries and secured the adjournment of the inquest for a week,[6] while in a fourth the sheriffs and coroner twice sent the jurors away to inform themselves about a homicide and were ultimately able to hold a fruitful inquest at the third attempt.[7] Elsewhere juries occasionally pleaded complete ignorance of a

---

[1] *Britton*, i.2.5; *The Mirror of Justices*, i. 13 (Selden Soc. vol. 7, p. 30).

[2] *Per temptacionem diaboli submersus fuit per infortunium* returned jurors of the city of York rather equivocally in 1355 (J.I.2/215, m. 5).

[3] *Britton*, i.2.5; *Fleta*, i. 25 (Selden Soc. vol. 72, p. 64); *The Mirror of Justices*, i. 13 (Selden Soc. vol. 7, p. 33).

[4] *Cal. Coroners Rolls of London*, pp. 118–19.

[5] *Ibid.* pp. 266–9.   [6] *Ibid.* pp. 158–60.

[7] K.B.27/476, Rex m. 31. I am indebted to Dr P. Chaplais for drawing my attention to this case.

fatality without the coroner taking any further action,[1] but twelve
Shropshire jurors, sitting on the body of a slain man, refused to return a verdict and were later tried, although acquitted, in King's
Bench.[2] Usually, however, the jurors were well informed, having
probably made inquiries immediately before the inquest.

Apart from discovering facts, the coroner's inquest usually entailed two other actions: the arrest or attachment by sureties of a
number of people, and the appraisal and committal to safe custody
of anything which might later be forfeited. Everyone indicted at the
inquest, whether of homicide or of aiding and abetting it, should
have been arrested. Ideally, they should have been arrested in the
hue and cry following the finding of the body and brought to the inquest, but this was rarely achieved. The majority of those who surrendered to the coroner had committed homicide accidentally or in
self-defence[3] and had little to lose by surrendering, their pardon being assured, and much to lose by flight.[4] The thirteenth-century rule
was that the coroner should deliver all arrested felons to the sheriff,
by whom they were committed to gaol,[5] but the later practice was for
the coroner to send them to gaol himself with a covering letter to the
gaoler ordering him to keep them in safe custody until the next gaol
delivery.[6] Another development was that, while imprisonment of the
principals was never dispensed with unless they were successful in an
inquisition *de odio et atia*, accessories came always to be allowed bail.[7]

Most felons fled as soon as they had committed the homicide, and
the coroner, on learning their names from his jury, had to order their
arrest. Such orders were given either to the sheriff or to the hundred
bailiff,[8] who could not act without the coroner's warrant.[9] The

[1] E.g. J.I.2/9, m. 1d.   [2] J.I.2/145, m. 12d.   [3] E.g. J.I.2/52, m. 9; 58, m. 3d.
[4] All their goods and chattels. See below, p. 29.
[5] Bracton, II, 342–3; *Officium Coronatoris* (*Statutes of the Realm*, I, 40).
[6] For such a letter see *Sx. Arch. Colls.* XCVI, 33–4.
[7] *Fleta*, i. 25 (Selden Soc. vol. 72, pp. 64–5); *The Mirror of Justices*, i. 13 (Selden Soc. vol. 7, p. 33). For the older rule see Bracton, II, 342–3. For the coroner's part in inquisitions *de odio et atia* see below, pp. 76–7.
[8] According to *Britton* (i.2.6) and *The Mirror of Justices* (i. 13: Selden Soc.
vol. 7, p. 33) the sheriff had to see to these arrests, but in practice the coroner
gave his orders either to the sheriff or to the hundred bailiff (e.g. *Select Coroners'
Rolls*, p. 38; J.I.2/6, m. 3). In Sussex, possibly because the hundreds were so
small, the bailiff of the rape was given these orders (e.g. J.I.1/921, m. 15d) and
the coroner might be amerced for using the hundred bailiff instead (e.g. J.I.1/
926, m. 1). In Wales after 1284 the coroner was required to deliver secretly to
the sheriff if he was present, otherwise to the bailiff of the commote, a written
order to arrest the indicted and keep them in gaol pending their trial (12 Edw. I,
c. 5).   [9] Selden Soc. vol. 24, p. 140.

jurors had to name the frankpledge tithings or mainpast of all the indicted in order that they might be amerced at the eyre if the felons
could not be found;[1] but this piece of information rarely appears on
the coroners' rolls after 1300.[2] The coroner had also to inquire where
the felons had gone and who had received them.[3] The harbourers
had also to be arrested.[4] In Oxford the jurors often said that the
felons had fled by night and that they therefore did not know where.[5]
This was because the town or township was amerced at the eyre if
the homicide had been committed in day-time and the felons escaped. The time of day at which the felony occurred was often recorded by the coroner,[6] but not until 1487 was he given statutory
authority to inquire about such day-light escapes at his inquest.[7]
Britton maintained that the coroner was supposed to inquire whether any of those indicted at his inquest had ever been bound over to
keep the peace towards the slain and, if they had, to record the names
of their sureties,[8] but no such entries appear on any of the extant
rolls.[9]

A great variety of people were liable to be attached by the coroner,
usually by two pledges, to appear both at the next county court,
when the townships had to present the fatality, and at the next
general eyre. Both the pledges and the pledged were amerced at the
eyre if the pledged defaulted. These attachments were mainly enforced for this and other financial reasons, few being strictly necessary for securing justice. Those who had to be attached included
the lord and whole household of any house in which a homicide or
death by misadventure had occurred or in which fatal wounds had
been given, even if the death had occurred elsewhere, and anyone
else present in it;[10] all witnesses of homicides and misadven-

---

[1] *The Mirror of Justices*, i. 13 (Selden Soc. vol. 7, p. 31).

[2] It is significant that in 1329 Nottinghamshire unsuccessfully tried to obtain
exemption from presenting the mainpast of felons (J.I.1/686, m. 3).

[3] *Fleta*, i. 25 (Selden Soc. vol. 72, p. 64); *The Mirror of Justices*, i. 13 (Selden
Soc. vol. 7, p. 31).

[4] E.g. J.I.1/926, m. 4d.   [5] E.g. *Records of Mediaeval Oxford*, pp. 22, 25.

[6] E.g. *Sx. Arch. Colls.* xcv, 56–8.   [7] By 3 Hen. VII, c. 2.

[8] i.2.6. Cf. the similar article of inquiry given by *The Mirror of Justices*, i. 13
(Selden Soc. vol. 7, pp. 30–1).

[9] This rule may, however, partly account for the fact that a few coroners recorded the binding over of men to keep the peace in the county court (e.g.
Select Coroners' Rolls, pp. 33–8).

[10] E.g. *Memorials of London and London Life in the XIIIth, XIVth and XVth
Centuries*, ed. H. T. Riley (1868), pp. 7–11. Hence the coroner always asked the
jurors where the death had occurred and whether inside a house or outside

tures;[1] the owner and everyone lodging in the house in which the felons had stayed the previous night;[2] and those who moved the body without the coroner's permission.[3] There was a *prima facie* case against some of these, although the primary motive behind their attachment was invariably financial. Thus witnesses of homicides, even if they had not been indicted before the coroner, had to be arraigned at the eyre; but the real reason for their attachment was because they were imprisoned at the eyre until they paid a fine if it was found that they had not raised the hue and cry after the felon and done their best to arrest him.[4] The fourteenth-century Buckinghamshire coroners were particularly thorough, attaching lords of bridges from which men accidentally fell to their death, lords of wells into which people accidentally fell to death, lords of mills and other things which were deodand, and lords or holders of houses in which people had died by misadventure.[5] Bedfordshire coroners of the previous century were equally meticulous in a different way. On at least three occasions when wounds had been inflicted during a quarrel and the wounded man had recovered and later died of some natural cause, the coroner attached the wounder;[6] and in a similar case the original striker fled and the coroner therefore caused the man from whose house he had come to find two sureties.[7] In 1262 judgment was passed against a Sussex coroner for not attaching the husband of a pregnant woman who died by misadventure,[8] while the wife of a man who fell down dead after being bled excessively was attached by the sheriffs and coroner of London[9] and after a sudden death in Norfolk the coroner ordered the attachment of both the widow and the man whom she had proceeded to marry.[10] If these last cases were unusual, there were three sets of people who were almost invariably attached: the 'first finder', the four nearest neighbours and, until the abolition of Englishry, those relatives of the deceased who presented Englishry.

(Bracton, II, 342–3; *Officium Coronatoris* (*Statutes of the Realm*, I, 40); *Fleta*, i. 25 (Selden Soc. vol. 72, p. 64); *Britton*, i.2.5). It is interesting that these authorities mention taverns, wrestling matches and other gatherings as likely places for sudden deaths.

[1] Even minors (Bracton, II, 342–4; *Officium Coronatoris* (*Statutes of the Realm*, I, 40–1); *Fleta*, i. 25 (Selden Soc. vol. 72, p. 64)).
[2] Bracton, II, 343; *Officium Coronatoris* (*Statutes of the Realm*, I, 40); *Fleta*, i. 25 (Selden Soc. vol. 72, pp. 64–5). E.g. *Memorials of London*, pp. 9–11.
[3] E.g. *ibid.* pp. 4–5.
[4] Selden Soc. vol. 24, p. 140. Sometimes they were merely amerced (e.g. J.I.1/930, m. 2d). [5] E.g. J.I.2/13; 14.
[6] *Select Coroners' Rolls*, pp. 4–5, 8, 24. [7] J.I.2/1, m. 3. [8] J.I.1/912A, m. 35d.
[9] *Memorials of London*, pp. 14–15. [10] J.I.2/266, m. 18d.

The 'first finder' of the body, male or female, of whatever age and whatever the cause of the death, had to be attached and his name and those of his sureties enrolled by the coroner,[1] unless the body was found within the verge[2] or the dead man had both received the last rites of the church and spoken between the wounding and death,[3] when he would presumably have exculpated the 'first finder'.[4] In practice, however, the 'first finder' was attached not in case he was the homicide, for if there was the slightest suspicion of that he would have been arrested, but in order that he might be amerced at the eyre if he had omitted to raise the hue and cry or amerced together with his sureties if, as frequently happened, he failed to attend the eyre.[5] The coroners conscientiously enrolled the names of the 'first finders' and their sureties throughout the thirteenth century, but most ceased to do so with the ending of the general eyre, although a few persisted to the end of the fourteenth century.[6] Kent was an exception to the normal custom of two sureties, 'first finders' there having to produce four.[7]

Whatever the cause of death, the coroner had to attach the four neighbours living nearest to the spot where the body was found, usually by two sureties each, and to enrol the names of both neighbours and sureties.[8] Only when the death had occurred within the verge were such attachments not required.[9] Elsewhere not even the receipt by the deceased of the last rites of the church excused them.[10]

---

[1] Bracton, II, 344; *Officium Coronatoris* (*Statutes of the Realm*, I, 41); *Britton*, i.2.10, 14; *Fleta*, i. 25 (Selden Soc. vol. 72, pp. 64–5); 12 Edw. I, c. 5. For examples see *Sx. Arch. Colls.* xcv, 48 (homicide); J.I.1/912A, m. 43 (suicide); J.I.2/10, m. 5 (misadventure).

[2] Selden Soc. vol. 24, lvi.

[3] *Ibid.* pp. 59, 112, 140. The coroner did not normally record the names of the 'first finder' and his pledges when the last rites had been received (e.g. *Sx. Arch. Colls.* xcv, 45–8). When he recorded their names and the receiving of the last rites (e.g. *Select Coroners' Rolls*, p. 38), a very infrequent occurrence, it must be assumed that the slain man had not spoken. One Worcestershire case contains no mention of the last rites, but states that there was no 'first finder' nor presentment of Englishry because the deceased had spoken after his fatal fall (J.I.2/258, m. 1).

[4] *Select Coroners' Rolls*, p. xxv.

[5] E.g. 'Roll of the Justices in Eyre at Bedford, 1227', ed. G. H. Fowler, *Beds. Hist. Rec. Soc.* III, 379. Townships might also be amerced for not presenting the 'first finder' at the inquest (e.g. *ibid.* no. 387).

[6] E.g. J.I.2/10, mm. 5–9; 35, mm. 11–12.

[7] Selden Soc. vol. 24, p. 59.

[8] Once again enrolment ceased in the fourteenth century with a few exceptions (e.g. J.I.2/35, mm. 11–12).

[9] Selden Soc. vol. 24, lvi.   [10] *Ibid.* p. 140.

Once again the original motive, the securing of possible suspects or witnesses, was soon subordinated to a purely financial one, the considerable chance of amercements for non-attendance at the eyre.[1] Some coroners allowed whole townships or tithings to go surety for the neighbours,[2] although strictly this was a punishable offence,[3] while in Buckinghamshire in the mid-fourteenth century the neighbours frequently went surety for each other.[4] A few towns had their own customs. In fourteenth-century Oxford only the two nearest neighbours had to find sureties,[5] while in London in the previous century either two or more might be required to do so. It was usually two, but when a man had been fatally wounded or had suffered a fatal accident in one place and had died in another, the two neighbours nearest to each place were attached;[6] and when a body was moved from the place where it had been found to another, the two nearest neighbours to each were attached.[7] Similarly, when a man fell dead in the street because he had been bled excessively, the two neighbours who lived next to him were attached as were the two who lived nearest to the spot where he was found.[8] In one exceptional case six neighbours had to find sureties after a homicide had been committed during a brawl: the two living nearest to the spot where the body lay, the two next to the place where the wounds had been given and the two next to the hostel from which the rioters had come.[9]

Some towns tried to establish special privileges in these matters. In 1262 the coroners and bailiffs of Chichester were found to have attached no 'first finders' or neighbours, but merely to have summoned them to appear before the justices, and the bailiffs pleaded that they had always done this;[10] but by 1279 Chichester was apparently attaching them normally.[11] Arundel's claims were yet more extreme and enduring. In 1262, 1279 and 1288 the borough claimed never to have attached or presented 'first finders' or neighbours in homicides or misadventures; it showed no warrant for this claim, but pleaded ancient usage, and the matter was not finally settled

---

[1] E.g. J.I.1/930, m. 10. Another frequent occasion of amercement at the eyre was the attendance of men who falsely presented themselves as neighbours, presumably in order to save their friends (e.g. J.I.1/909A, m. 22).

[2] E.g. *Select Coroners' Rolls*, p. 109.   [3] E.g. J.I.1/930, m. 10.

[4] E.g. J.I.2/12, mm. 6, 8, 10.

[5] E.g. *Records of Mediaeval Oxford*, p. 37.

[6] E.g. *Memorials of London*, pp. 15–17.   [7] E.g. *ibid.* pp. 4–5.

[8] *Ibid.* pp. 14–15.   [9] *Ibid.* pp. 9–11.

[10] J.I.1/912A, m. 25d.   [11] E.g. J.I.1/921, m. 26.

until 1288 when it was ordered to attach them in future.[1] It did so, and its coroners were entering the names of the 'first finder' and neighbours in their indictments long after most of the county coroners had ceased doing so.[2] By contrast, Southampton seems to have been completely successful in the thirteenth century in maintaining its claim to attach no neighbours unless they were suspected of causing the death.[3]

Originally introduced in order to safeguard the ascendant Norman minority, if not by the Danes yet earlier, and very possibly the original *raison d'être* of inquests upon dead bodies in England,[4] presentment of Englishry survived into the period of the coroner purely for financial reasons. Some counties, mainly those on the north and west marches, were exempt from it, and certain areas within other counties had either been granted or successfully claimed exemption.[5] Elsewhere, unless death had been caused by drowning in the sea, Englishry had to be presented at the coroner's inquest, at the following county court and finally to the justices in eyre. Failure to present it meant that the men of the neighbourhood, generally the hundred, incurred the *murdrum* fine. The requirements of proof of Englishry varied from county to county[6] but always one or more relatives of the deceased were required to come before the coroner and prove their relationship,[7] and in Wales at least, where the proof

[1] J.I.1/912A, m. 44d; 921, m. 21; 930, m. 18.   [2] *Sx. Arch. Colls.* xcv, 48.
[3] J.I.1/778, m. 60d; 780, m. 23d; 789, m. 36.
[4] As suggested by Havard, *op. cit.* pp. 11–13. For good accounts of Englishry and the *murdrum* fine, upon which much of this paragraph is based, see F. C. Hamil, 'Presentment of Englishry and the Murder Fine', *Speculum*, xii, 285–98; Somerset Rec. Soc. xi, pp. lviii–lxii.
[5] Arundel for long pleaded ancient custom and for some time, as in its fight against attaching 'first finders' and neighbours, successfully avoided presenting Englishry; its claim was queried in 1262 and 1279, but not until 1288 was the borough ordered to conform to the practice of the county (J.I.1/912A, m. 44d; 921, m. 21; 930, m. 18). Southampton, however, was again completely successful, although basing its claim on custom alone (J.I.1/778, m. 60d; 780, m. 23d; 789, m. 36).
[6] Variations included presentment by two paternal and two maternal relatives; by one paternal and one maternal; by two and one; and by two or one on one side only. In Gloucestershire women could not present it; in many counties it was not required for women, and in some neither for women nor for infant males.
[7] *Britton*, i.2.15; Selden Soc. vol. 24, p. 13. According to *Fleta* (i. 30) Englishry had to be presented before the burial of the body. Huntingdonshire successfully maintained in the 1230's that Englishry was presented there within fifteen days of the death either at the county court or to the coroners (J.I.1/341, m. 1), while the successful Hampshire claim forty years later that Englishry was presented there in full county court before the coroners (J.I.1/789, m. 1) seems to exclude a previous presentment at the inquest, but these were exceptional.

was of Welshry, and probably elsewhere, the jurors had to confirm it.[1] The coroner had to record either the names of the kinsmen and the sureties for their appearance before the justices or the fact that Englishry had not been presented.[2]

Considering the inevitably close relationships between the inhabitants of medieval villages and the comparative stability of the population, one would expect default of Englishry only when the dead man was a stranger. It is therefore surprising to find that *murdrum* was adjudged in twenty-one cases at the 1248 Sussex eyre, in fifty-one in 1279 and in ninety-two in 1288, or in about 12 per cent of presented cases of deaths in 1248 and in about 45 per cent in 1288.[3] These figures need to be explained because of both their size and their increase. The presenting kinsmen were required to attend the inquest, the county court and the eyre. If they attended the inquest but later defaulted they suffered financially,[4] but attendance at all three might well have proved equally costly, especially if they lived at a distance from the county court or the eyre. The alternative, to make no presentment at all, seems anti-social in that the hundred in which they lived would inevitably incur *murdrum*, but it is doubtful whether the number of defaults adjudged against it at the eyre made much difference to the hundred, which must have regarded the whole visitation as an elaborate system of taxation. Such it was, and just as there was a limit to the amount of money that a hundred could pay, so there was little doubt that the justices, with much cause or little, would reach that limit.[5] The kinsmen, as members of the hundred, would have to contribute to all fines and amercements imposed upon it. By presenting Englishry they would not have reduced the total amount appreciably, if at all; they would merely have inconvenienced and impoverished themselves. Only in this way is it possible to account for the very large number of failures to present Englishry, although the majority of the deceased were patently English.[6]

[1] 12 Edw. I, c. 5.   [2] *Ibid.*; *Britton*, i.2.15.
[3] J.I.1/909A; 921; 930.
[4] E.g. J.I.1/921, m. 12 (amercement of the kinsman, who had presented Englishry at the inquest, for failing to attend the eyre; *murdrum* imposed upon the hundred; and judgment passed against the coroner for not attaching the kinsman).
[5] Wilts. Arch. and Nat. Hist. Soc., Rec. Branch, XII, 72.
[6] Thus John the chaplain, son of John Baker of Chichester, was slain, and two men were killed in their father's barn, but in neither case was Englishry presented (J.I.1/926, mm. 18, 19d).

Even more surprising than the number of *murdrum* fines is the fact that their number increased during the second half of the thirteenth century, after their abolition in 1259 in cases of death by misadventure.[1] The increase may have been due partly to the determination of the justices to tighten up on procedure in order that no money might be lost by the provision of 1259 and partly to the growing consciousness of the local communities that the number of their defaults mattered little. Presentment of Englishry was ultimately abolished for all cases in 1340,[2] but only after the cessation of the general eyre had made it unprofitable and the war with France had made it yet more anachronistic.[3] For a few more years Englishry was occasionally presented at coroners' inquests, the last known instance being in a case of misadventure in Suffolk in 1362,[4] over a hundred years after it had been abolished for such cases.

Most coroners' juries had to appraise something. Potentially the most valuable were the lands and chattels of homicides and suicides and the chattels of anyone else who fled after an unnatural or sudden death. If homicide or suicide was ultimately adjudged, the king received the year, day and waste of the felon's free lands and his chattels were forfeited completely, as were those of all fugitives, although they were found not guilty.[5] In order to carry out the appraisal the

[1] Provisions of Westminster, c. 25, confirmed by the Statute of Marlborough (52 Hen. III), c. 25 (*Statutes of the Realm*, I, 11, 25). Despite this, *murdrum* occasionally followed neglect of Englishry in Sussex misadventures at the 1262 and 1279 eyres (e.g. J.I.1/912A, m. 35d; 921, m. 7d), the justices possibly taking advantage of a county which was so simple as to state on each occasion that Englishry had to be presented there both in homicides and misadventures (J.I.1/912A, m. 35; 921, m. 1). In 1288, however, no mention was made of misadventures in the initial presentment (J.I.1/926, m. 1) and in no case of misadventure in Sussex after 1279 was Englishry presented or did *murdrum* follow. Oxfordshire and Cambridgeshire had been much more shrewd and had taken precautions to ensure that the 1259 provision was not broken by the justices there by quoting it at the following eyres (J.I.1/701, m. 19; *The Assizes held at Cambridge, 1260*, pp. xiv–xv).
[2] 14 Edw. III, stat. 1, c. 4.
[3] *Speculum*, XII, 296–8; *Year Books 14 & 15 Edward III*, ed. L. O. Pike (Rolls Series, 1889), pp. xv–xvii.
[4] *Select Coroners' Rolls*, pp. xliii–xliv. In 1343, when an inquest was held by the coroner and bailiffs of Norwich on forty people who were drowned when an overloaded ship sank in the River Wensom, it was specifically stated that no Englishry was presented because Norwich was quit of it by a charter of Henry III (*The Records of the City of Norwich*, ed. W. Hudson and J. C. Tingey (1906), I, 222–4).
[5] For the appraisal of the lands and chattels of a fugitive who committed homicide in self-defence and of another who fled after a death by misadventure see *Sx. Arch. Colls.* XCV, 47; *Pleas of the Crown for Gloucester, 1221*, no. 415:

jury had naturally to adjourn to the land or house concerned,[1] where, according to *Fleta*, the sheriff and coroner had to inquire of the fugitive's neighbours whether he had fled on account of the death.[2] Neither lands nor chattels were forfeited until the case had been determined before the justices. After their appraisal the coroner had to commit the chattels to the safe keeping of the township in which they were found[3] or, less frequently, to one or more individuals.[4] The existing bailiffs were left in charge of any lands and had merely to find surety to answer for them before the justices.[5] Once the case had been determined the coroner's concern with the forfeitures ceased, either the sheriff or some franchisal official being ordered by the justices to account for them in the Exchequer.[6]

In practice, the value of the lands and chattels of felons and fugitives was rarely considerable, although there are indications that the coroners' juries tended to under-value them.[7] They found that very suicides' chattels were not forfeited if they had received the last rites of the church (Selden Soc. vol. 24, p. 81), but this was an extremely unlikely event.

[1] Bracton, II, 343; *Officium Coronatoris* (*Statutes of the Realm*, I, 40–1).

[2] i. 25 (Selden Soc. vol. 72, p. 65).

[3] *Ibid.*; Bracton, II, 343; *Officium Coronatoris* (*Statutes of the Realm*, I, 40); *Britton*, i.2.6. In Wales the committal was supposed to be made by view of the sheriff or bailiff and other faithful subjects (12 Edw. I, c. 5). For an example of the delivery of chattels to the four townships which constituted the coroner's jury see *Select Coroners' Rolls*, p. 100. Cf. *Sx. Arch. Colls.* xcv, 47, for a committal to one township.

[4] E.g. J.I.1/941A, m. 1. In the early thirteenth century five men undertook before the coroners and bailiffs of Bristol to produce both the chattels and the wife of a homicide before the justices (*Pleas of the Crown for Gloucester, 1221*, no. 497). In Oxford the chattels were often committed to the custody of the town bailiffs (e.g. Oxon. Hist. Soc. xviii, 164–5, 172). Occasionally the sheriff and coroners were ordered to restore a suicide bondman's chattels to his lord, provided that he found security to answer for them at the eyre if they were adjudged to the king (e.g. *Cal. Close Rolls, 1288–1296*, p. 227).

[5] *Britton*, i.2.6; *Fleta*, i. 26 (Selden Soc. vol. 72, p. 67); *De Catallis Felonum* (*Statutes of the Realm*, I, 230). As these authorities and *The Mirror of Justices* (i. 13: Selden Soc. vol. 7, p. 33) agree, the lands were technically taken into the king's hand by the sheriff, but those suspects who were arrested could be supported from their lands and chattels while they were in prison awaiting trial. In one case the Yorkshire coroners and serjeants attested at the eyre that a homicide had had some chattels but that 'he ate them in prison' (*Rolls of the Justices in Eyre for Yorkshire, 1218–19*, ed. D. M. Stenton (Selden Soc. vol. 56), no. 499).

[6] Only in the early thirteenth century, and then only occasionally, were the coroners made answerable for them (e.g. *Pleas of the Crown for Gloucester, 1221*, no. 486).

[7] In 1345 a Sussex inquest jury said that a fugitive had no chattels, but King's Bench had other information and ordered the sheriff to appraise them (K.B. 29/7, m. 47d). For a case in which the jurors were suspected of undervaluing and another inquiry was ordered by the justices see J.I.1/926, m. 23.

few felons had any lands, while it was unusual for their chattels to be valued at more than a pound. Many were found to have left no chattels at all, while those which were left were usually appraised at a few pence;[1] in one case the homicides left chattels worth three half-pence which were found near the body.[2] The fact that coroners were not concerned with any lands and chattels which were outside their bailiwicks only partly accounts for this. Thus borough and fran-chisal coroners ignored all lands and chattels which belonged to felons and fugitives indicted at their inquests but lay outside their boroughs and franchises,[3] and a coroner of the North Riding of Yorkshire could record that he knew nothing of the chattels of a man who had committed homicide in his bailiwick because he lived in the liberty of Whitby which had coroners of its own.[4] Occasionally the coroner recorded that a fugitive's chattels could not be found,[5] while in one Oxford case the inquest jurors appraised a homicide's chattels with the exception of a book pawned in the University Chest, the price of which they did not know because they could not gain access to it.[6]

In cases of homicide and suicide the coroner had to inquire with what weapon death had been inflicted. *The Mirror of Justices* men-tions staffs, stones and arms,[7] and in practice staffs, axes and knives of various kinds were most commonly employed. Although many indictments contain the words *insultu premeditato* or *ex malicia pre-cogitata*, most medieval homicides were committed during sudden fits of angry violence with whatever weapon the felon might happen to have in his hand. The coroner's jury had to appraise this weapon unless the felon had fled and taken it with him.[8] Normally, however, it was left behind and appraised, the most usual prices ranging from a halfpenny to a shilling.[9] The coroner then committed it to the township or borough,[10] or sometimes specifically to the constable or one or more men of the township,[11] to be kept until the next eyre and

<hr>

[1] E.g. *Sx. Arch. Colls.* xcv, 46–58. In the twenty-eight cases of homicide there only one felon had chattels of an appreciable value—three cart-loads of corn and six of oats worth four marks (*ibid.* p. 57). Only one had any lands at all and they were worth only two shillings a year (*ibid.* p. 47).
[2] J.I.1/921, m. 5d.   [3] E.g. *Sx. Arch. Colls.* xcv, 47–8, 57.
[4] J.I.2/209, m. 6.   [5] E.g. Oxon. Hist. Soc. xviii, 164–5.
[6] *Ibid.* p. 172.   [7] i. 13 (Selden Soc. vol. 7, p. 30).
[8] E.g. *Sx. Arch. Colls.* xcv, 54.
[9] E.g. *ibid.* pp. 48–58. For a large staff adjudged of no value and baslards appraised at two and four shillings see *ibid.* pp. 50–1, 54.
[10] E.g. *ibid.* pp. 50–1.   [11] E.g. *ibid.* p. 53 (constable).

then accounted for. In some places the weapon was called a deodand,[1] and it was undoubtedly confiscated originally for the same
reason as were deodands proper in cases of death by misadventure.

In misadventures the animal or object which caused the death was
forfeited as a deodand. The original theory was that its sin was ex-
piated by its subsequent dedication to the Church, but by 1194 the
practice was to regard deodands as just another source of royal revenue, although they were sometimes granted to lords of liberties
later.[2] The law concerning deodands was: *omnia quae movent ad*
mortem, deodanda sunt. Thus a mill-wheel was often deodand but
not the whole mill, a ship but not its cargo, or a branch and not the
whole tree.[3] Horses were frequently deodand,[4] and the law-books
also specifically mention trees, boats, carts and mills with good reason.[5] The coroner had to obtain full details concerning deodands, including who were their owners and into whose hands they had passed, and enrol them all.[6] Deodands were normally appraised by the
inquest jury, but there is an interesting Oxford case of 1305 in which
the inquest jury consisted of thirty men from four parishes whereas
the deodand was appraised by only twelve.[7] After appraisal, the deodand was usually committed until the eyre to the custody of one or
more townships,[8] but occasionally to the tithingman and his tithing.[9] When the deodand belonged to a very poor man or was essen-

---

[1] E.g. J.I.2/13, m. 2.

[2] E.g. G. Hill, *Treasure Trove in Law and Practice* (Oxford, 1936), pp. 244–51.

[3] *Britton,* i.2.12,14; *The Mirror of Justices,* i. 13 (Selden Soc. vol. 7, p. 31);
Year Books 30 & 31 Edward I, ed. A. J. Horwood (Rolls Series, 1863), p. 524;
Year Books 12 Richard II, ed. G. F. Deiser (Ames Foundation, 1914), pp. 19–20;
Selden Soc. vol. 24, pp. 89, 96.

[4] E.g. *ibid.* p. 89.

[5] *Officium Coronatoris* (*Statutes of the Realm,* 1, 41); *Britton,* i.8; *Fleta,* i. 25
(Selden Soc. vol. 72, p. 65); *The Mirror of Justices,* i. 13 (Selden Soc. vol. 7,
p. 31).

[6] *Britton,* i.2.12, 14.

[7] *Records of Mediaeval Oxford,* pp. 13–14.

[8] E.g. *Select Coroners' Rolls,* pp. 16–17; J.I.2/8, m. 4. This was laid down by
the *Officium Coronatoris* (*Statutes of the Realm,* 1, 41) and *Fleta* (i. 25: Selden
Soc. vol. 72, p. 65).

[9] E.g. Oxon. Hist. Soc. XVIII, 164; *Select Cases of Procedure Without Writ
under Henry III,* ed. H. G. Richardson and G. O. Sayles (Selden Soc. vol. 60),
p. ccii. As with homicides' chattels (see above, p. 30, n. 6), the eyre justices occasionally made coroners answerable at the Exchequer for deodands in the early
thirteenth century (e.g. *Pleas of the Crown for Gloucester, 1221,* no. 487), while
in 1384, although the order was soon cancelled, the Hull coroner was ordered to
sell all the deodands which he had taken into the king's hand and to answer for
the money at the Exchequer (*Cal. Close Rolls, 1381–1385,* p. 444).

tial for someone's livelihood, it was sometimes restored to him by a special writ, but, unless specifically excused, he was then obliged to account for it at the eyre.[1] Some other deodands were left with their owners perforce, as when the moving parts of a mill became deodand in Buckinghamshire; the coroner made the lord of the mill find sureties to appear before the justices and answer for their value.[2] William Barton, the coroner concerned, was particularly meticulous, for he not only attached by pledges the lords of most deodands, but normally did the same to lords of wells in which people had been drowned.[3]

Deodands caused the coroner much trouble. On the one hand, lords of liberties often made strenuous efforts not to forfeit deodands belonging to them,[4] and, on the other, the men of the townships or hundred often did their utmost to shield their unfortunate fellows who owned deodands. The coroner's jury was often amerced either for falsely appraising a deodand[5] or for not presenting it to the coroner at all.[6] It is clear from the wording of some inquests on the coroners' rolls that the coroner sometimes differed from his jurors as to what should be appraised as deodand, usually with good reason. In 1383 one of the wheels of a cart ran over a man, who later died. William de Ramenham, the Berkshire coroner, 'diligently inquired' of the jurors the value of the cart and horses and into whose hands they had come. The jurors, however, asserted that neither the cart nor the horses ought to be appraised and forfeited as the cause of death, but the wheel alone, which they valued at a mere twelvepence. But the horses and cart were all moving, and the fact that Ramenham enrolled the conversation in such detail proves that he

[1] E.g. *Cal. Close Rolls, 1272–1279*, p. 209; *1288–1296*, pp. 21, 58 (horses and carts).

[2] J.I.2/14, m. 2.   [3] E.g. J.I.2/13, m. 3; 14, m. 3.

[4] See below, p. 127.

[5] E.g. J.I.1/926, m. 21d. This is a remarkable case in that twelve townships and twelve jurors falsely appraised the deodand.

[6] E.g. Selden Soc. vol. 56, no. 826. The presenting jurors at the eyre might be similarly amerced. In one case they presented that a man had been drowned in the Severn after falling from a cliff, which would have entailed no deodand, whereas according to the coroners' rolls and the four townships he had fallen from a boat, which was accordingly adjudged deodand (*Pleas of the Crown for Gloucester, 1221*, no. 231). In a more remarkable Somerset case a township was amerced for presenting as deodand a vessel which had contained hot water into which a boy fell to his death and not adding, as did the coroners' rolls, that the boy had fallen in from fear of a dog which he was striking (Somerset Rec. Soc. XI, 935). The theory was probably that the dog, as 'moving to the death', should also have been deodand.

D

wished to dissociate himself from the jurors' decision.[1] At another
inquest the same coroner wished to award a barge as deodand, but
the jurors would not agree that it was moving to the death.[2] Finally,
in 1302 an Oxford coroner was at pains to enrol that a boat from
which a drunken man had been drowned was appraised at only a
shilling because it was in a very poor condition.[3]

Apart from the sealing of the written inquest by the jurors,[4] there
was nothing more to do at most inquests. But at those rare inquests
held after outlaws, fugitives and straying or returning abjurors of
the realm had been pursued and beheaded in the hue and cry, as by
law they should have been, the coroner had also to send the head to
the county gaol; in Northamptonshire he ordered the four townships to carry it to Northampton castle.[5] In cases of suicide the
coroner had to order the body to be buried in unhallowed ground.[6]
Finally, when, as frequently happened, anybody had been drowned
in a well, the coroner had to order it to be filled in. One version of the
rule, cited throughout the Middle Ages, was that the coroner should
order the tithingman and his tithing to fill in such wells and enrol the
order so that the tithing might be punished at the eyre if it defaulted.[7]
This may have been the early practice, but normally it was the lord
of the well who was ordered to fill it in at his own expense, and, according to *Fleta*, he had to pay an amercement at the eyre even if he
obeyed.[8] William Barton's attaching by sureties the lords of such
wells[9] was probably to ensure that they ultimately paid their amercements, while in 1334, when a woman's death had been caused by
falling into a well, the coroners and bailiffs of Oxford ordered the
owner to fill it up under a penalty of twenty shillings for default and
they also made him find two sureties.[10] Judgment had been passed
against an earlier Oxford coroner for not attaching a man in whose
court there was a well in which a drowning had occurred.[11] In one exceptional Gloucestershire case of 1372, instead of ordering the well
to be filled in, the coroner ordered it to be forfeited to the king as if
it were a normal deodand.[12] It was most frequently small children

---

[1] J.I.2/9, m. 5. [2] *Ibid.* m. 6.
[3] Oxon. Hist. Soc. XVIII, 164. [4] E.g. J.I.2/71, m. 1.
[5] E.g. *Select Coroners' Rolls*, pp. 75–6 (straying abjuror).
[6] E.g. J.I.2/191, m. 6d.
[7] E.g. Selden Soc. vol. 24, p. 87; British Museum, Harleian MS. 5145, f. 32b
(a corrupt fifteenth-century text of the *Officium Coronatoris*).
[8] i. 25 (Selden Soc. vol. 72, p. 65). [9] See above, pp. 24, 33.
[10] *Records of Mediaeval Oxford*, p. 31. [11] Oxon. Hist. Soc. XVIII, 197.
[12] J.I.2/35, m. 3.

and drunkards who fell into wells, but sometimes a man was drowned while trying to rescue another who had fallen in.[1] While most deaths in wells were from drowning, a few were caused by suffocation from the foul air.[2] That wells were filled only partly for safety and partly also for hygienic reasons is suggested by the absence of any such order after a Londoner's death by drowning when he fell through the rotten planks on which he had been sitting into a latrine.[3]

The author of *The Mirror of Justices* was guilty of wishful thinking when he wrote that coroners should hold inquests into homicides by false judgment or false evidence,[4] but correct in saying that they had to hold inquests into every death in prison.[5] According to *Britton*, if prisoners were buried without the coroner's view the townships where they were buried should be amerced.[6] In the fifteenth century it could be stated that the gaoler should suffer.[7] Both dicta were probably rash generalisations from the most common occurrences, for the plea rolls prove that whoever buried the body was amerced.[8] Only occasionally can one discover who sent for the coroner. It must usually have been the gaoler, but in 1348 it was the sheriff of Cambridgeshire when a man who was in his custody died.[9] The normal jury for inquests on dead prisoners consisted of twelve men,[10] although other forms are not unknown.[11]

The coroner had to inquire whether death had been caused by long imprisonment or torture,[12] and if he found that the gaoler or others had hastened death by harsh custody or pain inflicted on the prisoner they had to be arrested as homicides immediately.[13] Most prisoners, however, were found to have died naturally and the jurors

[1] E.g. J.I.2/11, m. 6.
[2] E.g. *Cal. Coroners Rolls of London*, pp. 198–9 (suffocation in foul air while cleaning a well); *Records of Mediaeval Oxford*, p. 48 (suffocation of two men for lack of air after descending a well—one to fetch a bucket which had fallen in and the other to help him). In 1344 an Oxford woman fell down a well while drawing water, climbed out by ladder and on her way home fell down in the street and died (*ibid.* p. 31).
[3] *Cal. Coroners Rolls of London*, pp. 167–8.
[4] i. 13 (Selden Soc. vol. 7, p. 31).
[5] *Ibid.* Even clerks had to be viewed, whether they were in a royal or an episcopal prison (Selden Soc. vol. 24, lvi, 141).
[6] i.21.5.   [7] *Year Books 9–10 Henry V*, p. 23.
[8] E.g. J.I.1/912A, m. 44d (steward); 926, m. 21d (chaplain).
[9] J.I.2/18, m. 20.   [10] E.g. *Select Coroners' Rolls*, pp. 79–81.
[11] E.g. the castle ward and twelve men (J.I.2/17, m. 29) and four townships, the castle ward and twelve men (J.I.2/18, m. 53).
[12] *The Mirror of Justices*, i. 13 (Selden Soc. vol. 7, p. 31).
[13] *Britton*, i.12.4; 21.5; *Fleta*, i. 26 (Selden Soc. vol. 72, p. 68).

usually specifically stated that death was not caused by duress or by default of custody.[1] When used of deaths in prison the term 'natural death' had a very wide connotation. Prisons, with their unhealthy conditions—men living together in considerable numbers with inadequate food and drink—were breeding grounds of plague and all sorts of infectious disease. Within a few months in 1425 Robert Scot, the lieutenant of John Holland, earl of Huntingdon, the constable and coroner of the Tower of London, held nine inquests on prisoners who died of the plague in the Tower;[2] and, as seven of these were hostages for King James I of Scotland and another was a bishop, it may be assumed that their environment compared favourably with that of the average felon in the county gaol. In just over two months of 1316 there were twenty-eight deaths in Wallingford gaol.[3] Deaths from disease, cold, hunger and thirst and from *peine forte et dure* were common to all gaols,[4] but they were all regarded as 'natural deaths'. In no case is a gaoler known to have been specifically indicted, probably through fear of what might happen if one of the jurors chanced to be imprisoned later. A coroner's jury found that a prisoner had died in Reading gaol from lack of food, but added that they did not know who ought to have provided it.[5] Another prisoner escaped from Canterbury gaol, was recaptured and flogged, and then died in gaol. The county coroner held an inquest and his jury returned a verdict of death from natural causes. The city coroner then held an independent inquest and his jury found that the flogging had caused the death. Nevertheless, the city jurors presented this at the eyre as a natural death.[6] Only rarely was a radically different verdict returned, as on the prisoner in Reading gaol who had been wounded in the hue and cry.[7]

---

[1] E.g. J.I.1/926, m. 21d; J.I.2/9, m. 1.   [2] E.163/7/10.
[3] *Hist. MSS. Comm., 6th Report*, App. p. 584. For other examples see M. Bassett, 'Newgate Prison in the Middle Ages', *Speculum*, XVIII, 245–6.
[4] E.g. J.I.2/61, m. 15; 108A, m. 1; 110, m. 3; 218, m. 56.
[5] J.I.2/9, m. 1.   [6] Selden Soc. vol. 24, lvi.   [7] J.I.2/9, m. 1d.

CHAPTER III

ABJURATIONS OF THE REALM

THERE were two types of sanctuaries in medieval England. Some abbeys and minsters had special rights of sanctuary, which usually extended for some distance, often a league, around the house.[1] Anyone who took refuge in such a sanctuary could remain there with impunity for life. These chartered sanctuaries were few, but every consecrated monastery, church or chapel with its graveyard could provide sanctuary for a limited period. The great majority of those who sought sanctuary there were either robbers or homicides, the former preponderating,[2] and many of them took sanctuary either when pursued by the hue and cry immediately after committing a felony[3] or after breaking out of prison, a frequent occurrence.[4] They could remain there unharmed for forty days.[5]

Cases of forcible extraction of felons from sanctuary were rare, since violation of sanctuary was an extremely serious offence.[6] It invariably resulted in excommunication if the offenders were laymen

---

[1] For details see J. C. Cox, *The Sanctuaries and Sanctuary Seekers of Mediaeval England* (1911), pp. 48–226.

[2] *Ibid.* pp. 287–301; H. M. Whitley, 'Sanctuary in Sussex', *Sx. Arch. Colls.* LXI, 85; R. M. Serjeantson, 'Sanctuary Seekers in Northamptonshire', *Associated Architectural Socs. Reports and Papers*, XXXII, 484.

[3] E.g. *Sx. Arch. Colls.* XCVI, 24.

[4] E.g. *Cal. Pat. Rolls, 1324–1327*, p. 178. Medieval gaols were very easily broken and Chichester gaol at one time lay open on the side which abutted upon the Friars Preachers' churchyard (*Cal. Inqs. Misc.* III, 520). In 1276 one man abjured the realm in Huntingdonshire after breaking two prisons (*Select Coroners' Rolls*, p. 36), and other escapes were made while the felons were being taken to gaol (e.g. *Ass. Arch. Socs.* XXXII, 195), or from the stocks (e.g. *ibid.* pp. 196–9). A Sussex man, who had been condemned to death at the court held outside the gate of Hastings castle, was rescued by armed men, including the castle chaplain, while he was confessing prior to execution, and escaped to the castle chapel (J.I.1/924, m. 45d). While a thief was being hanged at Petworth the rope broke, he escaped alive to a church and abjured the realm (J.I.1/921, m. 23d). Finally a hanged Somerset thief was *en route* for the cemetery to be buried when he came back to life, was carried to a church, completely recovered and later abjured (Cox, *Sanctuaries and Sanctuary Seekers*, pp. 297–8).

[5] According to *Britton* (i.17.2) the forty days were measurable from the day of the coroner's arrival at the church, but all other authorities agree that it was from the first day of sanctuary (e.g. Bracton, II, 383; *Fleta*, i. 29 (Selden Soc. vol. 72, p. 76)).

[6] Bracton, II, 383.

and the restoration of the felons to sanctuary.[1] Sanctuary was only denied to men who committed sacrilege, such as a felony while in sanctuary.[2] A Buckinghamshire thief, for example, was pursued to a church where he stole the vestry keys in order to try to escape. For this sacrilege he was extracted from the church and executed in the highway, an event which necessitated a coroner's inquest.[3] According to *The Mirror of Justices*, habitual, known or convicted felons could be dragged from sanctuary,[4] but practice did not conform to this. Even Bracton's more moderate statement that those who sought sanctuary after being condemned by the country, whether before or after judgment, or after being arrested in possession of stolen goods, could not stay in the church for forty days but had to leave on the arrival of the justices or coroners,[5] was a rarely realised ideal. There was one extraordinary Northamptonshire case in which a thief was hanged and his body carried to a church, where he revived and later abjured the realm. The eyre justices declared this abjuration to be illegal since the abjuror was outside the law,[6] but, strictly, so were very many men whose abjurations went unquestioned.[7] Normally, sanctuary seekers could exercise their right to abjure the realm before the coroner at any time within their forty days.

In thirteenth-century Sussex the number of recorded cases of sanctuary seeking averaged around thirty for each seven-year period,[8] which was certainly no higher than the number in other counties.[9] Thus, although abjurations of the realm cannot compare with inquests on dead bodies in the amount of trouble which they caused the coroner, they still added considerably to his burden. Both necessitated much travelling, especially in large counties.

[1] *Fleta*, i. 29 (Selden Soc. vol. 72, p. 76). E.g. J.I.3/111, m. 5; *Register of Bishop Robert Rede, 1397–1415*, ed. C. Deedes, I (Sx. Rec. Soc. VIII), 44–7; *Cal. Pat. Rolls, 1405–1408*, p. 191. In 1299 it was alleged that a Shropshire coroner had sent to Shrewsbury castle a clerk who had been dragged from sanctuary by Ludlow men; his restoration to sanctuary was ordered if the allegation was found to be true (*Cal. Close Rolls, 1296–1302*, p. 267).

[2] *The Mirror of Justices*, i. 13 (Selden Soc. vol. 7, p. 34).

[3] J.I.2/12, m. 5. But when a rector was killed in a churchyard and the felon took sanctuary, he was allowed to remain there for forty days although not to abjure the realm (H. M. Cam, *The Hundred and the Hundred Rolls* (1930), pp. 193–4).

[4] i. 13 (Selden Soc. vol. 7, pp. 33–4).   [5] II, 383.

[6] *Ass. Arch. Socs.* XXXII, 464.   [7] E.g. above, p. 37, n. 4.

[8] *Sx. Arch. Colls.* LXI, 85–9.

[9] There were 363 in Northamptonshire between 1275 and 1329 (*Ass. Arch. Socs.* XXXII, 484).

Abjurations could only be made from a consecrated church or chapel. If a felon took sanctuary in a church which had not been consecrated, he could be forcibly removed from it,[1] while both the coroner and the township or borough were amerced if they allowed a felon to abjure the realm from a place which had no sanctuary rights.[2] The coroner had to be summoned to any consecrated church or chapel whenever a sanctuary seeker asked for him, as the surviving records of abjurations prove,[3] and not as soon as the felon had taken sanctuary as *Fleta* believed;[4] and there is no record evidence to support *Britton's* inherently improbable assertion that the coroner was not obliged to go if he did not want to.[5] The fact that the felon could choose when to send for the coroner, coupled with his right to remain in sanctuary for forty days, accounts for the delays which often occurred between taking sanctuary and sending for the coroner. In one Sussex case the coroner arrived at the church exactly forty days after the felon had taken sanctuary.[6] The felons knew that they had nothing to lose by such delays and a fair chance of being able to escape—a chance which increased with the passage of time. The onerous duty of guarding churches in which felons had taken sanctuary was often performed inadequately.

Some local official must always have organised the guarding of felons in sanctuary before the coroner's arrival. In Norwich it was the bailiffs[7] and, at least sometimes, in Northamptonshire the chief constable of the hundred.[8] It probably depended on local custom and the size of the group responsible. Where, as in places in Sussex and Leicestershire, one township was responsible,[9] the village constable probably arranged the guard duty; when the frankpledge stood guard,[10] it must have been the tithingman; and when four townships did so,[11] it would have needed an hundredal official. It may well be wrong to see hard and fast local customs here. Those

---

[1] E.g. *Year Books 30 & 31 Edward I*, p. 541. In this case he unsuccessfully petitioned to be restored to it, but the justices seem to have regarded him as the victim of misfortune since they tried to persuade him to turn approver.

[2] E.g. E. A. Fuller, 'Pleas of the Crown at Bristol, 15 Edward I', *Trans. Bristol & Glos. Arch. Soc.* xxii, 163–4 (abjuration from a house of the tenure of the prior of St John of Jerusalem).

[3] E.g. *Sx. Arch. Colls.* xcvi, 24.   [4] i. 29 (Selden Soc. vol. 72, p. 76).

[5] i.17.1.   [6] J.I.1/926, m. 7d.

[7] *The Records of the City of Norwich*, I, 213.

[8] E.g. J.I.2/117B, m. 3.   [9] E.g. J.I.1/926, m. 12; J.I.2/49, m. 3.

[10] E.g. *Cal. Inqs. Misc.* I, 2254 (Leicestershire).

[11] E.g. J.I.1/690, m. 4 (Nottinghamshire).

participating in the hue and cry or the inhabitants of the immediate
neighbourhood of the church would obviously provide the guard
alone at the outset, but if the felon delayed sending for the coroner
they would naturally soon agitate to have neighbouring tithings and
townships called in to share the duty. That this was not the universal practice, however, is proved by amercements of single townships for the escape from sanctuary of felons who had been there for
a fortnight or more.[1]

The feelings of the localities on the subject of guarding churches
can sometimes be discovered. A captured thief who escaped to
Sompting church was allowed to come out, the whole tithing of
Storrington going surety for his appearance at the 1248 Sussex eyre.
As was inevitable, he did not appear then and the tithing was amerced[2]—an event which it must have anticipated and considered pre-
ferable to guarding the church. In 1305 Swansea declared itself not
bound to guard churches to which felons had fled; after a long
struggle London successfully maintained a similar claim; and in
1327 the abbot and convent of Bury St Edmunds released the aldermen and burgesses from this duty, undertaking to guard sanctuary
seekers at their own risk.[3] Apart from its obvious inconvenience, the
duty of guarding churches sometimes brought physical dangers,
since the forcible rescue of sanctuary seekers was not unknown.[4]
Hence the guarding of churches was frequently inadequate and,
although they inevitably meant an amercement for the township or other body responsible, escapes from sanctuary were
common.[5]

---

[1] E.g. J.I.1/926, m. 12.   [2] J.I.1/909A, m. 23d.

[3] Cox, *Sanctuaries and Sanctuary Seekers*, p. 241; *Cal. Coroners Rolls of London*, pp. xviii–xix.

[4] In 1311 a Norfolk coroner was prevented from taking an abjuration by men who beat those who were guarding the church and rescued the felon from sanctuary (*Cal. Pat. Rolls, 1307–1313*, p. 425). One of the men who were guard-ing a London church in which a robber had taken sanctuary, hearing a noise inside, went to a broken window through which he feared the robber might be escaping and was there fatally wounded by a clerk (*Memorials of London*, ed. Riley, pp. 16–17). Adam de Osegodby, a clerk, and others successfully secured the escape of one felon from an Oxford church in 1324, but within a week Osegodby was found dead in the High Street, having been killed by one of those who were guarding another felon in sanctuary, whom Osegodby had also pre-sumably been trying to release. The slayer fled out of fear. Later the death occurred of two other men, one a constable, whom Osegodby had wounded on the night of his death (*Records of Mediaeval Oxford*, pp. 22–3).

[5] E.g. J.I.1/926, m. 12 (township amerced). In the case mentioned above (p. 37, n. 4), in which a condemned thief escaped to the chapel of Hastings castle, he

Nevertheless, many sanctuary seekers sooner or later sent for the coroner, who was naturally summoned by representatives of the body which was guarding the church.[1] When summoned, the coroner was supposed to order the local bailiff, usually the hundred bailiff, to cause certain people to appear before him at the church on a certain day. According to *Britton* these people were the neighbours and the four neighbouring townships,[2] while the Statute of Wales called them 'the good and lawful men of the neighbourhood'.[3] There was a characteristic diversity in local practice. Sometimes the coroner summoned only those who had guarded the church. In fourteenth-century Nottinghamshire, for example, abjurations were commonly made before the coroner and the four townships which had summoned him,[4] and sometimes, as in Leicestershire, they took place before the coroner and one township.[5] But the area represented at abjurations was often greater than that responsible for guarding the church. In one Suffolk case, for example, the lawful men of the township summoned the coroner, but the neighbouring townships also attended the abjuration.[6]

The body which attended varied widely not only from county to county but also from year to year or from district to district within some counties. Within a period of twenty years in fourteenth-century Leicestershire there were abjurations before one, four and six townships,[7] four being the normal number, while during much the same period abjurations were made in Norfolk before either the men of the hundred and four townships, or twelve men.[8] If more details were available some development like that of the coroner's inquest jury would probably be found to have occurred in most counties, the responsibility for attending abjurations passing from the townships to the men of the hundred through an intermediate stage when the

was rescued from the chapel after eight days and helped to cross the Channel; the steward of the rape was fined ten marks for allowing the rescue and for not setting a guard round the chapel.

[1] E.g. *Cal. Inqs. Misc.* I, 2254 (frankpledge); J.I.1/690, m. 4 (four townships); J.I.2/9, m. 1d (men of Wallingford). According to *The Mirror of Justices* (i. 13: Selden Soc. vol. 7, p. 34) 'townships' had to guard felons throughout their period of sanctuary and to send for the coroner; there is no evidence to support the further statement that an order to this effect was given by Henry III at Clarendon.

[2] i.2.16. By 'neighbours' the author must have meant the men of the township in which the church was situated.

[3] 12 Edw. 1, c. 5. [4] E.g. J.I.1/690, m. 3d. [5] E.g. J.I.2/52, m. 5.

[6] *Select Coroners' Rolls*, p. 103. [7] J.I.2/52, m. 5; 59, mm. 12, 18.

[8] J.I.2/102, m. 23d; 105, m. 4.

presence of both was required.[1] Towns had their own peculiarities. The whole town was often required to attend, especially in the thirteenth century,[2] but in some places only certain wards or parishes were summoned,[3] while in Norwich abjurations were made in the presence of four parishes, knights and other men.[4] The exact constitution of the body seems never to have been queried either for county or borough abjurations, as long as there had been no disobedience to the coroner and a representative gathering of the community had attended. The abjuration ceremony was sufficiently colourful and entertaining to ensure a good attendance, and amercements for failure to attend were incomparably fewer than for failure to attend inquests.[5]

When the coroner arrived at the church he gave the felon in sanctuary the choice of either surrendering to the law or abjuring the realm.[6] Few adopted the first alternative, since it was usually because they were unwilling to stand their trial that felons took sanctuary. Many of those who surrendered were clerks, who did not have to face the death penalty even if they were convicted.[7] The coroner had to commit to gaol those who surrendered in order that they might stand their trial.[8] The Cambridgeshire coroners delivered such men to the constable of the township and the bailiffs of the hundred, who were given the duty of conducting them to the county gaol where they had to be kept.[9]

Those who refused to surrender and confessed their felonies to

---

[1] Sussex seems to show such a development (e.g. J.I.1/921, m. 17d; *Sx. Arch. Colls.* xcvi, 24); the twelve free men of the hundred there sometimes included two constables of the hundred (*ibid.*). The townships were probably represented as at coroners' inquests. Some Northamptonshire abjurations were held before four townships and by view of twenty-four lawful men (e.g. *Ass. Arch. Socs.* xxxii, 225).

[2] E.g. J.I.1/923, m. 21d (Arundel); J.I.2/50, m. 1 (14th-century Leicester).

[3] E.g. *Bristol & Glos. Arch. Soc.* xxii, 163–4 (five wards).

[4] E.g. J.I.2/102, m. 26d.

[5] For examples of such occasional amercements see J.I.1/912A, m. 36d; 921, m. 17d. The coroners noted any defaults (e.g. *Ass. Arch. Socs.* xxxii, 208).

[6] *Bracton*, II, 382; *Britton*, i.17.1; *Fleta*, i. 29 (Selden Soc. vol. 72, p. 76); *The Mirror of Justices*, i. 13 (Selden Soc. vol. 7, p. 34).

[7] When the clergy protested that clerks who were found in the realm after their abjuration were put to death, they were naturally told that anyone in sanctuary who asserted his clergy could not be compelled to abjure but could enjoy benefit of clergy if he surrendered (9 Edw. II, stat. 1 (*Articuli Cleri*), c. 15).

[8] *The Mirror of Justices*, i. 13 (Selden Soc. vol. 7, p. 34). E.g. J.I.2/117B, m. 3; 180, m. 1d.

[9] E.g. J.I.2/18, mm. 32, 38. Cf. J.I.2/117B, m. 3.

the coroner were given the further choice of either abjuring at once or remaining in the church for a further period not exceeding forty days from their first arrival. While many abjured on the day of the coroner's arrival,[1] many others, presumably having second thoughts when given the choice, elected to wait. The latter were wise, especially those who told the coroner that they would not abjure until the fortieth day,[2] for escape was still a strong possibility, despite the coroner's having to order the church to be guarded for as long as the felon remained in sanctuary. According to *Britton* the townships had to guard the church, the coroner giving the order to the constables,[3] but practice was again fluid; there are examples of coroners ordering one and four townships to guard the church.[4] In towns the usual practice was for the coroners to order the town bailiffs to appoint the guard.[5]

Escapes after the coroner's first arrival were fairly common, but the townships were amerced for escapes and there may therefore have been some justification for the clerical complaint, remedied by the *Articuli Cleri*, that sanctuary seekers were guarded so closely by armed men that they were allowed neither to leave hallowed ground to relieve nature nor to have the necessaries of life brought to them. For zealous watchmen, however, the remedy had an almost nullifying 'saving clause': the guard was not to stay in the churchyard unless peril of escape made it essential.[6] Over-strict guarding may well account for those frequent cases, otherwise difficult to explain, when abjurations were made only a few days after the coroner's first arrival and long before the expiry of the forty days.[7] It was also in the guard's interest to capture any sanctuary seekers who escaped. Their attempts may account for some of the examples of felons taking sanctuary but refusing to abjure, escaping, later taking sanctuary in another church, confessing again before the same coroner and abjuring the realm.[8]

If the felon refused to abjure or to surrender to justice at the end of his forty days in sanctuary, his privileged position came to an end.

[1] E.g. *Sx. Arch. Colls.* xcvi, 23–5.
[2] E.g. *Ass. Arch. Socs.* xxxii, 226–7. In one of these two cases the felon escaped before the fortieth day.
[3] i.17.2.   [4] E.g. *Ass. Arch. Socs.* xxxii, 215 (one); J.I.2/236, m. 1 (four).
[5] E.g. J.I. 2/33A, m. 10; 178, m. 15; *Ass. Arch. Socs.* xxxii, 226–7; *Records of Mediaeval Oxford*, pp. 30, 38.
[6] 9 Edw. II, stat. 1, c. 10.
[7] E.g. *Sx. Arch. Colls.* xcvi, 25; *Records of Mediaeval Oxford*, p. 38.
[8] E.g. *Ass. Arch. Socs.* xxxii, 215.

He still could not be forcibly removed, but from being a duty it became an offence to provide him with food and drink.[1] *Britton* gave the penalties for providing for or communicating with such men as hanging for laymen and banishment for clergy,[2] and in 1464 a Norwich coroner publicly proclaimed that nobody was to give, send or throw food to one such man under penalty of a charge of felony.[3] Such men were tantamount to outlaws.[4] They still had to be guarded because they had to be imprisoned on their surrender.[5] Only a few desperate men refused to abjure on the fortieth day, for there was much less chance of escape with their declining strength thereafter than there had been before; seeing a term to its labours and with the hourly expectation of an attempted flight, the guard would be doubly alert. In 1344 a sanctuary seeker confessed to homicide before a Nottinghamshire coroner but refused to abjure or to surrender. After forty days he was still obdurate. The coroner therefore ordered all the doors to be guarded and withdrew. Five days later the felon died in the church.[6]

In the great majority of cases, however, taking sanctuary was followed sooner or later by abjuration of the realm before the coroner and the assembled representatives of the neighbourhood. The ceremony most commonly took place at the gate or stile of the churchyard.[7] The first essential was a confession, and in those cases in which the abjuror had confessed on the coroner's first arrival and then delayed his abjuration, the confession probably had to be repeated. Despite *Britton's* statement that men guilty of trespass might abjure the realm,[8] the abjuror had to confess that he had committed a felony. In 1241, for example, judgment was passed against a Berkshire coroner for causing a man to abjure the realm 'for petty larceny, namely for corn worth sixpence';[9] stealing less than a shilling did not constitute a felony. It is probable that a number of the

---

[1] Bracton, II, 383; *Fleta*, i. 29 (Selden Soc. vol. 72, p. 76); *The Mirror of Justices*, i. 13 (Selden Soc. vol. 7, p. 35).

[2] i.17.5.   [3] Cox, *Sanctuaries and Sanctuary Seekers*, pp. 239–40.

[4] *Britton*, i.17.2.

[5] *Britton* undoubtedly exaggerated when saying that the whole county was charged with their custody (*ibid.*).

[6] J.I.1/690, m. 4.

[7] *Britton*, i.17.3; *The Mirror of Justices*, i. 13 (Selden Soc. vol. 7, p. 34); *Tractatus de Officiis Coronatorum* (*Statutes of the Realm*, I, 250). In Rye the abjuror sat on the churchyard stile (*Borough Customs*, ed. M. Bateson, II (Selden Soc. vol. 21), 38, n. 4).

[8] i.17.8.   [9] J.I.1/37, m. 29.

felonies confessed by abjurors were invented for the occasion under
the inspiration of fear. As an example, a Leicestershire chaplain,
who was committing adultery with a woman, saw her husband's
father approaching the house. He first hid in a chest, but, fearing that
the father would kill him, he got out and fled to the church. Still
fearing for his life, he refused to surrender at the coroner's request,
but the coroner rightly refused to allow him to abjure the realm unless he confessed to a felony. He therefore confessed to stealing
eightpence from the chest in which he had hidden and abjured,[1] although he had still not confessed to a felony. His abjuration was later
pardoned, as was that of John Brambylle, an Etchingham labourer,
who, although guiltless, had confessed to a robbery and a homicide
and abjured before a Sussex coroner after taking sanctuary in Tice-
hurst church because he feared the enmity of a certain John Palmer
and after others had encouraged this fear by telling him that Palmer
would go to considerable lengths to secure his death.[2] These pardons
were in accordance with the law-book precept that when a man abjured through fear and it was proved that he was innocent of the
felony which he had confessed, he might return; his heirs were not
to be disinherited, but his chattels had to remain forfeited on account of his flight.[3] *Fleta* urged that coroners should exercise great
care to discover whether fear had inspired false confessions.[4] This
can rarely have been possible, but the rolls of one Sussex coroner
proved that the abjuration of a man, whose horse had accidentally
killed a woman, had been due to fear and not to any felony, and the
justices therefore quashed it.[5]

After confessing, the abjuror had to take the oath of abjuration.[6]
He swore on the Gospels to leave the realm of England and never return except with the express permission of the king or his heirs;[7] to
hasten by the direct road to his port, not leaving the king's highway
under pain of arrest as a felon nor staying at any one place for more
than one night; on arriving at the port, to seek diligently for passage

---

[1] *Cal. Inqs. Misc.* I, 2254.   [2] *Cal. Pat. Rolls, 1441–1446*, pp. 190–1.
[3] *Britton*, i.17.6.   [4] i. 29 (Selden Soc. vol. 72, p. 77).
[5] J.I.1/921, m. 14.
[6] For slightly differing forms of the oath see Bracton, II, 382; *Britton*, i.17.3;
Fleta, i. 29 (Selden Soc. vol. 72, p. 77); *The Mirror of Justices*, i. 13 (Selden Soc.
vol. 7, p. 34); *Abjuratio et Juramentum Latronum* (*Statutes of the Realm*, I, 250);
Ass. Arch. Socs. XXXII, 193.
[7] *The Mirror of Justices* (i. 13: Selden Soc. vol. 7, p. 34) wrongly implies that
the abjuror could return without permission after the death of the reigning
king.

across the sea, delaying only one tide if possible; if he could not secure a passage, to walk into the sea up to his knees every day as a
token of his desire to cross it; and, if he was still unsuccessful at the
end of forty days, to take sanctuary again at the port.

The word 'port' was given a wide interpretation. Abjurors did not
abjure all the king's territories, but only the kingdom of England.[1]
They therefore did not need to have a sea-port for crossing to
France, but could go to Ireland from a west-coast port or to Scotland via a Border town. Although Channel ports were much the most
popular, with Dover well in the lead, some abjurors left England by
Berwick-upon-Tweed for Scotland. Useful analyses have been
made for some counties of the ports for which the abjurors set out
and the number of days assigned by the coroners for the journeys,[2]
for the coroners had to name the places on the route at which the abjurors were allowed to spend the night. The number of days allowed
for the journey depended on the physical condition of the abjuror,[3]
and many coroners made generous allowances for sickness and infirmity, even occasionally allowing a stay of two nights at one place.[4]
According to Fleta, the coroner could supply the abjuror with a
'schedule' containing the name of the port and details of the journey,[5] but there is no evidence that this was ever done.

During the first half of the thirteenth century, abjurors could
choose their own ports of embarkation.[6] Bracton regarded this as an
established rule,[7] and as late as the 1240's the justices queried as-
signments of ports by coroners.[8] Britton[9] and Fleta[10] follow Bracton,
but The Mirror of Justices, while agreeing that by law abjurors had
the choice, called it an abuse that they were not allowed this right
but had their ports assigned and journeys delimited by the coroners.[11]
Indeed, before this time many coroners had adopted the practice of
assigning ports[12] and in 1279 judgment had been given against the

[1] Bracton, II, 382–3.
[2] Cox, Sanctuaries and Sanctuary Seekers, pp. 25–31; Cal. Coroners Rolls of
London, p. xxi; J. C. Cox, 'The Sanctuaries and Sanctuary Seekers of Yorkshire', Arch. Journ. 2nd ser. XVIII, 289–90.
[3] Fleta, i. 29 (Selden Soc. vol. 72, p. 77).
[4] E.g. J.I.2/104, mm. 19d, 20d, 31, 49d; Cox, Sanctuaries and Sanctuary
Seekers, p. 30.
[5] i. 29 (Selden Soc. vol. 72, p. 77). [6] E.g. Curia Regis Rolls, XIV, 464.
[7] II, 382. [8] E.g. Somerset Rec. Soc. XI, 804.
[9] i.17.4. [10] i. 29 (Selden Soc. vol. 72, p. 77).
[11] i. 13; v. i. 23 (Selden Soc. vol. 7, pp. 34, 157–8).
[12] E.g. Select Coroners' Rolls, p. 38.

Arundel coroner for allowing an abjuror to choose his own port and not assigning one to him.[1] In 1284 the custom of coroners assigning ports was imposed by statute upon Wales,[2] while it was popularised for England by treatises which ultimately gained the force of statutes,[3] and shortly after 1300 the royal justices were maintaining that abjurors were to take the port assigned by the coroner and none other.[4] It was probably because the law-books and statutes showed such an equal division of opinion on the subject that, although in the majority of cases abjurors were assigned ports, throughout the Middle Ages a considerable number were still allowed a choice.[5]

Some coroners obeyed the letter of both laws by allowing the abjurors to choose their ports and then assigning them to them.[6] Others regularly allowed them to choose one port only to assign them another lying in the opposite direction,[7] the monumental example being a Northamptonshire one: abjuration to Scotland was requested and the coroner thereupon assigned Dover.[8] Such coroners, though few, were wise. They were not merely indulging a perverted sense of humour, but must have guessed that the law's interests were not best served by allowing abjurors to take a route of their choice. Similarly, when two or more felons abjured from one church on the same day, the wise course was to assign to each a different port.[9] There is no known authority for the judgment given at the 1313–14 Kent eyre against a coroner for assigning Portsmouth to an abjuror when he might have assigned a much nearer port[10]—an extraordinary judgment considering the large number of Yorkshire abjurors who were regularly assigned Dover.[11]

In order that he might be distinguished from the ordinary wayfarer, the abjuror had to undertake his journey carrying a wooden

[1] J.I.1/923, m. 21d.   [2] 12 Edw. I, c. 5.
[3] E.g. *Abjuratio et Juramentum Latronum*; *Tractatus de Officiis Coronatorum* (*Statutes of the Realm*, I, 250).
[4] E.g. *Year Books 30 & 31 Edward I*, p. 508.
[5] For the variations in the Sussex practice see *Sx. Arch. Colls.* XCVI, 19. The Cinque Ports always allowed free choice (Selden Soc. vol. 21, p. 38).
[6] E.g. *Sx. Arch. Colls.* XCVI, 25.
[7] E.g. J.I.2/115, mm. 3, 11, 13; 134, m. 3; 138, m. 4.   [8] J.I.2/119B, m. 2.
[9] E.g. *Ass. Arch. Socs.* XXXII, 196. One Sussex coroner unwisely allowed four confederate thieves to leave for the same port on the same day (*Sx. Arch. Colls.* XCVI, 23–4).
[10] Selden Soc. vol. 24, p. 112.
[11] *Arch. Journ.* 2nd ser. XVIII, 289. The Sussex practice of assigning near-by ports was unusual (*Sx. Arch. Colls.* XCVI, 18–19).

cross in his hand, as a sign of the Church's protection,[1] and in distinctive dress. Originally the dress was a single garment of sackcloth,[2] but from the late thirteenth century onwards he seems normally to have been allowed his shirt, coat and breeches, his other clothing being forfeited;[3] when the coroners' rolls mention his dress at all, they merely note that his head and feet were uncovered.[4] The change was probably made to lessen the township's burden. It must always have had to construct the cross, but it no longer had to provide the sackcloth garment. Having handed the abjuror his cross, the coroner had to lead him to the highway, give him a final warning not to stray from it and see him off in the right direction.[5] In the Cinque Ports those officials who acted as coroner had publicly to threaten with loss of life and limbs anyone who molested the abjuror on the highway,[6] and such warnings may well have been given elsewhere. When a felon abjured the realm in the bishopric of Durham, the coroner handed him over to the nearest constable, who passed him on to the next, and so he was transferred from constable to constable until he reached his port.[7] This practice could well have been extended to the rest of the country, where there was no rule that abjurors should be watched on their journey. In one case the township in which an abjuror left the highway was amerced,[8] as his mainpast or tithing should also have been,[9] but any vigilance thereby inspired cannot have extended many miles from the sanctuary.

It would be surprising to discover that more than a minute proportion of all abjurors ever left the kingdom or even reached their

[1] *Britton*, i.17.4; *Fleta*, i. 29 (Selden Soc. vol. 72, p. 77); *The Mirror of Justices*, i. 13 (Selden Soc. vol. 7, p. 34); 12 Edw. I, c. 5; *Tractatus de Officiis Coronatorum* (*Statutes of the Realm*, 1, 250); Selden Soc. vol. 21, p. 38. E.g. *Sx. Arch. Colls.* XCVI, 25.

[2] Cox, *Sanctuaries and Sanctuary Seekers*, p. 32.

[3] *Britton* (i.17.4) and *Fleta* (i. 29: Selden Soc. vol. 72, p. 77) say a coat only, and *The Mirror of Justices* (i. 13: Selden Soc. vol. 7, p. 34) a coat or shirt. Most versions of the *Officium Coronatoris* ignore the topic of sanctuary and abjuration altogether, but a fifteenth-century version contains an interpolation to the effect that abjurors were to travel in their shirt, coat and breeches, all their other clothes being confiscated by the coroner, but not as a perquisite of his office (Harleian MS. 5145, f. 32b).

[4] E.g. J.I.2/119C, m. 3d.   [5] E.g. J.I.2/71, m. 4d; 73, m. 2; 139, m. 3.

[6] Selden Soc. vol. 21, p. 38.

[7] G. T. Lapsley, *The County Palatine of Durham* (Harvard Hist. Studies, VIII, 1900), p. 253.

[8] Selden Soc. vol. 24, lxx, 134.

[9] *Ibid.* p. 102. Abjurors' tithings had always to be presented at the eyre (e.g. J.I.1/912A, m. 35).

ports. Dover,[1] Sandwich, Portsmouth and the other popular ports would have had to make special arrangements if all who chose to leave from them had arrived. The few who wished to cross the sea probably did so, for there is no known instance of an abjuror taking sanctuary again after forty days of fruitless searching for a passage.[2] Indeed, sea-port churches seem generally to have done no greater trade in sanctuary seekers than any others.[3] What must have happened in the vast majority of cases is that the abjurors sooner or later left the highway and took up residence unmolested elsewhere.[4] They could easily do so, for, with no escort and in dress not radically different from that of other men, they had only to jettison their cross when on a lonely stretch of road. This they would be encouraged to do both by a natural reluctance to live overseas and by the knowledge that even the protection of the Church did not save all abjurors. Despite the penalties attaching to those who molested lawful abjurors who kept to the highway, there are recorded cases of the pursuit and decapitation of such abjurors both on the highway and after they had been forced from it.[5] The reason for such violence was undoubtedly that somewhere near the sanctuary lived the family which had been robbed, bereaved or otherwise injured by the abjuror, whom they were unwilling to see escape with virtual impunity. Many of the victims, however, would not have dared to slay lawful abjurors, and it was therefore most rash for abjurors to leave the highway too near the place of sanctuary, since straying abjurors had to be arrested, or, failing that, could be beheaded with impunity.[6] To

---

[1] Two abjurors embarked from Shoreham for Normandy, but they had previously been pirates; they were thrown out of the boat in mid-Channel (*Cal. Pat. Rolls, 1354–1358*, p. 202).   [2] Selden Soc. vol. 24, lxxiii.

[3] *Sx. Arch. Colls.* XCVI, 17. Lostwithiel and Padstow were minor exceptions (Cox, *Sanctuaries and Sanctuary Seekers*, pp. 299–300).

[4] A. Réville, 'L'"Abjuratio Regni" ', *Revue Historique*, L, 26–7.

[5] E.g. *Select Coroners' Rolls*, p. 9; *Arch. Journ.* 2nd ser. XVIII, 287. That these were not isolated cases is proved by the warnings against such homicides in the law-books (e.g. *Britton*, i.17.4) and by the complaint of the clergy that abjurors were taken by enemies from the highway and hanged or beheaded (9 Edw. II, stat. 1, c. 10).

[6] Bracton was alone, and either wrong or outmoded, in saying that abjurors might leave the highway out of great necessity or in order to be entertained (II, 382). The author of *The Mirror of Justices* regarded it as an abuse that they were not allowed to use footpaths running beside the highway or to use the roads and hospices as pilgrims (v. 1. 24: Selden Soc. vol. 7. p. 158). *Britton* maintained that straying abjurors were not to be slain if they could be arrested (i.17.4), but *Fleta* emphasised that they might be beheaded with impunity, only secondly mentioning that if arrested they were to be sent to gaol (i. 29: Selden Soc. vol. 72, p. 77).

E

leave the highway too soon was therefore to provide one's enemies
with a perfect excuse for wreaking their vengeance and the coroner
with the duty of holding an inquest shortly after receiving an abjuration and sending the head to the county gaol.[1] It was equally legitimate to decapitate an abjuror who returned to the kingdom without
specific permission,[2] although those whom the plea rolls so describe
had rarely left England but had merely ventured too near to the
place of their abjuration after a spell elsewhere.

When abjurors who had 'returned' without permission were arrested, there was usually little that they could say in their defence
and they were invariably hanged when the coroner produced his
record of their abjuration.[3] Some abjurors who were arrested shortly
after leaving the highway could give no explanation of their straying
and were also hanged,[4] but many others recited the standard defence: that they had been forced from the highway by men whom
they did not know. A jury of the neighbourhood was then summoned
and almost always said that no force had been employed, whereupon
the abjurors were hanged.[5] In one exceptional Sussex case, however,
this story was upheld by the jury, and the sheriff and county coroners
were then summoned to King's Bench to receive the abjurors concerned, take a new oath of abjuration from them and replace them
on the highway at the point where they had been forced from it.[6]

It has been argued that coroners did not hold inquests in connection with abjurations.[7] It is true that the ceremony of abjuration,
although taking place before a body of local men, was not in itself

[1] E.g. *Select Coroners' Rolls*, pp. 75–6. In at least one case in which the
abjuror left the highway very soon he had been followed by a man of the township in which he had abjured, who raised the hue and cry; the whole township
followed it and the abjuror was beheaded (*ibid.* p. 37). The man who raised the
hue may have been a personal enemy of the abjuror, or a representative of the
township deputed to see that the abjuror kept to the highway and that the township thus incurred no amercement, or both.
[2] *Fleta*, i. 29 (Selden Soc. vol. 72, p. 77).
[3] E.g. J.I.3/111, m. 10d; 163, m. 10d. This was even the fate of an abjuror who
produced a charter pardoning his original felonies but not his consequent
abjuration (*Year Books 19 Edward III*, ed. L. O. Pike (Rolls Series, 1906),
pp. 174–6).
[4] E.g. Selden Soc. vol. 24, p. 102.   [5] E.g. *Sx. Arch. Colls.* XCVI, 25.
[6] *Ibid.* p. 24. Dr H. M. Cam has drawn my attention to a case which had a
similar ending (J.I.1/1187, m. 14d). In this case it was the sheriff's serjeants who
forced the abjuror from the highway, although the sheriff pleaded that he had
sent them to conduct the abjuror and only to arrest him if they found him off the
highway.
[7] I. L. Langbein, 'The Jury of Presentment and the Coroner', *Columbia Law
Rev.* XXXIII, 1357–8.

an inquest, but many abjurations entailed inquests at one stage or another. There are cases on the coroners' rolls of coroners holding inquests concerning the truth of confessions made by abjurors. Langbein maintained that they are not true inquests, but merely repetitions and validations of those parts of the abjurors' confessions which incriminated associates; that the abjurors, being outside the law, could not appeal associates, who therefore could not be arrested without the 'verdict' of good and lawful men; and that this did not constitute an inquest, because they did not provide the coroner with any new information and did not speak from their own knowledge.[1] This argument is indefensible. There is no reason to assume that these men were always more personally ignorant of the felonies confessed than any other inquest jurors were of the subject of their inquest. There is no justification for saying that an inquest could not be called by that name if it failed to produce new information: at some coroners' inquests upon dead bodies the juries confessed their complete ignorance of the facts of the case.[2] Moreover, in one of the two cases on which Langbein based his argument, the word 'inquest' is used to describe the inquiry.[3] Although both cases support his thesis that such presentments were only made when associates were implicated, there are other cases in which this was not so. Twelve men, before whom an abjuror had confessed to theft in Sussex, were sworn in by the coroner and confirmed that the confession was true in all respects, but added that the value of the stolen goods was three shillings.[4] Again, there are some Northamptonshire cases in which the abjurors were found by jurors to have committed felonies other than those to which they had confessed.[5] Two further cases are illuminating. In both a felon took sanctuary and, on the coroner's arrival, turned approver and appealed associates; one then escaped from sanctuary and the other abjured the realm, but in neither case did the coroner record that an inquest was held to validate the appeals.[6] Langbein's theory therefore lacks support. These inquests probably developed from the 'diligent examination' which *Fleta* advocated to ensure that only men guilty of felony abjured the realm.[7] They may have been very common, but would usually only

[1] Langbein, *loc. cit.* n. 109. [2] Above, pp. 21–2.
[3] *Select Coroners' Rolls*, p. 103. [4] *Sx. Arch. Colls.* XCVI, 24–5.
[5] E.g. *Ass. Arch. Socs.* XXXII, 199–200. [6] J.I.2/157, m. 4; 167, m. 5d.
[7] i. 29 (Selden Soc. vol. 72, p. 77). After at least one Wilton abjuration the borough coroner and constable held an inquest into the circumstances with a jury of twelve (J.I.2/196, m. 1).

be recorded when the findings differed from the confession. They would have given little trouble since every abjuration was followed by an inquest concerning the lands, goods and chattels of the abjuror, and the practice of combining the two inquests was probably normal.[1]

Langbein agreed that townships sometimes appraised abjurors' chattels, but held that an appraisal did not necessarily imply an inquest and that there is no evidence of any inquests.[2] This is merely a verbal quibble and not even an accurate one, for there are many instances in the coroners' rolls where the appraisal is definitely termed an 'inquest'.[3] All abjurors forfeited their goods and chattels to the king, who also had the year, day and waste of their lands unless they had abjured through fear.[4] The coroners had also to inquire concerning the goods and lands of those sanctuary seekers who surrendered and were sent to gaol[5] and of those who refused both to confess and to surrender.[6] Very few sanctuary seekers had any lands and not many had chattels worth more than a few pence. The possessions of many abjurors consisted largely or entirely of articles of clothing, such as caps and girdles with purses, which were additional to their requirements for their journey.[7] After the appraisal, the coroner committed the goods and chattels to the custody of the township until the next eyre.[8]

Any stolen goods in an abjuror's possession had also to be safeguarded. An interesting London case occurred in 1289. A man who called himself a chaplain stole sixteen silver dishes, took sanctuary and confessed before the city coroner and warden, the victim and others. The coroner then delivered the dishes to one of the sheriffs to be kept by him under the owner's seal. Two days later at the king's command they were unsealed in the Guildhall and delivered by the sheriff to the coroner, who restored them to the owner in the presence of the warden and others.[9] Stolen goods could only be restored by a special writ. About the same time a Cornish coroner was de-

---

[1] E.g. *Ass. Arch. Socs.* xxxii, 222; *Select Coroners' Rolls*, p. 103.
[2] *Columbia Law Rev.* xxxiii, 1357–8.
[3] E.g. *Select Coroners' Rolls*, p. 36.
[4] *Britton*, i.17.6. *Britton*'s rule that men who abjured on account of trespasses only forfeited their chattels (i.17.8) could only rarely have been applied, since such men should not have been allowed to abjure. *Britton* alone would have allowed them to (see above, p. 44).
[5] E.g. J.I.2/18, m. 32.   [6] *Britton*, i.17.1.
[7] E.g. *Ass. Arch. Socs.* xxxii, 194–5, 198.
[8] *Britton*, i.17.1. E.g. *Sx. Arch. Colls.* xcvi, 23–4.
[9] *Memorials of London*, ed. Riley, pp. 24–5.

nounced as foolish by the eyre justices for delivering chattels stolen by an abjuror to their owners because they had pursued him and tried to arrest him until he took sanctuary.[1] The coroner's only other duty was to enrol full details of the abjuration, including the appraisal of lands and chattels.[2]

These inquests concerning the circumstances of abjurations and the abjurors' lands and chattels were held by the usual variety of coroners' juries.[3] It was not always the men who had witnessed the abjuration who held the inquest, although it sometimes was.[4] In some cases, for example, the abjuration took place before the coroner and four townships and the inquest was made either by a jury of twelve men[5] or by twelve jurors together with the four townships.[6] The number of different groups of local men which could be involved in abjurations is exemplified by a Suffolk case of 1356. The lawful men of the township summoned the coroner to the church, and had presumably guarded the felon during his ten days in sanctuary; the abjuration took place before the coroner and the lawful men of this township and of the neighbouring townships; and the inquest concerning the abjuror's felonies and chattels was made by twelve jurors.[7]

Finally, coroners sometimes held inquests concerning escapes from sanctuary,[8] although into only a small proportion of them. They probably held them *ex officio*, for in no case is it stated that they acted on a writ. It was nevertheless illegal for coroners to hold such inquests *ex officio*. When the Chichester coroners held one by a jury of twelve men, the inquest was summoned to King's Bench where the justices held that coroners could only hold them on a special warrant.[9] That they nevertheless held them can have only one explanation: they wished to exculpate themselves. So did the jurors, and the verdict was therefore usually suspect. In this Chichester case, for example, the jurors found that the escape was not through

---

[1] *Year Books 30 & 31 Edward I*, p. 526.

[2] As early as 1201 the Cornish coroners were amerced for failing to enrol an abjuror's chattels (Selden Soc. vol. 68, no. 244).

[3] E.g. three townships (e.g. *Select Coroners' Rolls*, p. 36); four townships by the oath of twelve men (e.g. J.I.2/81, m. 1); four townships and twelve men (e.g. *Ass. Arch. Socs.* XXXII, 216); the township, the four neighbouring townships and twelve men (e.g. J.I.2/18, mm. 32, 38); and twelve free men (e.g. above, p. 51). For the amercement of a township for not appearing at a coroner's inquest into an abjuror's chattels see *Ass. Arch. Socs.* XXXII, 432.

[4] E.g. above, p. 51.

[5] E.g. *Ass. Arch. Socs.* XXXII, 222.

[6] E.g. *ibid.* p. 200.

[7] *Select Coroners' Rolls*, p. 103.

[8] E.g. J.I.2/64 m. 3 (*bis*); 178, m. 15.

[9] *Sx. Arch. Colls.* XCVI, 26.

lack of guarding but was contrived by two friars, from whose church it was made. An Oxford inquest, held a month after the escape of two men from sanctuary, was unusual in that the verdict was that their escape had been due to defective guarding by night.[1] The juries used in these cases were usually of the same type as those used for inquests on dead bodies. The Oxford jury consisted of twelve men from three parishes; one other parish had failed to attend. Sometimes, as in Ipswich, the same jurors both made a presentment concerning the escape and appraised the felon's chattels,[2] while two Ipswich coroners held an inquest by twelve jurors in the presence of the town bailiffs into the capture of two men who had previously abjured the realm before two former Ipswich coroners.[3] Finally, it was probably after an inquest that a man who had led a homicide to sanctuary in Shrewsbury was committed to prison by the town coroner.[4]

The lack of coroners' rolls for the fifteenth century makes it impossible to discover whether there was any decline in the number of abjurations of the realm, but the probability is that there was not. There was certainly no radical alteration in their procedure during the Middle Ages. This only came with the Tudors, who must have particularly disliked a privilege of the Church which was a permanent affront to law and order. Henry VIII introduced the branding of abjuring felons on the thumb with the letter 'A'. Another of his statutes required abjurors, instead of leaving the realm, to go to one of certain precisely defined sanctuaries and remain there for life, on pain of death if they should leave it. Privilege of sanctuary was denied to those guilty of murder, rape, burglary, robbery, arson and sacrilege, but this limitation was modified by an act of Edward VI.

The new system of sanctuary introduced by Henry VIII's legislation did not work well and was abrogated in 1603. But the restoration of the common law was opposed to the public opinion of the seventeenth century, and so the privilege was completely abolished by a statute of James I in 1623/4.[5]

[1] *Records of Mediaeval Oxford*, p. 30.   [2] J.I.2/178, m. 15.   [3] *Ibid.* m. 13.
[4] *Hist. MSS. Comm., 15th Report*, App. x, p. 26.
[5] This statement is based on a fuller account in W. S. Holdsworth, *A History of English Law*, III (3rd ed. 1923), 306-7. For further details see I. D. Thornley, 'The Destruction of Sanctuary', in *Tudor Studies presented . . . to Pollard*, ed. R. W. Seton-Watson (1924), pp. 182-207. Some coroners' records of abjurations of the realm by branded felons and abjurations to jurisdictional sanctuaries can be found among King's Bench Ancient Indictments (e.g. K.B.9/519, m. 147; 521, mm. 82-4).

CHAPTER IV

APPEALS AND OUTLAWRIES

In the early years of the coroner's life nearly every felony resulted in an appeal,[1] but during the thirteenth century the number of appeals rapidly declined for two reasons. Firstly, the justices did their utmost to discourage them, because, if successfully maintained, they resulted in the archaic practice of trial by battle. The justices therefore rigidly insisted that every variation between the appeal as made in the county court and as made before them, however minute, invalidated it.[2] Secondly, the appellor had little to gain from his appeal. The most he could hope for was the chance of personal vengeance in battle, with the equal prospect of failure. But the chances of reaching that stage were very small; he was far more likely to be imprisoned until he paid a fine for neglecting or varying his appeal.[3] Instead of exposing himself to these hazards, he had the choice, if the felony were homicide, of allowing the case to be brought before the justices on the indictment of the coroner's inquest jury; and in the event of one of the other felonies, he could proceed by writ of trespass or by bill and obtain damages if successful.[4] Appeals continued to be made throughout the Middle Ages, but were never again more than a small proportion of the total number of felonies.

The coroner was concerned with all appeals when they reached the county court and in the first half of the thirteenth century, although probably not later, he was concerned with many of them at an earlier stage. The intending appellor had to take every possible step to bring the felony to the notice of the authorities. Whatever the felony, he had to raise the hue and cry and see that it was followed to the neighbouring townships, then to the bailiff or serjeant of the hundred, from him to the coroners and finally to the next county court.[5] It was sometimes possible to leave out a stage or two. Bracton allowed that the hue should be made to the serjeants 'if they

[1] Linc. Rec. Soc. XXII, xlix.   [2] *Ibid.* pp. lix–lx; Bracton, II, 386, 394–6.
[3] *Britton*, i.26.2.
[4] Selden Soc. vol. 60, Introduction; Wilts. Arch. & Nat. Hist. Soc., Rec. Branch, XII, 59. *Britton* advocated proceeding by writ of trespass rather than by appeal in such felonies as wounds (i.26.2).
[5] Bracton, II, 394. E.g. *Select Coroners' Rolls*, pp. 18, 65.

could be found', and that if the county court was due to be held on
either of the two days following the felony, suit to the serjeant and
coroners could be omitted as they would be going to the county
court.[1] There are many instances of the by-passing of either the
bailiff or the coroners, which seems never to have invalidated the
appeals.[2] The fact that coroners were not absolutely essential to appeals before the county court stage was reached must largely account for their gradually confining themselves solely to that stage in
the later thirteenth century. This was not questioned, provided that
the coroners testified that the hue had been raised and that 'sufficient
and reasonable' suit had been made.[3] If the hue had not been raised
as soon as possible after the felony, the appeal was quashed.[4]

There were two distinct elements to the hue and cry. Its immediate purpose was the pursuit and capture of the felon by the townships. The bailiff and coroners would be concerned with this, but
they had also to look ahead to the proceedings in the county court
and the appellor therefore often made his initial accusation before
one or other of them. Appellors often claimed that they had made
suit from township to township, thence to the bailiff and from him
to the coroners, before whom they made their appeals.[5] Many appeals were first made in the hundred or wapentake courts and the
coroner's presence there was often specifically noted.[6] *The Mirror of
Justices* regarded it as an abuse for appeals to begin elsewhere than
before the county coroner,[7] but many were nevertheless first made
before town and franchisal coroners.[8] This initial hearing, however,
cannot compare in importance to the county court stage. It was the
county court version of the appeal which was enrolled by the coroners and used to check the appeal as made before the justices, and it
was probably in the county court that it was first made in all its formal and technical phraseology. Word perfection would hardly have

[1] II, 394.
[2] E.g. *Curia Regis Rolls*, VI, 264; J.I.1/926, m. 26d; J.I.2/3, m. 11d.
[3] Bracton, II, 406.
[4] In normal circumstances a delay of a fortnight was fatal to the appeal (e.g.
J.I.1/912A, m. 43d; 926, m. 26d), but if the appellor had been incapacitated by
the felony a delay was allowed (e.g. Selden Soc. vol. 60, ccii).
[5] E.g. K.B. 27/257, Rex m. 18d.
[6] E.g. *Curia Regis Rolls*, VII, 169–70.
[7] v. I. 45.
[8] E.g. *Sx. Arch. Colls.* XCVI, 26–7 (Arundel coroner); *Records of Mediaeval
Oxford*, p. 27 (Oxford coroners and bailiffs); J.I.2/93, m. 1 (mayor, coroners and
bailiffs of Lincoln); 199, m. 3d (Salisbury coroner and the steward of the dean
and chapter).

been expected within hours of the felony and there is evidence that the appellor's suit to the bailiff and coroners was of the most informal nature. This is suggested by the use of the word *querela* or *querimonia* to describe this stage of the appeal,[1] and the fact that the appellor only made a 'plaint' then did not disqualify him from making his formal appeal in the county court.[2] A man who began to make an appeal of treason before the mayor and bailiffs of Chichester at a view of frankpledge in 1441 was delayed until the city coroners had been called in and then made his appeal in short, breathless sentences, couched in colloquial terms which defied translation into Latin and were only evoked by continual questioning;[3] it provides a complete contrast to the formal appeal required in the county court.

The coroner was thus concerned in the initial stages of many appeals, but he had extra duties in appeals of rape, mayhem and wounds, as well as in appeals of homicide when he had to hold inquests on the dead bodies. These duties, although never abolished, seem only to have been performed in the first half of the thirteenth century. A raped woman, who wished to lodge an appeal, had not only to raise the hue and cry but also, if possible, to produce material signs of the offence—a flow of blood, or torn or blood-stained clothes. These signs had to be shown to the men of the neighbouring townships, the bailiff of the hundred and the coroners. They were important because they made it necessary for the appellee to find four or more sureties for his appearance at the eyre in the early thirteenth century and later disqualified him from bail, whereas he had to find only two sureties in the absence of such signs.[4] Thus in 1202 a Lincolnshire coroner, to whom a woman, who brought an appeal of rape, had gone as soon as the appellee had released her two days after the offence, bore witness that she came to him 'bloodstained and disgracefully treated'.[5]

In appeals of wounds or mayhem the wounds should have been exhibited at every stage up to and including the first appearance in the county court. The coroners were supposed to measure them for length, breadth and depth and their exact position on the body and to find with what weapon they had been inflicted. This had to be

[1] *Trans. R. Hist. Soc.* 5th ser. VIII, 96.
[2] E.g. Linc. Rec. Soc. XXII, 916.
[3] R. F. Hunnisett, 'Treason by Words', *Sx. Notes & Queries*, XIV, 117–18.
[4] Bracton, II, 344–5, 415; *Officium Coronatoris* (*Statutes of the Realm*, I, 41); *Fleta*, i. 25 (Selden Soc. vol. 72, p. 66).
[5] Linc. Rec. Soc. XXII, 590.

done either during the hue and cry at what Bracton called an 'inquest', with or without the sheriff, or in the county court.[1] Appeals were often quashed if the coroners attested that no wound had been shown either to them personally or in the county court,[2] and it was a valid exception to an appeal of wounds or mayhem that a recent and open wound had not been shown to the coroners.[3] The presence of blood was not enough by itself to justify an appeal. Thus in a Yorkshire appeal of wounds a serjeant witnessed to recent blood and one flow but no wound and the coroners and county court to dry blood but no wound; the appeal was accordingly quashed.[4] But when the coroners said that reasonable suit had been made and that they had seen recent wounds, the appeal was considered good.[5] The appellor who was found to have shown recent wounds both to the town coroners in Gloucester and before the county coroners in the county court was in this respect in an unassailable position.[6] The normal form of the appeal gives the impression that the appellor had to seek the coroner out in order to show his injuries, but this was not necessarily so. The coroners sometimes attended hundred or wapentake courts to view them,[7] and there is at least one instance of the amercement of a township which confessed that it had not sent for the coroners during the life of the wounded man. His death turned what would have been an appeal of wounds or mayhem into an appeal of homicide.[8]

A very unusual case was the appeal, made in King's Bench, of the circumcision of a Christian boy aged five by Jews in Norwich in 1240. The boy had been rescued by neighbours, who showed him immediately to the Official, the archdeacon and the city coroners, who all agreed to the circumcision and considerable swelling. A jury of the coroners and thirty-six citizens found that the offence was as stated, but the justices decided that it was not strictly a felony as the boy had been neither wounded nor maimed; it was, however, an affront to the Church and so was handed over to the ecclesiastical authorities.[9]

[1] Bracton, II, 345; *Officium Coronatoris* (*Statutes of the Realm*, I, 41).
[2] E.g. Linc. Rec. Soc. XXII, 899.
[3] Bracton, II, 407, 409. E.g. Selden Soc. vol. 56, no. 581.
[4] E.g. *ibid.* no. 476.
[5] E.g. *ibid.* no. 911; *Pleas of the Crown for Gloucester, 1221,* no. 87.
[6] *Ibid.* no. 434.   [7] E.g. Selden Soc. vol. 56, no. 724.
[8] K.B.26/117, m. 6. For other examples of coroners' travelling to view wounds see *Select Coroners' Rolls,* p. 22; *The Court Baron,* ed. F. W. Maitland and W. P. Baildon (Selden Soc. vol. 4), pp. 85–6.
[9] F. Blomefield, *History of Norfolk,* III (1806), 44–5.

The immediate fate of an appellee depended on the view of the wounds by the coroners or in the county court. If they appeared likely to prove fatal, he had to be arrested and detained until it was known whether or not the wounded man would live. If he died, the appellee was kept in prison until the case came before the justices, but if he recovered the appellee could go free provided that he found two or more sureties according to the gravity of the injury.[1] An appellee who was a stranger from distant parts or lacked friends and therefore could find no sureties had to remain in gaol, but as a safeguard and not as a punishment.[2] The law-books and statutes deal with the arrest or attachment of appellees in connection with the coroner and this must certainly have been his duty, especially when the next county court was not immediately due. When one or more coroners were amerced by themselves at the eyre for not attaching appellees,[3] their default had probably been committed outside the county court. Bracton, however, only visualised the joint negligence of sheriff and coroners in the county court,[4] and they were frequently amerced together for dismissing appealed men without pledges[5] or for attaching them by poor pledges.[6] During the 1218–19 Yorkshire eyre, one sheriff and the county coroners of his time were in trouble for making practically no attachments in appeals.[7]

Only a small proportion of those appealed gave themselves up either at once or during the course of the appeal in the county court, and if they did not appear they could not be attached. All appellors, however, had to find two sureties who undertook to be responsible for the due prosecution of their appeal in all its stages. Only very poor people were excused and they had to pledge their faith that they would prosecute.[8] The law-books agree that the pledges to prosecute had to be found at the first county court,[9] and this was normally the practice, except that in boroughs they were often found in the presence of the borough coroners before the appeal reached the county court.[10] It was a dangerous undertaking to go surety for an

---

[1] Bracton, II, 345; *Officium Coronatoris* (*Statutes of the Realm*, I, 41); *Fleta*, i. 25 (Selden Soc. vol. 72, p. 66).

[2] Bracton, II, 345.   [3] E.g. Linc. Rec. Soc. XXII, 623.

[4] II, 420.   [5] E.g. Selden Soc. vol. 68, no. 733.

[6] E.g. Beds. Hist. Rec. Soc. XXI, 676. Like the appellors, they should probably have been attached by men who were distrainable by the sheriff (*Britton*, i.2.7).

[7] Selden Soc. vol. 56, no. 835. Cf. no. 1085.

[8] E.g. Selden Soc. vol. 60, ccii, cciii; vol. 56, no. 510.

[9] *Britton*, i.2.7; 24.1; *Fleta*, i. 25 (Selden Soc. vol. 72, p. 66).

[10] E.g. *Records of Mediaeval Oxford*, p. 27.

appeal. Very many appeals were withdrawn or discontinued sooner or later, and in that event the appellor was arrested and his pledges were amerced.[1]

Except that town coroners often heard appeals initially throughout the Middle Ages,[2] the coroner's duties in appeals were usually confined to the county court stage after the first half of the thirteenth century. There are several reasons for this. The county court stage was all-important and he had to attend that. Secondly, the earlier stages entailed much travelling and the coroner had other important duties which also involved him in considerable travelling. Finally, the coroner's attendance at the earlier stages had never been absolutely essential, and this was basically because he had inherited his duties in connection with appeals outside the county court from the hundred serjeants and the take-over had never been complete. There are early thirteenth-century examples of serjeants hearing appeals and viewing the signs of rape,[3] while the viewing of wounds on which appeals were based showed much diversity. Although a man who brought an appeal before the *Curia Regis* as early as Easter 1198 could plead that he had shown his wound to one of the county coroners,[4] it for long sufficed that wounds were shown to the serjeant, coroners, sheriff or specially assigned knights of no official position, to any combination of two or more of them, or in the county court.[5]

A few exceptional appeals were removed to King's Bench before they had reached the county court. One such, probably because it was an appeal of treason, was removed from the Chichester view of frankpledge in 1441.[6] A few important franchises had exceptional

[1] E.g. J.I.1/912A, m. 44; K.B. 29/5, m. 45.   [2] See above, p. 56.
[3] *Trans. R. Hist. Soc.* 5th ser. VIII, 96.
[4] *Curia Regis Rolls*, I, 39.
[5] Linc. Rec. Soc. XXII, xlv, 644. Cf. Selden Soc. vol. 68, no. 353 (knights); *Curia Regis Rolls*, IV, 163 (sheriff, coroners and hundred serjeant); Linc. Rec. Soc. XXII, 625 (serjeant, coroners, sheriff and county court), 647 (sheriff and coroners), 650 (serjeant and two knights). A beadle—probably the beadle of the hundred who earlier sometimes viewed wounds (e.g. *Three Rolls of the King's Court in the reign of Richard I, 1194–1195*, ed. F. W. Maitland (Pipe Roll Soc. XIV), p. 100)—attested at the 1202 Lincolnshire eyre, when a man brought an appeal of wounds given to his wife and the killing of her unborn child, that he had seen a recent wound and blood in the wapentake court. But the appeal was quashed and the beadle was amerced for false testimony, because the serjeant of the riding, the coroners and twelve knights all maintained that they had seen neither wound nor blood (Linc. Rec. Soc. XXII, 629).
[6] *Sx. Notes & Queries*, XIV, 117.

rights,[1] but the overwhelming majority of appeals were prosecuted in the county court. Only before the county coroners in the county court was the appeal formally made and recorded and could the exigent normally be awarded.[2] In 1343 the Oxford town coroners made an indenture with the sheriff of Oxfordshire, testifying that they had delivered to him the record of an appeal made before them and the town bailiffs. The appellor had found his two pledges to prosecute before the town coroners and bailiffs, but the serious business of exigent was reserved for the county court.[3]

In the county court the coroners' duties in respect of appeals were twofold. Firstly, they had to enrol them verbatim in the stereotyped form in which they were made, with every detail of time, place and circumstance and the names of the two pledges to prosecute. This was to allow legitimate exceptions later when their rolls were the final arbiters.[4] Secondly, they had to legalise and record any subsequent exactions and outlawries.

The exigent was the most solemn and awesome part of medieval mesne process. Outlawry was its culmination, but even outlawry was not in itself a punishment. The whole process of exigent was concerned solely with securing the attendance of an appellee or defendant in court and his submission to justice, inability to get men to stand their trial being a characteristic feature of all types of plea in the Middle Ages. The exigent could only be operated in the county court, where alone outlawries could be promulgated. The exigent consisted of exactions or public demands made at four successive county courts that the man concerned appear and surrender to justice. If he still absented himself on the fourth exaction he was outlawed, unless one or two men pledged themselves to secure his attendance at the fifth county court. If he did not appear then after three well-spaced calls had been made for him, outlawry could be delayed no longer and his sureties could look confidently forward to

[1] Some claimed the right to decide appeals by battle in their courts if both appellor and appellee were men of the liberty (e.g. J.I.1/818, m. 53: liberty of the abbot of Bury St Edmunds), while all appeals arising in the liberty of Cockermouth were prosecuted until outlawry in the three-weekly court of the liberty and then the record was sent by the coroner and four suitors to the county court for the promulgation of outlawry (C.145/254, no. 13).

[2] *The Mirror of Justices*, i. 13 (Selden Soc. vol. 7, p. 29).

[3] *Records of Mediaeval Oxford*, p. 27.

[4] Bracton, II, 394–6; *Britton*, i.24.1, 3; *Fleta*, i. 25 (Selden Soc. vol. 72, p. 66). E.g. *Select Coroners' Rolls*, pp. 18–23.

an amercement at the next eyre.[1] Women and children under twelve could not be outlawed because they were technically not under the law, never having been sworn to it and not being in a frankpledge tithing; but women could be exacted and waived, which amounted to outlawry.[2]

The county coroners had to attend all exactions and outlawries, both to legalise and to record them. It was impossible to promulgate an outlawry if no coroner attended the county court, as happened in Sussex in 1321 when the suitors refused to outlaw those who were then exacted for the fifth time.[3] This case suggests that it was the suitors who promulgated outlawries. This is supported by *Britton*[4] and outlawries were most commonly said to be promulgated 'by consideration of the whole county and in the presence of the coroners'.[5] Occasionally, however, the outlawry was said to be 'by consideration of the coroners and the whole county'[6] or even 'by the county coroners',[7] and *The Mirror of Justices* maintained that the coroners gave judgment of outlawry.[8] What probably happened was that the coroners sometimes formally proclaimed the outlawry, but in doing so merely acted as the mouthpiece of the whole body of suitors by whose 'consideration' the exacted man was technically outlawed.

The process of exigent could be started in two ways: either by an appeal or by a writ of exigent. The coroner was more closely connected with the first. When an appellor had made his appeal in the county court one of two things could happen. The appellee or appellees might appear, in which case the sheriff would either arrest them or attach them by sureties and the appeal would then await the justices.[9] But if, as more frequently happened, they did not attend the coroners had to order the sheriff or bailiff of the area in which the felony had been committed to have them at the next county court.[10] If they did not appear then they were placed in the exigent and

---

[1] E.g. *Sx. Arch. Colls.* XCVI, 33.

[2] Selden Soc. vol. 24, pp. 106, 108. Similarly women could abjure the realm, but children under twelve could not (e.g. *Pleas of the Crown for Gloucester, 1221*, no. 150).

[3] *Sx. Arch. Colls.* XCVI, 21-2.   [4] i.14.6.

[5] E.g. *Sx. Arch. Colls.* XCVI, 33.   [6] E.g. J.I.2/110, m. 1.

[7] E.g. *Mediaeval Archives of the University of Oxford*, ed. H. E. Salter, II (Oxon. Hist. Soc. LXXIII), 76.

[8] i. 13; ii. 8 (Selden Soc. vol. 7, pp. 29, 51).

[9] E.g. J.I.1/912A, m. 42d. The appellee came to the first county court *et sponte posuit se in prisonam domini regis*.   [10] *Britton*, i.2.7, 8.

exacted for the first time. When an appeal of homicide was launched in the county court at Derby in 1335, the appellor found pledges to prosecute and the county coroners ordered the sheriff to arrest the appellees and have them at the next county court. The sheriff then reported that they had not been found and the coroners repeated their order. Only on the receipt of a second *non sunt inventi* at the third county court was the exigent awarded.[1] There must have been special circumstances attaching to this appeal, for in all other cases the exigent was awarded at the second county court of the appeal.

The county court not only could but was obliged to award the exigent in appeals originating there. It is uncertain whether the suitors or the coroners awarded it. *The Mirror of Justices* says that the coroners did,[2] but if so they were probably only acting on behalf of the suitors and declaring their decision, as when promulgating outlawries and issuing writs of *capias* to the sheriff before the award of the exigent. Once awarded, the exigent continued until outlawry unless one of several things happened. Firstly, the appellee could appear in court at any stage prior to outlawry. If he did, he was either committed to gaol or had to find sureties.[3] Secondly, the exigent automatically lapsed if the appellor failed to prosecute his appeal at any county court before outlawry. This was always a possibility, especially if there were several appellees, when a separate appeal had to be made against each;[4] and if some were appealed as principals and others as accessories, the exigent could not be awarded against the accessories until the principals had appeared or been outlawed,[5] which meant that anyone bringing such an appeal was faced with the prospect of prosecuting at successive county courts for almost a year. Once an appeal had lapsed it could only be revived if the appellor was allowed to initiate a fresh appeal[6] or, failing that, at the initiation of the justices after the next general eyre if the appellee had

---

[1] *Year Books 12 & 13 Edward III*, ed. L. O. Pike (Rolls Series, 1885), pp. 152–4.

[2] i. 13 (Selden Soc. vol. 7, p. 29).

[3] E.g. J.I.1/926, m. 11d. At the 1279 Sussex eyre the coroners' rolls proved that when certain men who were appealed of assault and robbery appeared at the fifth county court and were delivered to the custody of the sheriff, he allowed them to go free without sureties. Judgment was therefore passed against the sheriff and the appellor was allowed to prosecute her appeal in the county court until outlawry (J.I.1/921, m. 5).

[4] *Britton*, i.2.8. E.g. J.I.1/926, m. 26d. Each appeal had to have separate pledges for its prosecution. [5] *Britton*, i.2.9.

[6] E.g. *Year Books 20 & 21 Edward I*, ed. A. J. Horwood (Rolls Series, 1866), p. 396.

failed to attend to answer at the king's suit.[1] Thirdly, the exigent ceased if the appellee abjured the realm, since abjuration was tantamount to outlawry; an appeal could be dropped at any stage with impunity to the appellor and his sureties if abjuration was proved.[2] Fourthly, exceptional circumstances, such as civil war, were sometimes held to justify the temporary discontinuance of an appeal.[3] A fifth contingency was that the appellee might obtain a pardon and either produce it in the county court, or get a *supersedeas* on the strength of it.[4] Finally, a royal writ sometimes removed an appeal to King's Bench or set up a special commission of oyer and terminer to deal with it before the stage of outlawry had been reached in order to determine it without delay.[5] This must usually have been at the instance of the appellees, since without any guarantee that they would attend it would have been pointless: the appeal could not have been tried and the outlawry would merely have been delayed. One such writ even ordered the removal of an appeal to Westminster if the appellees 'request it and not otherwise'.[6] In 1272, however, a writ ordered the removal of an appeal from the Bedfordshire county court to Westminster because one of the coroners was the appellor's kinsman and was said to favour her.[7]

Despite all these possibilities, the vast majority of exactions resulted in outlawries. Even with the promulgation and recording of the outlawry, the coroners' duties were not complete. They had to inquire in whose tithing or mainpast the outlaw had been and enrol it, in order that it might be amerced at the eyre for his flight,[8] and also to appraise his lands and chattels—a matter which will be discussed below.[9]

---

[1] *Britton*, i.2.8. E.g. J.I.1/926, m. 23.   [2] E.g. *ibid*. m. 19.

[3] E.g. Selden Soc. vol. 56, no. 740 (war and pilgrimage).

[4] In Edward II's reign the Sussex county court fell into a trap. The exigent had been awarded in an appeal of burglary and rape. At the fifth exaction a pardon was produced and the process therefore ceased. The pardon, however, related to the burglary only and King's Bench therefore passed judgment against the whole county and ordered the exigent to be resumed at the point at which it had stopped. Outlawry was duly promulgated, only to be reversed because the appellee had been in Colchester gaol at the time of the fifth exaction and so had had no opportunity of attending (K.B. 27/240, Rex m. 7).

[5] E.g. J.I.1/926, m. 8d (commission of oyer and terminer).

[6] *Select Coroners' Rolls*, pp. 65–6. They presumably did, for there is a note on the coroners' roll that nothing more was done in the county court.

[7] *Ibid*. pp. 20–1. For another example see J.I.2/266, m. 28.

[8] *Britton*, i.2.9; *The Mirror of Justices*, i. 13 (Selden Soc. vol. 7, p. 29). E.g. J.I.1/909A, m. 26d.

[9] Pp. 66–7.

Because appeals were not the only type of action in which difficulty was experienced in securing attendance in court, the process of
exigent was gradually extended from appeals to felonies in general
and to cases brought by writ of trespass, and then it began to be preferred to the process of distraint in civil actions, especially debt.[1]
Since appeals were made in the county court, the coroners or suitors
could award consequent exigents there orally. But in order to initiate the exigent in other pleas, the justices concerned had to send a
writ of *exigi facias* or exigent to the sheriff of the county in which the
felony or other offence had been perpetrated, ordering him to exact
the defendant from county court to county court until his appearance or outlawry and, if he appeared, to produce him before them.[2]
The coroners were thus slightly less important in such exactions than
in those arising from appeals when they initiated the process; but
their presence was still essential and they still had to enrol full details.

There were special writs of exigent with which the coroners were
rather more closely concerned. At the end of a general eyre the justices entered in two rolls the names of all fugitives who had failed to
come before them to answer concerning the felonies of which they
were suspected. One roll they delivered to the Exchequer and the
other to the sheriff and coroners of the county. These exigent rolls
were only glorified writs of exigent, since all named in them had to
be exacted at the first county court after the eyre and in successive
county courts until their outlawry.[3] In some counties the justices
gave the exigent roll to the coroners alone, as in Cambridgeshire
where on one occasion, for some unexplained reason, they were
given the exigent rolls of the eyre which had just finished and of
the previous one which had been held thirteen years before.[4]

[1] M. Hastings, *The Court of Common Pleas in Fifteenth Century England* (New
York, 1947), pp. 169–70.
[2] For the use of writs of exigent by the court of Common Pleas and by J. P.'s
see *ibid.* pp. 169–79; *Proceedings before the Justices of the Peace in the Fourteenth
and Fifteenth Centuries*, ed. B. H. Putnam (Ames Foundation, 1938), pp. ciii–civ.
They used them only after *non est inventus* had been returned on one or more
writs of *capias*, which in their turn had often not issued until after the failure of
a *venire facias* and *distringas* or *attachies*.
[3] *Britton*, i.27.14. E.g. J.I.1/1387, m. 1; *Cal. Inqs. Misc.* I, 2186. Some eyre
rolls contain copies of these rolls (e.g. J.I.1/635, mm. 82–87d; 653, mm. 36–36d;
686, mm. 96–96d).
[4] J.I.1/96, m. 54. Trailbaston justices and other justices of oyer and terminer
left normal writs of exigent addressed to the sheriff, often containing hundreds
of names, at the end of their visitations (e.g. J.I.2/256/24–28; J.I.1/941A, mm.
58–58d).

F

The process initiated by writ of exigent was naturally more certain to result in the outlawry or appearance of the men exacted than exactions dependent upon the ability and desire of an individual to prosecute his appeal at five county courts. The only way in which the execution of a writ of exigent could be stayed, apart from the appearance of the defendant or, temporarily, by the non-attendance of the coroners, was by a writ of *supersedeas* addressed either to the sheriff or to the sheriff and coroners.[1] A *supersedeas* could in its turn be quashed and the process of exigent recommenced, generally at the stage at which it had been stopped, by a writ of *de novo exigi facias* addressed to the sheriff.[2]

Outlaws' goods and chattels were forfeited to the king unless specifically granted away, and the king also obtained the year, day and waste of any lands. The method of appraisal depended upon whether the outlawry had followed an appeal or had resulted from a writ of exigent. In the first case the coroners had to proceed to the appraisal of the lands and chattels in their bailiwick immediately after the outlawry and also to inquire whether and where they had any more.[3] At the 1221 Warwickshire eyre it was stated that the coroners had sealed with their seal a chest which constituted the chattels of a man who had been outlawed on an appeal of homicide.[4] In Warwickshire at this time the sheriff and coroners or their heirs were sometimes made answerable for outlaws' lands and chattels,[5] but this was exceptional.

When outlawries resulted from the exigent order given by the justices at the end of an eyre, no further action concerning the lands and chattels was necessary in the case of felons, because the justices had already adjudged them to be forfeited and caused them to be appraised on account of their flight.[6] But the appraisal of the pos-

---

[1] E.g. *Select Coroners' Rolls*, pp. 78–9 (sheriff); *Cal. Close Rolls, 1302–1307*, p. 398 (sheriff and coroners).

[2] E.g. *Select Coroners' Rolls*, pp. 77–9; K.B. 27/240, Rex m. 7.

[3] *Britton*, i.2.9. There is no evidence to support the statement in *The Mirror of Justices* (ii. 8) that at the first county court of an appeal and before the exigent the coroners had not only to order the arrest of the appellees but also the taking of all their goods and chattels into the king's hand. Normally, if the appellees surrendered at any of the five exactions they suffered no forfeiture unless and until they were found guilty before the justices. In one Kent case, however, the justices decided that because the coroner had recorded that the appellees had not appeared until the fifth county court their chattels should be forfeited (Selden Soc. vol. 24, p. 106).

[4] Selden Soc. vol. 59, no. 930.   [5] E.g. *ibid.* no. 935.

[6] E.g. J.I.1/1387, m. 1.

sessions of those who were put in the exigent for trespasses awaited outlawry, as with a normal writ of exigent.[1] When outlawry resulted from the execution of a writ of exigent, no automatic appraisal of lands and chattels followed. Not until the court which was hearing the case had received the sheriff's return to the writ of exigent did it order, by another writ, an inquest to appraise the outlaw's lands and chattels. From an early date such writs were usually addressed to the sheriff and coroners, who were jointly responsible for holding the inquest, and ordered them to inquire diligently by the oath of good and lawful men what goods and chattels, lands and tenements the outlaws had in their county on the day of their outlawry and to whose hands they had come.[2] Sometimes these writs were sent to the coroners alone, and in one case the coroners held the inquisition although the writ had been addressed to the sheriff alone.[3] A Bedfordshire case of 1267 shows an equitable but unusual division of labour. The sheriff held an inquisition in execution of a writ and appraised the annual value of an outlaw's house and garden, the waste of his grove and his rents of assize, adding in his return that the growing crops had been valued in the coroner's roll.[4] In franchises which had the return of writs, inquisitions into the possessions of men outlawed on writs of exigent were held by franchisal officials.[5]

There remains the question: what happened to the vast multitude of medieval outlaws? Strictly they bore 'wolves' heads' which could be cut off with impunity by anyone,[6] and under Richard I five shillings were paid to serjeants by royal writ for an outlaw's head.[7] There were very few such cases of later date. A Yorkshire coroner's roll records an inquest on the body of an outlaw who was slain in trying to avoid arrest in 1355. There had been a considerable change in attitude since the reign of Richard I; far from receiving a reward, the homicides—the bailiff of the wapentake and his subordinates—had to appear in King's Bench before they were acquitted.[8] At this date the summary execution of outlaws was very exceptional, but if outlaws were arrested and found to be outlaws from the coroners' rolls they should strictly have been hanged,[9] and there are instances of the hanging of outlaws on the testimony of the coroners' rolls

[1] Selden Soc. vol. 24, pp. 95, 134.
[2] E.g. K.B.27/240, Rex m. 7; 250, Rex m. 14.
[3] *Cal. Inqs. Misc.* I, 523.   [4] *Ibid.* no. 587.
[5] E.g. K.B.27/226, m. 137.   [6] *Fleta*, i. 27 (Selden Soc. vol. 72, p. 70).
[7] *Pipe Roll 9 Richard I* (Pipe Roll Soc. N.S. VIII), p. 169.
[8] J.I.2/215, m. 29.   [9] *Britton*, i.13.4.

from the early thirteenth century to the fifteenth.[1] But in all these cases the outlaws were felons. Although in theory there were no degrees of outlawry, in practice men who had been outlawed for not appearing to answer writs of trespass and, more especially, defaulting defendants in debt actions need never have feared execution. When the sheriff had returned the writ of exigent and certified the outlawry, the court which was hearing the case issued him with a writ of *capias utlagatum*, whereupon one of three things would happen. As already noted, a few outlaws were arrested. Many more, possibly a majority of those who were outlawed for civil offences and trespasses, ultimately surrendered, bought their pardons, with which the Patent and Pardon Rolls abound, and stood their trial. A large number of outlawed felons also either bought or, by serving for a term in the king's service, 'worked' their pardons of both their outlawry and their original felony; such men had their peace proclaimed in the county court before the sheriff and coroners,[2] as did men whose outlawries were quashed for any reason.[3] A third possibility was that most outlaws could, if they chose, continue their old existence with impunity. In 1445, for example, the sheriff of Sussex was ordered to have another county coroner elected in place of John Veske who was and had long been an outlaw.[4] When outlaws could hold such positions for any length of time, there can be little doubt that lesser, non-official men were rarely affected by outlawry. It would only have been the disorderly, felonious outlaws against whom petitions were made to Parliament—men like Friar Tuck who lurked in the Weald to the detriment of the district.[5]

Exactions and outlawries and the county court stages of appeals were essentially the concern of the county coroners, although there are occasional examples of the outlawry of men in the county court in the presence of the coroners of the borough in which they had lived.[6] Confessions and approvers' appeals, however, could be made equally well before any coroner.

Hearing and recording confessions was an important part of the coroner's work. Felons had to confess before the coroner before they

---

[1] E.g. Selden Soc. vol. 56, no. 876; J.I.1/1339, m. 6; K.B.9/164, m. 107d.
[2] See below, p. 78.
[3] E.g. K.B.29/7, m. 62 (quashed because in gaol at time of outlawry).
[4] *Sx. Arch. Colls.* xcvi, 22.
[5] E.g. *Cal. Pat. Rolls, 1416–1422*, p. 84; *Rotuli Parliamentorum*, I, 379.
[6] E.g. J.I.2/123, m. 4.

were allowed to abjure the realm or to turn approver, and the coroner also inherited from the hundred serjeant the right to hear confessions of felony when neither abjuration nor turning approver was contemplated.[1] Simple confessions, which had to be made in the presence of witnesses,[2] were very rare, because the felons had nothing to gain by making them and they could never subsequently deny them, but were summarily hanged on the production of the coroner's record.[3] Their number may have been even smaller than at first appears, for what seem to be simple confessions may sometimes have merely been the prelude to turning approver. Thieves captured with the mainour were the most common confessors,[4] and capture may well have preceded some confessions which seem from the records to have been the result of conscience.[5] Normally, the coroner's only other immediate duty was to commit the confessed felon to gaol, unless he was there already, sending with him a letter to the gaoler relating the nature of the confession.[6] In one Oxford case, however, a thief who was arrested and imprisoned in the town gaol confessed before the mayor and one of the coroners that he had hidden £11 underground and the two officials thereupon went and found the money.[7]

An approver was a medieval 'king's evidence'. A felon himself, if he successfully maintained his appeals against a certain number of others who had committed felonies in his company and secured their conviction, he escaped hanging and was allowed either perpetual imprisonment or to abjure the realm.[8] But before he could appeal others he had to confess his own felony or felonies.[9]

Whereas ordinary appeals had to be made in the county court of the county in which the felony had been committed, approvers could make their appeals in any county and at any place within the county.[10] The original rule was merely that they had to be made before a coroner in the presence of witnesses.[11] There is one case in

---

[1] *Trans. R. Hist. Soc.* 5th ser. VIII, 95.

[2] Bracton, II, 425; *The Mirror of Justices*, i. 13 (Selden Soc. vol. 7, p. 35). E.g. *Curia Regis Rolls*, VI, 10; VIII, 215.

[3] Bracton, II, 425. E.g. J.I.2/199, m. 4d; J.I.3/91, m. 2d.

[4] E.g. *ibid.*   [5] E.g. *Sx. Arch. Colls.* XCVI, 34.

[6] E.g. *ibid.*   [7] Oxon. Hist. Soc. XVIII, 209.

[8] *Fleta*, i. 36 (Selden Soc. vol. 72, p. 94).

[9] *Year Books 9–10 Henry V*, p. 22; F. C. Hamil, 'The King's Approvers', *Speculum*, XI, 240.

[10] W. Staundford, *Les Plees del Corone* (1607), ff. 52v, 53.

[11] *The Mirror of Justices*, i. 13 (Selden Soc. vol. 7, p. 35).

which a felon is said to have come before a Sussex coroner, confessed to theft and turned approver. Why he did so is not clear. The wording suggests that he acted voluntarily, but he may have done so to escape arrest or after arrest. Felons at large did not voluntarily seek a coroner, for very few appeals of approvers succeeded, and this Sussex approver withdrew his appeal at the Guildford gaol delivery and was hanged.[1] A few felons turned approver in sanctuary and then either abjured the realm or escaped from the church.[2] They had no real need to incriminate others, unlike Thomas Trippe, a thief who fled for sanctuary to St James's church near Chichester. Finding the door shut, he held on to the ring but was forcibly removed by his pursuers and committed to Chichester gaol. While there he turned approver and appealed an associate as an alternative safeguard. At the gaol delivery his petition to be restored to sanctuary was allowed, and when his abjuration was attested in court the justices allowed the appellee to go free, the abjuration having invalidated the appeal and the king having no suit in such cases.[3] In another case a man was appealed of burglary before the Arundel coroner and then immediately turned approver and appealed three associates.[4] This was contrary to the general rule that only men indicted and not appealed of felony could turn approver.[5] Another man turned approver before a Sussex coroner either at the inquest on the body of the man of whose death he was indicted or shortly afterwards.[6] These were very early stages at which to turn approver. More, although still only a few, turned approver in the county court.[7] Normally, however, it was only oppression or the imminence of conviction and death which encouraged felons to make this last desperate attempt to save their lives, and the great majority therefore turned approver either in gaol pending their trial or during the trial.

Many felons turned approver when their cases came up at gaol deliveries or in King's Bench, but it became increasingly popular to turn approver before justices of the peace because they had no power to determine such appeals and had to return the approver to prison until the next gaol delivery. It was only too well known that

---

[1] J.I.3/129, m. 62d.
[2] E.g. J.I.2/157, m. 4; 167, m. 5d; *Records of Mediaeval Oxford*, pp. 49–50.
[3] J.I.3/111, m. 5.   [4] *Sx. Arch. Colls.* XCVI, 26–7.
[5] *Speculum*, XI, 240.
[6] He later pleaded clergy but was found to be illiterate and was hanged (J.I.3/129, m. 61).   [7] E.g. J.I.1/690, m. 7; J.I.2/164, m. 9.

in the meantime such approvers would do their utmost to escape or
buy a pardon,[1] and it was to counteract this evil that the Commons
petitioned, unsuccessfully, in 1468 that J.P.'s be given 'full auctorite
and power, to assigne to every such Provers a Coroner or Coroners,
to here the seid Prover is appelle; and the same Justices to have
theruppon like power and auctorite, to here and determyn, doo and
execute all thyng growyng and to come theruppon, as youre seid
Commissioners for the delyveraunce of youre said Gailles have, as
by the lawe afore tyme have had and used'.[2] This petition implies
not only that J.P.'s could not determine approvers' appeals but also
that they could not even assign coroners to hear them, and this was
the legal position.[3] Nevertheless, from the late fourteenth century
onwards J.P.'s habitually assigned coroners to felons indicted before
them who wished to turn approver.[4]

Turning approver entailed the same procedure before J.P.'s, at
gaol deliveries and in King's Bench. The felon had first to plead
guilty and confess the felony or felonies of which he had been indicted. He could then ask for a coroner to be assigned to him 'for the
king's profit'. The justices next consulted as to whether this might
lawfully and profitably be done, invariably decided that it could,
made the felon swear on the Gospels that he would appeal all those
who were guilty of the same offence as he, omitting none for favour
and adding none through malice, warned him that he would be
hanged if he broke his oath, and finally assigned the approver one or
more of the coroners present in court to hear, record and report
whatever he had to say on one or more of the days specifically appointed for the hearing of the appeals. The approver was mean-
while returned to gaol.[5] That many such felons turned approver
merely to gain time in which to save their lives is proved by the fact
that many withdrew their appeals when they were due to be determined. Equally significantly, a Yorkshire felon who had been indicted before the West Riding J.P.'s and then turned approver, having thus gained his respite, refused to appeal anyone on any of the
three days allowed, as the coroner's letter to the J.P.'s relates.[6]

---

[1] *Speculum*, XI, 253–4.   [2] *Rotuli Parliamentorum*, V, 621.
[3] *Speculum*, XI, 239, n. 7; *Proceedings before the Justices of the Peace in the
Fourteenth and Fifteenth Centuries*, pp. cvi–cvii.
[4] E.g. *ibid.* pp. civ, cvi–cvii; *Sx. Arch. Colls.* XCVI, 28–9.
[5] *Speculum*, XI, 240; *Year Books 9–10 Henry V*, p. 22. E.g. *Sx. Arch. Colls.*
XCVI, 28–32.
[6] J.I.2/250, m. 2d.

Although many felons turned approver in court, more did so in gaol. Approvers were hanged on their confessions if they failed to prove their appeals and those who turned approver in gaol therefore faced trial and almost certain death sooner than if they had delayed turning approver until the next gaol delivery. Delay thus meant at worst a rather longer life, but also during that extended period a correspondingly greater chance of escaping from gaol. The only possible explanation of the fact that so many prisoners turned approver is that they were forced to do so. *The Mirror of Justices* gave, in its list of abuses, the compelling of felons to turn approver,[1] while it is significant that a large number of men who had turned approver in gaol withdrew their appeals at the gaol delivery.[2]

Sheriffs and gaolers forced prisoners to turn approver most frequently.[3] They had the greatest opportunity and also the most to gain since they were thereby provided with a chance of extortion from the appellees. It was against the compelling and procuring of approvers' appeals by sheriffs and gaolers that petitions and enactments were made throughout the fourteenth century,[4] but coroners were sometimes guilty,[5] as were some justices. In 1338 an approver disavowed his appeal, maintaining that it had been forced from him by a justice. The coroner asserted that there had been no compulsion and that the approver had made his appeal of his own free will. The approver, however, replied that he had been so distressed before the coroner's arrival and so afraid that his plight might become worse after he had gone, that he did not know what to say to him. The justices seem to have noted a ring of truth in this and ordered an inquiry into the circumstances by the approver's neighbours, although strictly he could have been condemned by the coroner's record.[6] It is significant that many coroners felt it necessary to record that approvers made their appeals of their own free will and unconstrained.[7]

As a result of this prevalent corruption there was a universal dis-

[1] v. 1. 18.

[2] *Speculum*, XI, 251; *The English Government at Work*, III, 161–2.

[3] E.g. *ibid.*

[4] E.g. *Rotuli Parliamentorum Anglie Hactenus Inediti*, ed. H. G. Richardson and G. O. Sayles (Camden 3rd ser. LI), p. 124; *Rotuli Parliamentorum*, II, 9, 266–7; 1 Edw. III, stat. 1, c. 7; 14 Edw. III, stat. 1, c. 10.

[5] See below, pp. 125–6.

[6] *Year Books 11 & 12 Edward III*, ed. A. J. Horwood (Rolls Series, 1883), p. 626.

[7] E.g. J.I.2/9, m. 2; 14, m. 19d.

trust of all approvers' appeals, many of which were withdrawn before the justices when the compulsion was removed, and an almost indiscriminate acquittal of the vast majority of appellees and consequent hanging of the approvers. Yet the number of felons turning approver remained fairly constant until well into the fifteenth century, when there was a rapid decline and such appeals virtually ceased.[1]

The coroner's duties in connection with approvers consisted of receiving their oaths,[2] recording their appeals verbatim, since, as with ordinary appeals, form and detail were all-important and any variation was fatal,[3] and ordering the sheriff to arrest and imprison the appellees. Borough coroners instructed borough officials to arrest any appellees living within the borough and the sheriff any living outside,[4] but no coroners had the power to order sheriffs of other counties to arrest appellees living outside the county in which the appeal was made.[5] It is probable that the amount of work brought upon the coroner by approvers increased after 1311 when the time allowed for their appeals was limited to three days.[6] This was intended to prevent local officials forcing false appeals out of approvers at widely separated times and was probably beneficial. But whereas previously most approvers had made all their appeals on the same day, it was the practice after 1311 for the justices or, in the event of appeals in gaol, the coroners themselves to assign three successive days for hearing them.[7] All three days were often not needed, but this seems not to have excused the coroner three visits to the gaol. A conscientious Coventry coroner, for example, recorded that on the two days following an approver's appeal he went to him and asked him whether he wished to say anything more, but he did not.[8] Nevertheless, a surprisingly large number of approvers used all three days, possibly in some cases inspired to greater feats of memory by the coroner, while a Sussex case of 1481 was very exceptional in that after the approver had made one long series of appeals at the gaol delivery and these had been reported to the justices, he said that

---

[1] *Speculum*, XI, 257.   [2] E.g. J.I.2/14, m. 19d.
[3] *Speculum*, XI, 242–3.
[4] E.g. J.I.2/110, m. 6d; Oxon. Hist. Soc. XVIII, 195–6.
[5] *Speculum*, XI, 241.   [6] 5 Edw. II (Ordinances), c. 34.
[7] E.g. J.I.2/111, m. 7; 164, m. 3; 250, m. 2d; K.B.9/271, m. 42; *Year Books 9–10 Henry V*, p. 22. Occasionally even when the justices had assigned a coroner it was the coroner who appointed the days (e.g. J.I.3/163, m. 12).
[8] J.I.2/191, m. 5. Cf. J.I.2/250, m. 2d (none of the three days used).

he had more to say and was assigned four more days although he probably used only one.[1] It is surprising that approvers were not required to make all their appeals on a single day. If this was because of a hope that some might disavow on the second and third days any false appeals made on the first, it seems never to have been gratified. In 1388, however, an approver in Newgate gaol threatened to appeal two wealthy men unless they paid him money; both took a coroner to the gaol and obtained the approver's confession of his attempted blackmail.[2]

[1] *Sx. Arch. Colls.* xcvi, 29–32.
[2] *Calendar of Letter-Books of the City of London: Letter-Book H*, ed. R. R. Sharpe (1907), pp. 328–30.

CHAPTER V

MISCELLANEOUS DUTIES

THE medieval coroner was no less busy and important than the law-books and statutes imply. His ignoring of felonies as such, treasure trove and wreck of the sea was counterbalanced by many other duties not generally described. Firstly, some coroners felt themselves obliged to take steps to help preserve the peace in emergencies, even if it meant that they were exceeding the normal bounds of their office without a special warrant to do so. A plaintiff alleged that in 1255, on their withdrawal from the county court at Chichester, the Sussex county coroners found his wife besieged in Manhood church, in which she had taken sanctuary two days before, after his house had been burgled, his servants assaulted and his maid beaten and thrown into a ditch. The coroners rescued her from the church and escorted her safely back to her home. The defendant was acquitted of all the charges, since it was found that he was the bishop of Chichester's bailiff and that he had merely distrained the husband to do suit at the hundred court, but the account of the church episode is so circumstantial as to ring true.[1] Even if it was untrue, it shows that coroners were not expected to ignore manifest breaches of the peace.

Secondly, the coroner's attendance at the county court meant that he witnessed matters with which he was otherwise not concerned, and his presence possibly prevented some shrieval oppression. In the thirteenth century such matters occasionally came to be entered on the coroners' rolls, probably because the clerks were not exactly certain where the boundary-line lay. A Devon roll of 1229 has several entries concerning the finding of sureties in the county court by felons of various kinds, while one Bedfordshire roll contains the case of a man suspected of stealing a sheep who was dealt with in the county court and another contains many cases of men coming to the county court and seeking the king's peace against others who had threatened them.[2] Such plaintiffs had to produce two sureties, and,

[1] J.I.1/911, m. 8d.
[2] Hunnisett, 'An Early Coroner's Roll', *Bull. Inst. Hist. Research*, XXX, 228–31; *Select Coroners' Rolls*, pp. 31, 33–8. These cases may be compared with the enrolment by the Gloucestershire coroners before 1221 of the finding of

if their enemies were not present, it was ordered that they be attached to come to the next county court to wage their peace towards the
plaintiffs. This they did by producing two sureties who guaranteed
that they would keep the peace in future. Although coroners' rolls
only rarely record such matters, these few examples suggest that the
coroner exercised general supervisory powers over all matters touching the king's peace which arose in the county court.

Thirdly, the coroner performed a large number of miscellaneous
duties of an administrative or judicial nature on the receipt of
special writs. Some of these duties, such as those connected with inquisitions *de odio et atia*, derived from his attendance in the county
court. Very occasionally the question whether or not an appeal was
malicious was not raised until it reached the justices. The coroner
was not concerned with such cases, the sheriff alone having to summon a jury.[1] From the beginning of the thirteenth century, however,
anyone who was imprisoned for homicide could apply to Chancery
for a writ *de odio et atia*,[2] which by the terms of *Magna Carta* was
free and could not be denied.[3] At first such writs were almost always
obtained to decide whether appeals were malicious, but with the decline in the popularity of appeals they were increasingly sought by
men indicted of homicide, and a large number of indictments were
found to have been maliciously procured. If hate and spite were established by the inquisition, the prisoner was released on bail until
his trial, which was still necessary.[4] In the 1250's the writ *de odio et
atia* underwent a slight change of form.[5] Previously, it had merely
ordered the sheriff to hold the inquiry by the oath of good and lawful
men of his county.[6] In practice, however, the county coroners often
attended these inquisitions, at least from the 1220's onwards, presumably because the sheriff found it convenient to hold them in the
county court, and by the 1230's this practice had become almost in-

---

sureties by a man imprisoned for homicide who was acquitted by the ordeal by
water (*Pleas of the Crown for Gloucester*, 1221, no. 383). This may have taken
place at the ordeal or later in the county court.
    [1] E.g. K.B.26/111, m. 7d.   [2] E.g. *Curia Regis Rolls*, IV, 275.
    [3] C.36 (*Select Charters*, p. 297). The author of *The Mirror of Justices* con-
sidered it to be an abuse that the writ was only obtainable in cases of homicide
(v. I. 59).
    [4] *Fleta*, i. 26 (Selden Soc. vol. 72, p. 67).
    [5] The developments discussed in this paragraph can be seen in the large
number of writs and inquisitions *de odio et atia* among Chancery, Criminal
Inquisitions (C. 144), which are too drastically calendared in *Cal. Inqs. Misc.* I–II.
    [6] E.g. Bracton, II, 346.

variable.[1] In the 1250's the writ was modified to make this essential, and the sheriff was thereafter always required to hold the inquisition in full county court *assumptis tecum custodibus placitorum corone nostre*.[2] The heyday of these inquisitions coincided with that of the general eyre. When gaol deliveries became frequent and regular[3] they became less necessary, and their numbers declined rapidly during the second half of Edward II's reign. They were eventually abolished in 1354.[4]

From about 1256, although a writ was always needed before they could be held, all inquisitions *de odio et atia* took place in the presence of the coroners. There were many similar inquisitions, also held pursuant to writs, which were often, but not invariably, held in their presence. With very few exceptions only the king could pardon felonies, abjurations and outlawries.[5] In the thirteenth century pardons were invariably granted to men who had committed homicide in self-defence, accidentally or while insane, and sometimes to other felons at a magnate's request. The original coroner's inquest was not usually regarded as sufficient by itself to justify the grant of a pardon to those who had committed homicide accidentally or in self-defence. A further inquiry was normally ordered to ensure that there had been no malice or evil intent. Although sometimes held by other special commissioners,[6] these second inquisitions were more frequently held by the sheriff. The writs ordering them were usually addressed to the sheriff alone, but, as with inquisitions *de odio et atia*, he probably held them in the county court on most occasions, with the result that in the later thirteenth century he was generally ordered to hold them there *assumptis tecum custodibus placitorum corone nostre*.[7] Practice varied, however, and some such inquisitions were held by a special commissioner together with the sheriff and county coroners[8] and some by one or more of the coroners

[1] C. T. Flower, *Introduction to the Curia Regis Rolls, 1199–1230* (Selden Soc. vol. 62), pp. 301–2.

[2] As in *Registrum Omnium Brevium: Originalium* (1634, ed.), f. 133v.

[3] See below, p. 112.   [4] 28 Edw. III, c. 9.

[5] Exceptions included the abbot of Battle and, for homicides committed in self-defence, the Cinque Ports (E. Turner, 'Battel Abbey', *Sx. Arch. Colls.* XVII, 42; Selden Soc. vol. 21, xl–xli).

[6] E.g. *Cal. Pat. Rolls, 1258–1266*, pp. 625, 639, 669.

[7] E.g. *Cal. Inqs. Misc.* I, 2099, 2204. Possibly this was one of the ultimate results of c. 14 of the Articles of the Barons, which was not included in *Magna Carta: Ut nullus vicecomes intromittat se de placitis ad coronam pertinentibus sine coronatoribus* (*Select Charters*, p. 287).

[8] E.g. *Cal. Inqs. Misc.* I, 2097.

alone.[1] Coroners of boroughs and liberties were not exempt from
these duties. In 1300, for example, although the writ originally
issued to the sheriff and coroners of Suffolk, the steward and coroners of Bury St Edmunds held the inquisition to discover whether or
not a homicide had been committed accidentally and, if it had,
whether the slayer was of good repute.[2]

During the period 1293–1301, when Edward I's French and
Scottish wars made pardons very numerous, many inquisitions were
held to discover both the nature of the homicide and the reputation
of the slayer.[3] There were also innumerable inquisitions held by the
sheriff and coroners on special writs concerning reputation alone,[4]
although these inquisitions *de gestu et fama* were later held before
the J.P.'s instead.[5] Details of outlawries, appeals and abjurations
were frequently demanded and might be obtained either from the
coroners' rolls[6] or, almost as frequently, especially if additional facts
were required with a view to issuing a pardon, from inquisitions in
the county court before the sheriff and coroners.[7] Thus it was sometimes found that an outlaw had been overseas at the time of the
promulgation of his outlawry[8] or an appellee at the time of the appeal.[9] In 1282 the adulterous Leicestershire chaplain, whose abjuration in 1270 is described above,[10] was granted a pardon, but before
this could be done a *certiorari* issued to the sheriff and coroners for
the cause of his abjuration. An inquisition was then held in the
county court because both county coroners of the time of the abjuration were dead and the sheriff was unable to certify from their
rolls.[11]

Pardons involved the county coroners in further duties. The
sheriff and coroners of the counties in which the felonies had been
committed had to proclaim the peace of the pardoned men, as they
similarly did when outlawries were for any reason quashed.[12] The
coroner's connection with pardons became even closer in 1336,
when pardons seem to have been granted indiscriminately to felons

[1] E.g. *Cal. Inqs. Misc.* I, 2368. In this case one Bedfordshire coroner acted on a privy seal writ in 1300.
[2] *Ibid.* no. 2382.   [3] E.g. *ibid.* nos. 2338–2408.
[4] E.g. *ibid.* nos. 2345–2361.   [5] E.g. *Sx. Notes & Queries*, XIV, 119.
[6] See below, pp. 99, 195.
[7] E.g. *Cal. Inqs. Misc.* I, 1361, 1838 (outlawries), 1052 (appeal and outlawry), 2270 (abjuration).
[8] E.g. *ibid.* nos.1264, 2259.   [9] E.g. *ibid.* no. 2248.
[10] P. 45.   [11] *Cal. Inqs. Misc.* I, 2254.
[12] E.g. K.B.29/7, m. 62; J.I.2/16, m. 5d.

and outlaws of all kinds provided that they surrendered to gaol, undertook to serve in the king's forces and found six men who would go surety for their future good behaviour. There had been a similar increase in the number of pardons in the 1290's, when soldiers were required for Gascony and Scotland, and at that time the sureties had to be produced in Chancery.[1] In 1336, however, it was decreed that they had to be produced instead in the county in which the felony had been committed before the sheriff and coroners, who were made responsible for seeing that the sureties were 'good and sufficient'. This new procedure was established for all felons pardoned in future; they had to find their sureties within three months of obtaining their pardons.[2] For some years after 1336 all sheriffs received numerous writs, stating that for the good service which a certain man of their county had given the king in Scotland, Flanders or elsewhere, the king had pardoned him his suit for all felonies and trespasses and any consequent outlawry and had granted him his firm peace, provided that he answer any other individual who might sue him for any of his offences; and ordering the sheriff to take surety from him for his good behaviour according to the statute and then to have the pardon read in full county court and his peace publicly proclaimed. After executing these writs, the sheriff endorsed them with a brief note to that effect, naming the coroners who had been present, and returned them to Chancery with the manucaption, which was sealed by all six sureties.[3] After a few years, however, the sheriff merely returned the writ with a detailed endorsement of its execution, only the Yorkshire and Lincolnshire sheriffs continuing to send a separate manucaption.

The number of pardons remained large during the rest of the Middle Ages. The sureties, usually six but occasionally only four, were found in the county court before the sheriff and coroners until towards the end of Edward III's reign, when the use of Chancery began to become popular again. By the early fifteenth century sureties were very rarely found in the county court, and as many writs to take sureties of pardoned men and proclaim their peace were issued to the J.P.'s as to the sheriff. So infrequent had the use of the county court become by the early 1460's that when the Lincolnshire sheriff

[1] C.202D/1-2.
[2] 10 Edw. III, stat. 1, c. 3.
[3] E.g. C.202D/3-5, *passim*. For the developments discussed in this and the next paragraph see C.202D/6-54, *passim*.

returned a manucaption to Chancery he felt it necessary to explain that a statute had allowed the alternatives of finding sureties either in Chancery or before the sheriff and coroners.[1]

It was not only pardons which led to writs to the sheriff and coroners to inquire concerning felonies. When appeals were discontinued in King's Bench the sheriff was sometimes ordered to inquire concerning all the details of the felonies with the county coroners,[2] although the sheriff and coroners were more frequently required merely to send any relevant appeals or indictments of the appellees that they might have.[3] During the hearing of a burglary case in Council in 1243, the accused put themselves on the verdict of the country. The sheriff of Sussex was therefore ordered to hold an inquisition with the county coroners in the county court to discover whether or not the burglary had been committed.[4] For such and similar reasons details concerning felonies of all kinds were frequently required in Chancery and the central courts of law, and the sheriff and coroners were continually ordered to provide them by holding inquisitions, especially in the thirteenth century.[5]

Forfeitures to the king were another constant cause of writs to the sheriff and coroners, although the writs for the appraisal of the lands and chattels of men outlawed on writs of exigent were the only ones normally issued to them.[6] When they were ordered to appraise the chattels of a fugitive homicide or a deodand, the implication is that the coroner, who should have appraised them unordered, had either done so inadequately or not at all.[7] Similar writs issued ordering the sheriff and coroners to inquire whether or not the possessions of homicides and abjurors were the king's escheat,[8] and on at least one occasion to restore goods to a man whose homicide was pardoned,[9] while in 1252 the sheriff and coroners of Lincolnshire were ordered to restore to its owner any stolen money found on certain hanged thieves.[10] The state of mind in which a man had taken his own life was important from the aspect of forfeiture, and in 1383 the sheriff

[1] In file C.202D/43.   [2] E.g. K.B.29/3, m. 55d.
[3] See below, p. 195.   [4] K.B.26/125, mm. 10, 14.
[5] E.g. Cal. Inqs. Misc. I, 1842 (theft), 2084 (robbery and imprisonment), 2192 (wounds); II, 436 (rape).
[6] See above, p. 67.
[7] E.g. Close Rolls, 1227–1231, p. 558; 1231–1234, p. 200.
[8] E.g. Cal. Inqs. Misc. I, 1190, 2184.
[9] Close Rolls, 1254–1256, p. 233.   [10] Close Rolls, 1251–1253, p. 248.

and coroners of Berkshire held an inquisition to discover whether or not a suicide had been insane.[1]

The sheriff and coroners were frequently ordered to inquire about the lands and chattels of felons of all kinds,[2] but inquisitions concerning treasure trove and wreck of the sea were normally held either by special commissioners or by the escheator.[3] In the event of a wreck, however, the sheriff was sometimes ordered to hold an inquisition,[4] and in 1280 the sheriff and coroners of Lincolnshire jointly inquired whether a wrecked ship and the goods in it ought to belong to the king,[5] while in 1331 another inquisition was held before the Lincolnshire sheriff and coroners concerning the seizure of a small whale which had come to land.[6]

Escheats of all kinds could be made the subject of inquisitions held before coroners by special writs. In 1220 all the sheriffs of England were ordered to make diligent inquiry in full county court as to what demesne lands were in John's hand at the beginning of the recent war and what escheats and lands of Normans had fallen to the king and who held them in 1220. The returns were to be made under the seals of the sheriffs and county coroners.[7] Most inquisitions were of a narrower nature, providing necessary information in particular cases. Many concerned escheated lands and goods,[8] and some were inquisitions *post mortem* and *ad quod damnum*.[9] The sheriff and coroners were frequently ordered to inquire into tenurial matters by themselves,[10] but the escheator was sometimes associated with them[11] or just with one or more of the coroners,[12] and in 1253 an inquisition concerning a warren was held before the sheriff, county coroners, escheator and the bailiff of Somerton.[13]

---

[1] *Cal. Inqs. Misc.* IV, 231.   [2] E.g. *ibid.* I, 1680, 2237.
[3] *Bull. Inst. Hist. Research*, XXXII, 135–6.
[4] E.g. *Cal. Inqs. Misc.* I, 1867, 2412.
[5] *Ibid.* no. 1199.   [6] *Ibid.* II, 1267.
[7] *Rotuli Litterarum Clausarum*, ed. T. D. Hardy (Rec. Comm. 1833–44), I, 437.
[8] E.g. *Cal. Inqs. Misc.* I, 211, 219, 310; *Victoria County History: Wiltshire*, V, 15.
[9] E.g. *Yorkshire Inquisitions*, I, ed. W. Brown (Yorks. Arch. Soc., Rec. Ser. XII), pp. 85–7; *Cal. Pat. Rolls, 1247–1258*, p. 473.
[10] E.g. *Cal. Inqs. Misc.* I, 140 (lands of aliens), 181 (custody of and election to vacant abbey), 196 (valuation of lands alienated from serjeanty without licence), 398 (suit of court), 2094 (lands entered upon by Cistercians).
[11] E.g. Yorks. Arch. Soc., Rec. Ser. XII, 45–6 (inquisition *ad quod dammum* held in full county court); *Cal. Inqs. Misc.* I, 179 (in this case the writ was issued to the escheator).
[12] E.g. *ibid.* no. 290; *Close Rolls, 1264–1268*, p. 2 (in full county court).
[13] *Cal. Inqs. Misc.* I, 172.

Most of the inquisitions so far cited were required in Chancery, but it was not only Chancery which ordered them. Any matter of fact upon which issue was joined by parties to a suit in the courts of King's Bench, Common Pleas or the Exchequer of Pleas might be resolved before the sheriff and coroners. When the parties submitted to the verdict of the country in the thirteenth century, one of two courses was followed. A jury of the neighbourhood might be summoned to Westminster or wherever the court was sitting—a course which often entailed great delays. Alternatively a writ could be sent to the sheriff of the county in which the dispute had originated, ordering him to hold an inquisition and make a return. The writ often contained the phrase *assumptis tecum custodibus placitorum corone nostre* and the return was made to the court from which the writ had issued, usually under the seals of the sheriff and coroners.[1] The commonest types of fact required concerned such matters as the seisin and descent of lands, grants by charter, dower, distraint, waste and trespass, to name but a few,[2] but their variety was considerable and on one occasion the sheriff and coroners had even to discover whether or not a man had the right to have a bull and a boar roaming at large in a village.[3]

Many writs ordered the inquisitions to be held in the county court, and there can be little doubt that that was where they were normally held. The Statute of Marlborough, for example, assumed that inquisitions arising out of writs of dower and *quare impedit* and assizes of darrein presentment, among others, would often be held before the sheriff and coroners in the county court.[4] In the majority of cases there was no advantage in going to the actual site of the dispute, whereas the sheriff and coroners regularly attended the county court and would have had little difficulty in securing the attendance of a jury there and, when charters were in dispute, their witnesses also.[5] In 1348, however, an inquisition was held by the sheriff and two Kent coroners not in the county court but at Shinglewell, where, as they found, an accidental fire had burned many houses, including

---

[1] E.g. *Curia Regis Rolls*, XII, 903. Sometimes two or more of those by whose oath the inquisition had been held had also to go to Westminster to bear the record of it (e.g. *ibid.* no. 1728).

[2] E.g. *Bracton's Note Book*, ed. F. W. Maitland (1887), nos. 332, 669 (grants by charters), 497, 608, 751 (land tenure, customs and services), 547 (seisin of lands), 540 (waste), 1131 (wardship and marriage).

[3] *Ibid.* no. 881.   [4] 52 Hen. III, c. 13.

[5] E.g. *Bracton's Note Book*, no. 332.

that of Michael de Ifeld, a coroner, which was burnt down together with a chapel in which was a chest containing his rolls and other official documents.[1] Inquisitions concerning felonies were also sometimes held away from the county court,[2] but these were exceptional. Unless the writ specifically ordered the sheriff and coroners to go to the land in question they rarely did so. All writs of redisseisin, however, which could be obtained by anyone who had recovered seisin of his freehold by an assize of novel disseisin or mort d'ancestor and was later disseised of it again by the same persons, ordered the sheriff to take the coroners and other lawful knights to the land in dispute and there hold an inquisition by the first jurors and others.[3] Also, when inquiry was made into the waste or destruction of lands and tenements, the writ often ordered it to be held on the spot.[4]

Although never completely untroubled by them, the sheriff and coroners were never again required to hold as many inquisitions as during the thirteenth century. Inquisitions *de odio et atia* died out, those concerning escheats were normally assigned to the escheators[5] and those relating to the facts at issue in cases in the central law courts came often to be taken locally before justices of *nisi prius*.[6] By contrast, the number of administrative duties which the sheriff and coroners were ordered to perform remained much more constant throughout the Middle Ages.

These more often involved activity outside the county court, although not always. Whereas in 1257 the sheriff of Norfolk received a writ ordering him to take the coroners and four discreet knights of the county to visit a woman who was said to be insane,[7] in 1223 the sheriff of Wiltshire was ordered to produce a widow at the next county court when she was to be viewed by discreet and lawful knights and viewed and touched on the breasts and womb by discreet and lawful women before a special commissioner and the county coroners in order to discover whether or not she was pregnant, as she alleged.[8] When error was alleged in a county court plea, a writ of *recordari facias* issued to the sheriff, ordering him to record the plea in full county court *assumptis tecum custodibus placitorum corone nostre* and to have the record, as well as four of the lawful men

---

[1] *Cal. Inqs. Misc.* III, 7.   [2] E.g. C.47/81/6, no. 173 (homicide).
[3] 20 Hen. III (Statute of Merton), c. 3. E.g. *Cal. Inqs. Misc.* IV, 372.
[4] E.g. K.B.26/121, m. 30d.   [5] *Cal. Inqs. Misc.* III–IV, *passim*.
[6] Plucknett, *A Concise History of the Common Law*, pp. 29, 157–8.
[7] *Cal. Inqs. Misc.* I, 2095.   [8] *Bracton's Note Book*, no. 1605.

who were present at its making, before the justices.[1] In 1239 the sheriff of Hertfordshire was ordered to see that one man paid money due to another before the coroners in the county court,[2] and in 1300 the sheriff and coroners of every county were ordered to see to the election in the county court of knights to go to York to deliberate about the observation of *Magna Carta* and the Forest Charter.[3] But when the inhabitants of Shrewsbury complained in 1224 that a weir had been constructed on the Severn, which was a royal and public waterway, without the king's consent and to the hindrance of navigation, the sheriff was ordered to go to the weir with the county coroners and other lawful men and, if the position was found to be as described, to cause it to be destroyed.[4] Thirty years later the sheriff and coroners of Herefordshire were required to measure all weirs on the rivers in their bailiwick and reduce them to their former size, and to destroy all fish traps and small nets found in the rivers.[5]

The sheriff and coroners were often given important financial duties, especially in Henry III's reign. On one occasion those of Shropshire and Staffordshire were specially commissioned to assess a tallage,[6] and on another those of Somerset and Dorset had to inquire about the king's debts.[7] In 1354 the sheriff and coroners of Hertfordshire were ordered to assess the amount of money needed to rebuild or repair Hertford gaol, to apportion it among the men of the county, levy it from them and apply it to the work.[8] This writ must have been executed partly in and partly outside the county court. On four similar occasions in the fourteenth century, when the sheriff of Wiltshire was authorised to spend money on the repair of buildings in or near the castle of Old Sarum, one or more of the county coroners were appointed to view, control and testify to the expenditure.[9] This is another reminder that coroners had originally been created to act as a check upon the sheriff, especially in financial matters. Indeed, the fact that they were so often associated with the

---

[1] E.g. Surtees Soc. LXXXVIII, 195.   [2] K.B.26/120, m. 27d.
[3] *Cal. Close Rolls, 1296-1302*, pp. 387-8.
[4] *Rotuli Litterarum Clausarum*, I, 622, 648.
[5] *Close Rolls, 1254-1256*, p. 7.   [6] C.60/38, m. 8.
[7] E.368/11, m. 4.   [8] *Cal. Close Rolls, 1354-1360*, p. 11.
[9] *Cal. Close Rolls, 1346-1349*, p. 430; *1349-1354*, p. 310; *1354-1360*, p. 468; *1360-1364*, p. 34. On the second occasion a second person was associated with the coroner. In earlier cases of repairs to the same castle in this period other men were appointed to supervise the work and expenditure (e.g. *Cal. Close Rolls, 1333-1337*, p. 254; *1337-1339*, p. 558).

sheriff in the execution of writs testifies to their continuing value as checks.

The fifteenth-century teaching was that it appeared from the terms of the writ of redisseisin, and because any *certiorari* would be directed to him alone, that the sheriff was the 'sole judge' and the coroners were merely witnesses or assistants.[1] If this is so, it is true of all inquisitions held on special writs addressed to the sheriff and containing the words *assumptis tecum custodibus placitorum corone nostre*, but in all cases the attendance of the coroners was essential. Their absence invalidated them.[2] Thus an inquisition into a Kent outlawry was delayed for one county court in 1274 because no coroner attended.[3] In 1327 a plaintiff, who had a writ of redisseisin, alleged in the Exchequer of Pleas that, although the sheriff and all the others necessary were present on the agreed day and the inquisition could have been held, the sheriff postponed it out of favour for the defendant and in the meantime the plaintiff had suffered damage which he estimated at £40. The sheriff replied that he could not proceed to execution because the coroners, 'without whom nothing should be done in this matter', did not attend on the appointed day.[4] Whoever was speaking the truth, the coroners' presence was clearly regarded as essential.

The coroners were always ordered to collect and pay amercements suffered by the sheriff and any other debts which he owed,[5] but the check exercised by the coroners on the sheriff became more regular and effective with the Exchequer reforms towards the end of Edward II's reign. One of the new arrangements was for long notice to be given of the sheriff's day of account and for writs to issue to the county coroners who had to warn the sheriff to attend on the

---

[1] *Readings and Moots at the Inns of Court in the Fifteenth Century*, ed. S. E. Thorne, I (Selden Soc. vol. 71), 53. [2] E.g. *ibid*.

[3] *Cal. Inqs. Misc.* I, 2186. In 1231 a case concerning customs and services was adjourned and a *sicut alias* was sent to the sheriff of Wiltshire when one of the parties complained before the justices that the inquisition which they had ordered had not been held before the sheriff and coroners nor in the county court nor by knights (*Bracton's Note Book*, no. 585). This may be compared with a case of 1235, when the sheriff of Sussex was ordered to make record of an appeal of homicide before the coroners in full county court and return it under his and the coroners' seals. It was successfully maintained against the record, when sent, that it was not made in full county court but elsewhere in secret and before the coroners alone, who were the appellor's enemies (K.B.26/115B, m. 25d).

[4] E.13/54, m. 1.

[5] W. A. Morris in *The English Government at Work, 1327–1336*, II, ed. W. A. Morris and J. R. Strayer (Cambridge, Mass. 1947), p. 64, n. 8.

appointed day. The coroners had also to have it announced in the county court that bailiffs of liberties, who answered personally concerning the king's dues, should attend on the same day, and in the county court and elsewhere that those who had Exchequer tallies for which allowance had not been made, those who claimed allowance or quittance of debts and, most important, those who wished to complain of any oppressions by the sheriff or bailiffs should all appear at the account. This order by Exchequer writ to the coroners became a normal annual practice from 1326 onwards.[1] It may be compared with the order given to all coroners in 1309 to proclaim that all persons aggrieved in prisage matters should appear before special commissioners of inquiry.[2]

In the fifteenth century, at least, the clerk of the warrants and estreats, an official of the court of Common Pleas, made up a list of estreats for each county from the De Banco roll every term and delivered it by way of the clerk of the assizes to the coroners, who assessed the amercements and returned the list to the clerk of the warrants and estreats, who was then able to compile his Estreat Roll for the use of the Exchequer.[3] Another recurring duty was given to the coroners by statute in 1444. Writs had previously issued to the sheriff to levy the wages of the knights of the shire for the time of their attendance in Parliament. In 1444 it was alleged that they had habitually levied more money than was due to the knights, retaining the surplus for themselves. The statute aimed at remedying this by ordaining that in future the sheriffs were to proclaim openly in the county court following the receipt of such writs that all the coroners, chief constables of the peace and hundred and wapentake bailiffs of the county should be at the next county court to assess the wages, which the sheriff would then levy and pay to the knights.[4] An even stricter control of the sheriff by the coroners had been introduced in 1338, when the coroners and knights of all counties were ordered to see to the election of sheriffs in full county court and to make their return under the seals of the coroners and four of the knights.[5] These

[1] *The English Government at Work*, II, 90–1. The writs were always enrolled on the L.T.R. Memoranda Rolls among the *brevia retornabilia* (e.g. E.368/191, m. 131; 194, m. 112).
[2] *Cal. Pat. Rolls, 1307–1313*, p. 249.
[3] Hastings, *The Court of Common Pleas in Fifteenth Century England*, pp. 148–9.   [4] 23 Hen. VI, c. 10.
[5] *Cal. Close Rolls, 1337–1339*, p. 463; *1339–1341*, p. 193. Cf. *Cal. Fine Rolls*, V, 94, 154.

same coroners and knights had also to undertake on behalf of the county that they would be answerable for the sheriffs whose election they had supervised.[1] These orders, however, were obeyed in only a few counties and the system was replaced in 1340 by the annual appointment of sheriffs in the Exchequer.[2]

The writs described in the last paragraph form a natural and convenient bridge between those cases in which the coroners acted as a check upon the sheriff by being associated with him and those in which they exercised yet greater control by acting in place of him. When ordered by a special writ, the county coroners could take over any of the sheriff's duties, and they were frequently required to do so. When the sheriff was a party to a law suit, writs relating to it, which would otherwise have been addressed to him, issued instead to the coroners. The same happened if the sheriff was suspected of partiality towards one of the parties, if he had deliberately or through negligence impeded the course of justice by delaying action, or if he was accused of making a false return. The rule seems to have been that when the sheriff was disqualified from acting in a particular case the coroners were ordered to deal with it instead, whereas if he was temporarily incapacitated the under-sheriff acted for him in all cases.[3] The distinction is due to the fact that the under-sheriff was the sheriff's subordinate, whereas the coroners were largely independent of him. Orders were only given to the coroners during the period of office of the partial or defaulting sheriff. The 1414 statute against riots and unlawful assemblies, for example, ordered that if the sheriff defaulted a commission should be appointed to inquire into such disturbances and the default, and that the county coroners should impanel the jury while the defaulting sheriff remained in office; but if he had been replaced before the inquiry was held, the new sheriff and not the coroners had to impanel the jury.[4] In 1470, however, Littleton decided that when an array of jurors had been quashed by the sheriff's default and the *venire facias* and *habeas*

---

[1] In 1339 those of Sussex omitted to do this and they were therefore ordered to make a second return to that effect (*Cal. Close Rolls, 1339–1341*, pp. 335–6).

[2] 14 Edw. III, stat. 1, c. 7. For the failure of the 1338 experiment see T. F. Tout, *Chapters in the Administrative History of Mediaeval England* (Manchester, 1920–33), III, 93–5.

[3] *The English Government at Work*, III, 164. According to *Britton* (iii.7.9) if the sheriff neglected to allot the parcels of land in a partition, either a writ should issue to the coroners or a special justice should be commissioned to act.

[4] 2 Hen. V, stat. 1, c. 8.

corpus had been awarded to the coroners and the case had then gone *sine die*, in the event of a resummons the order should go directly to the coroners.[1]

The dictum of the justices in 1340, that when the sheriff was a party the plaintiff might have a writ directed to the coroners if necessary and if he wished,[2] is true of all types of plea. As early as 1228 the coroners of the North and West Ridings were ordered to have twenty-four jurors before the justices at Ripon when the sheriff of Yorkshire was accused of usurping the liberties of the church of St Peter and St Wilfrid there.[3] In 1309 the order to summon the jury, by whom commissioners were to inquire concerning the removal of Templars' goods in Yorkshire, was given to the county coroners because the sheriff was one of those who had carried them off, and the same coroners were ordered to have the recognitors in a case of darrein presentment at Westminster in 1313 because the sheriff was one of the principals.[4] In 1327 the sheriff of Staffordshire reported to King's Bench that one of those, whom a woman was appealing of the death of her husband, had been arrested and imprisoned but was too ill to be brought to court. The woman thereupon maintained that this appellee was none other than the sheriff himself, and the county coroners were therefore ordered to attach him and produce him in court.[5] In Devon Nicholas Tewkesbury, on being given a pound, allowed a captured thief to escape with the mainour. The sheriff was ordered to extend Nicholas's lands, and process continued to issue to the sheriff until Nicholas himself became sheriff, when it issued to the coroners instead.[6] A slightly different variation occurred in 1223, when the sheriff of Buckinghamshire was accused of unjust distraint. The knights of the county were ordered to record, in the presence of the coroners, whether the plaintiff had fined with the sheriff for his beasts, and other details.[7]

[1] *Year Books 10 Edward IV and 49 Henry VI*, ed. N. Neilson (Selden Soc. vol. 47), p. 119.

[2] *Year Books 14 Edward III*, ed. L. O. Pike (Rolls Series, 1888), p. 36.

[3] *Memorials of the Church of SS Peter and Wilfrid, Ripon*, ed. J. T. Fowler, 1 (Surtees Soc. LXXIV), pp. 56–7. The first order was ineffective but it was successfully repeated.

[4] *Cal. Chancery Warrants*, 1, 304; *Year Books 6 Edward II*, ed. P. Vinogradoff and L. Ehrlich (Selden Soc. vol. 34), p. 56.

[5] 'Extracts from the Plea Rolls of the reign of Edward III', ed. G. Wrottesley, *Wm Salt Arch. Soc.* XIV, 3.

[6] *Placitorum Abbreviatio*, ed. W. Illingworth (Rec. Comm. 1811), p. 312.

[7] *Bracton's Note Book*, no. 1623.

Finally, when the sheriff failed to render his account at the Exchequer, the county coroners were always ordered to distrain and attach him.[1]

This use of the coroners was sometimes abused. It was alleged in 1433 that it was a common practice for men to get their assizes of novel disseisin directed to the coroners by naming the sheriff as one of the disseisors, although he neither was nor ever had been disseisor or tenant. This practice was injurious not only to the sheriff but also to the tenants, who often remained ignorant of the assizes, not finding any against them in the sheriff's file, and so they frequently lost their tenements by default. A statute of the same year attempted to meet this complaint by ordering that such writs be quashed and the plaintiffs be 'in the grievous mercy of the king' when the tenants averred that the sheriff had never been disseisor or tenant of the lands concerned,[2] but this was not a complete remedy in that it provided no means of overcoming the tenants' ignorance of the writs.

It was often alleged that the sheriff was partial. In his return to a writ of exigent the sheriff of Warwickshire stated that the exacted woman appeared at the fifth county court when he took her prisoner, but that he could not produce her in court because she was pregnant and to do so would endanger the lives of the woman and her child. It was testified, however, that she was in good health and capable of appearing, that the sheriff had taken her to his manor where she was at liberty and that he had made this return out of favour for her. The sheriff was therefore ordered to produce her in court and the county coroners to attach the sheriff and have him in King's Bench on the same day.[3] In a similar case the Derbyshire coroners were ordered to inquire about the abduction of an heir from Lichfield and, if they could find him, to keep him in safe custody and produce him in court. When they returned that they could not find him and it was stated that he was with the sheriff, they were ordered to produce him later.[4]

The Sussex sheriffs of Edward II's reign seem to have been

---

[1] E.g. *The English Government at Work*, III, 154; T. Madox, *The History and Antiquities of the Exchequer of the Kings of England* (1769), II, 238.
[2] 11 Hen. VI, c. 2.
[3] 'Extracts from the Plea Rolls of the reign of Edward II', ed. G. Wrottesley, *Wm Salt Arch. Soc.* x, 34.
[4] 'Extracts from the Plea Rolls of the reign of Edward I, 1293–1307', ed. G. Wrottesley, *ibid.* VII, 63.

particularly prone to partiality. At Horsham in July 1315 the justices
of assize observed that two writs of novel disseisin returned by Peter
de Vienne, the sheriff, were not in Chancery form and style nor were
they written in the recognisable hand of any Chancery clerk. They
therefore ordered the coroners to attach the sheriff and those of his
clerks who dealt with royal writs, as well as the demandants, and produce them at Westminster.[1] The justices obviously suspected the
sheriff of forgery, probably with good reason, for at the same session
a tenant in several assizes of novel disseisin complained that in all of
them he had secured the return of partial recognitors. The justices
accordingly gave the coroners the further duty of summoning other
recognitors for each of these assizes and also of viewing the disputed
tenements.[2] In another case, which dragged on during much of the
reign, William de Henle, a Sussex sheriff, ignored the *capias* for
William de Beaule, who was wanted in King's Bench to answer for
his ransom for a trespass; instead, out of favour, the sheriff allowed
him to wander at large in the county and falsely returned a *non est
inventus*. The county coroners were ordered to arrest Beaule and
either attach or arrest Henle and have them in court.[3] The third
Sussex sheriff to default in this reign was Henry Husee. He correctly
passed to the bailiff of a liberty a writ ordering the defendants in a
plea of trespass to be distrained to appear in King's Bench. The
bailiff executed it and made his return to the sheriff, who then delayed his return and the coroners were accordingly ordered to attach
him by sureties. This they did, but he failed to appear in court and
they were therefore ordered to distrain him to secure his appearance.[4]

In 1341 when a writ to the coroners was sought because the sheriff
was aiding one of the parties in a *quare impedit*, the justices maintained that first some default had to be found in the sheriff.[5] They probably meant that some particular default had to be specified, although
in some cases the coroners were used merely to guard against the
possibility of partiality. In 1307, for example, in a case in which the
treasurer was the defendant, the *venire facias* issued to the coroners

[1] Hunnisett, 'Mediaeval Diplomatic', *Sx. Notes & Queries*, XIV, 95–6.
[2] J.I.1/936, m. 10.
[3] K.B.27/216, m. 103; 222, m. 148; 228, m. 123; 232, m. 121(2); 234, m. 130d;
236, m. 111d; 238, Rex m. 13d. Cf. 240, Rex m. 2; 242, Rex m. 4; 244, Rex
m. 4d.
[4] *Ibid.* Rex m. 14d.
[5] *Year Books 15 Edward III*, ed. L. O. Pike (Rolls Ser. 1891), p. 162.

because the plaintiff claimed that the sheriff was 'subject to the treasurer by reason of his account and for other reasons'.[1] Similarly, process issued to the coroners when issue was joined on a question of fact when error was alleged in connection with a presentment at the sheriff's tourn,[2] and in 1254 the Herefordshire coroners were appointed by writ to inquire about certain privileges claimed by two hundreds concerning the tourn.[3] With this may be compared the *recordari facias*, which issued to the coroners when false judgment was alleged in the county court only after the sheriff had failed to execute a similar writ. They were then ordered both to record the plea and to summon the sheriff to answer for his default.[4]

Partiality must often have been the root cause of shrieval negligence or malpractice. The Register of Writs contains a number of writs to the coroners on the complaint by the plaintiff of default by the sheriff. A *venire facias vicecomitem* issued to them when the sheriff was accused of making a false return, such as that the writ directed to him had arrived too late for execution,[5] or when he was alleged to have suppressed or delayed action on writs returnable on a given day.[6] This ordered the coroners to have the sheriff at Westminster on a certain day to answer the king and the plaintiff; they were sometimes also required to see that the plaintiff found sureties for the prosecution of his claim and to return their names.[7] Other common writs ordered the coroners to attach the sheriff when he was accused of impanelling unfit jurors or of taking the beaupleader fine contrary to the Statute of Marlborough.[8] Before 1285 there was another writ *de cursu* which was directed to the coroners when the sheriff failed to return a *pone*; they had to deliver another *pone* to him personally and make return of the day of its delivery and the names of those present.[9] This writ became obsolete with the new procedure introduced by the second Statute of Westminster,[10] but the others were frequently used throughout the Middle Ages, just as some of them had been from the earliest years of the thirteenth century.[11]

[1] *Placitorum Abbreviatio*, p. 260. [2] *Year Books 14 Edward III*, p. 306.
[3] *Cal. Inqs. Misc.* I, 207. [4] E.g. *Bracton's Note Book*, no. 1019.
[5] *Registrum Omnium Brevium: Judicialium*, ff. 31v, 82–82v. Cf. ff. 67–67v.
[6] *Ibid.* f. 32. [7] *Ibid.* ff. 82–82v. [8] *Ibid.: Originalium*, ff. 178v, 179.
[9] *Ibid.* ff. 83–83v, 85v–86. [10] 13 Edw. I, c. 39.
[11] E.g. *Curia Regis Rolls*, v, 18; *Placita de Quo Warranto*, p. 685; *Placitorum Abbreviatio*, p. 294; *Year Books 5 Edward II*, ed. G. J. Turner and T. F. T. Plucknett (Selden Soc. vol. 63), p. 270; *Year Books 13 & 14 Edward III*, ed. L. O. Pike (Rolls Ser. 1886), p. 302; *Year Books 14 Edward III*, p. 238.

So frequently were coroners called upon to act in place of the sheriff in civil pleas and administrative matters that statutes dealing with these subjects often mentioned them. In 1436, for example, the statute concerning the type of person to sit on attaint juries assumed that such juries were empanelled by sheriffs, bailiffs of franchises and coroners, while in 1468 the statute against liveries assumed that either the sheriff or the coroners would distrain the defendants.[1] Normal county coroners, however, performed no such duties without a writ, despite Bracton. He regarded it as a general rule that a plaintiff could arrest an essoinee who was found wandering at large if he took the hundred serjeant and other lawful men of the neighbourhood with him. If the plaintiff could not take the serjeant he could still arrest the essoinee with the hue and cry, so that, if necessary, the men of the neighbourhood would be able to bear witness to what they had seen. He should then send for the coroners and serjeants so that they might also bear witness, and their record could only be traversed if the essoinee produced clear proofs to the contrary.[2] Bracton apparently considered that coroners acted *ex officio* in such cases, but there is no proof that they ever did so. Their only known connections with essoins were when they were required by special writ to hold inquisitions with the sheriff about details of particular essoins[3] or when they were ordered, after defaults by the sheriff and again by writ, to send four knights to view essoinees *de malo lecti*, give them a day for answering their plea if they were found not to be ill, and to summon the sheriff to hear judgment passed on him for his default.[4]

Borough coroners were sometimes ordered by writ to act in place of the bailiffs if the latter defaulted. In 1334, for example, a writ issued to the bailiffs of Great Yarmouth for indictments of a William Man, who had been indicted before the bailiffs and coroners, and the bailiffs replied that they had none. This return was regarded as insufficient, the bailiffs were amerced and a similar writ issued to the coroners.[5] Generally, however, borough coroners had less to do on special writs than county coroners. This was partly because they were concerned with a smaller area and partly because it was often thought wise to use county officials to discover facts relating to bor-

---

[1] 15 Hen. VI, c. 5; 8 Edw. IV, c. 2.   [2] Bracton, IV, 128.
[3] E.g. *Curia Regis Rolls*, XII, 1728.
[4] E.g. *Bracton's Note Book*, no. 1016.
[5] H. Swinden, *The History and Antiquities of the Ancient Burgh of Great Yarmouth* (Norwich, 1772), pp. 259–64.

oughs, especially if their liberties or finances were at stake. Thus in
1280 the sheriff and coroners of Lincolnshire held an inquiry into
the cloth industry of the city of Lincoln.[1] On other occasions commissions consisting of county and borough officials were appointed
to hold inquisitions concerning boroughs, as in 1256 when the
sheriff and coroners of the county of Oxford and the mayor of the
town found by inquisition that a homicide had been committed in
self-defence.[2] Such joint action was probably designed to overcome
any opposition by the burgesses to the county officials. In 1304,
however, when the sheriff and coroners of Northumberland were
ordered to inquire concerning a homicide's chattels which were in
Newcastle-upon-Tyne, they returned that they had no authority
within the borough.[3] Thereafter writs relating to boroughs which
had their own coroners were not normally addressed to county
officials. In 1384, for example, after the innkeepers of Northampton
had petitioned to be allowed to bake bread of legal measure in their
houses according to custom, the mayor and bailiffs were ordered to
allow them to do so. They replied that despite the writ they had forbidden the practice, since no innholder had ever had the right to
bake even horse-bread in his house and that this would be to the
detriment of the bakers and the whole town. Another writ therefore
issued, upon which an inquisition was held before the mayor, one of
the coroners, two bailiffs and other burgesses of Northampton which
confirmed the previous return.[4]

Although having less to do on special writs, many town coroners
had certain *ex officio* duties of an administrative or judicial nature
which the county coroners did not have. The Bristol coroners, for
example, were more closely connected with wagings of peace than
were the county coroners in the county court.[5] Complaints of
threats were usually made before one of the town coroners and one
of the bailiffs, not necessarily in a court. These officials then ordered
the arrest of those complained of and ultimately, if they were found,
received their sureties for their future good behaviour.[6] The Scarborough coroners kept crown pleas and tried others,[7] while many
borough coroners sat with other borough officials to hear pleas of
various kinds in the local courts, presumably in accordance with

---

[1] *Cal. Inqs. Misc.* I, 1202.   [2] *Cal. Pat. Rolls, 1247–1258*, p. 495.
[3] *Cal. Inqs. Misc.* I, 2415.   [4] *Ibid.* IV, 258.
[5] See above, pp. 75–6.   [6] E.g. J.I.2/34, mm. 2, 3d, 4.
[7] A. Ballard and J. Tait, *British Borough Charters 1216–1307* (Cambridge,
1923), p. 359.

their oath to see that the reeves dealt justly with both rich and poor;[1] this may be compared with the check which the county coroners kept on the sheriff in the county court. It was probably in the borough court that the borough officials, sometimes including the coroners, attested local deeds in their official capacity.[2] In 1382, when the mayor of Northampton died in office, it was the borough coroners and bailiffs who wrote to the treasurer and barons of the Exchequer asking for confirmation of the election of a certain Henry Lavenden for the remainder of the year.[3] The Ipswich coroners were even more intricately connected with borough administration. According to the constitution established in 1200, after the burgesses had elected two bailiffs and four coroners these officials nominated four men from each parish who elected the twelve portmen to help them to govern the town. This happened annually, and in 1200 after the first elections the bailiffs, coroners and portmen jointly prepared a set of ordinances for the government of the town, to which all the burgesses agreed.[4]

Some borough coroners were permanently assigned specific duties not normally belonging to the office. In 1221 the Worcester coroners were put in charge of the assize of wine, in 1389 the Shrewsbury coroners were made superintendents of all the town works, for which they were each allowed sixpence a week, and in 1451 the coroner of Coventry was made clerk for taking all future recognizances of debts by statutes merchant.[5] In 1462 Ludlow was exempted

---

[1] For some details see *Bull. Inst. Hist. Research*, XXXII, 124–5, 128–9. H. E. Salter has described the existence of two borough courts in Oxford, one meeting on Mondays at which the bailiffs heard cases initiated by Chancery writs and the other meeting occasionally on Saturdays when cases initiated by bill, especially cases concerning intrusion and fresh force, were heard by the bailiffs and coroners (*Munimenta Civitatis Oxonie*, ed. H. E. Salter (Oxon. Hist. Soc. LXXI), pp. xlv–xlvi). His distinction rests on comparatively few cases, while there is no evidence to support his guess, made before the recent work on procedure by bill, that the bills were obtained from the coroners.

[2] E.g. *City and County of Kingston upon Hull. Calendar of the Ancient Deeds, Letters, Miscellaneous Old Documents, etc., in the Archives of the Corporation*, ed. L. M. Stanewell (Kingston upon Hull, 1951), p. 5; *Hist. MSS. Comm., 14th Report*, App. Pt. VIII, p. 257. Similarly it was probably in the county court that the sheriff and county coroners witnessed deeds (e.g. *The Register of the Priory of Wetherhal*, ed. J. E. Prescott (Cumberland & Westmorland Antiq. & Arch. Soc., Rec. Ser. I), pp. 154–7), although they did so comparatively infrequently.

[3] S.C.1/43, no. 85.

[4] C. Gross, *The Gild Merchant* (Oxford, 1890), I, 23–6; II, 116–23.

[5] Above, p. 8; H. Owen and J. B. Blakeway, *A History of Shrewsbury* (1825), I, 173; *Cal. Charter Rolls*, VI, 116–17.

from normal gaol deliveries, the bailiffs and recorder or steward being empowered to deliver the town gaol instead. Because of this the
town coroner was given the duty, normally executed by the bailiffs,
of empanelling juries, making attachments and doing all other necessary things in connection with the gaol deliveries 'as the sheriffs of
the realm do', making their returns to the bailiffs and recorder or
steward.[1] In 1468 Wenlock received a charter containing the same
provisions,[2] but these two Shropshire boroughs were exceptional.
The only other gaol delivery at which coroners had any duties other
than attending with their rolls and memoranda and hearing approvers' appeals was that of Bedford gaol in 1230, when the county
coroners were appointed, with one other, as justices of gaol delivery.[3]

Coroners of liberties were not required to perform administrative
duties on special writs as frequently as their county and borough
counterparts, but they were not entirely exempt. In 1431, for example, the bishop of Hereford ordered the steward and his lieutenant, the two bailiffs and two coroners of the liberty of Mont-
gomery to arrest an excommunicate under pain of ecclesiastical cen-
sure.[4] And just as some franchisal coroners combined that office with
another,[5] so others regularly performed duties by virtue of their
office of coroner which were only performed on special writs elsewhere. The Durham coroners were very much the bishop's ministers. They took possession of escheats for the bishop and kept accounts, some of which survive. These include details of rents and
issues of the bishop's escheats, for which they were answerable at
the palatine Exchequer.[6] The coroners of the palatinate of Chester
and Flintshire also had special duties, which can only be paralleled
outside of franchises by those belonging to the coroners of Cornwall
and Northumberland, whose history presents so many differences
from that of the rest of England.[7]

[1] *Cal. Charter Rolls*, vi, 159.   [2] *Ibid.* p. 232.
[3] *Close Rolls, 1227–1231*, p. 397.
[4] *Registrum Thome Spofford Episcopi Herefordensis, 1422–1448*, ed. A. T.
Bannister (Canterbury & York Soc. XXIII), pp. 131–2.
[5] See below, p. 162.
[6] Lapsley, *The County Palatine of Durham*, pp. 87, n.1, 88, 271. The only
other coroner's account known to survive belonged to the Caernarvonshire
coroners of 20–21 Edw. III (E.101/507/29), although on at least one occasion a
Northumberland coroner not only appraised treasure trove but also delivered it
into the Wardrobe (*Cal. Pat. Rolls, 1281–1292*, p. 504).
[7] *Bull. Inst. Hist. Research*, XXXII, 124, 133.

CHAPTER VI

THE CORONERS' ROLLS

THE custody of crown pleas inevitably entailed keeping written records. When the coroner was called upon to act on a special writ, it was usually because information was urgently required or something had to be done at once. The return of the writ ended the matter as far as he was concerned and he kept no record of it. The duties which he performed *ex officio*, however, had to be recorded and the record kept until royal justices had dealt with the cases.

The fact that coroners kept written records entailed their attendance at many courts and greatly added to their travelling, as if inquests and abjurations did not involve them in enough. The courts were of two kinds: at some they recorded proceedings and in others they presented their rolls and other records when the cases were tried. The county court, held every four or six weeks, was much the most important of those in the first category, since the county coroners' attendance was obligatory throughout the Middle Ages in order to record appeals, exactions and outlawries and probably to check presentments of unnatural deaths also.[1] The county court was a twofold institution, with one court for civil pleas, which was not a court of record, although the sheriff kept a roll of its proceedings,[2] and one for pleas of the crown, whose proceedings both the sheriff and the coroners enrolled, although only the coroners' rolls were considered to be 'of record'.[3] *Britton* maintained that the coroners and suitors held the county court in its second aspect,[4] but the sheriff seems generally to have taken charge[5] except on rare occasions as

---

[1] The townships and hundreds were amerced at the eyre if the coroners' rolls showed that they had delayed presenting unnatural deaths in the county court (Selden Soc. vol. 24, pp. 75, 140; *Fleta*, i. 27 (Selden Soc. vol. 72, pp. 68–9)). There is no evidence to support the statement that the coroner presented his rolls at the county court (*The English Government at Work*, III, 160); indeed, many based their rolls entirely on the county court proceedings (see Hunnisett, 'The Medieval Coroners' Rolls', *Am. Journ. Leg. Hist.* III, 104–5).

[2] *Britton*, i.28.1; *Rolls from the Office of the Sheriff of Beds. and Bucks., 1332–1334*, ed. G. H. Fowler (Quarto Memoirs of the Beds. Hist. Rec. Soc. III).

[3] *Britton*, i.28.1. For the sheriff's 'counter-rolls' see below, pp. 104–6, 194–5.

[4] i.28.1.

[5] Writs of exigent and *de odio et atia* issued to him, for example (see above, pp. 65, 76–7).

when the coroners had to see to the election of a sheriff there.[1] Even
in small counties, attending the county court must often have meant
a long journey for at least one of the coroners, and one Yorkshire
coroner was removed from office because he lived in parts remote
from the county court.[2] By contrast the borough coroners lived a
very static life, merely attending the borough court.[3]

In the fourteenth and fifteenth centuries the coroners were always
summoned to attend the quarter sessions held by the justices of the
peace, just as they had been summoned to the sessions of their forerunners, the keepers of the peace, in the early fourteenth century.[4]
Their presence was needed in order that they might hear, record and
report the appeals of any who wished to turn approver there[5] and
also because the J.P.'s came to exercise control over them and jurisdiction over their misdeeds.[6] The J.P.'s ordered the sheriff to proclaim the session and to warn the coroners and others to attend,[7] but
normally only one coroner seems to have done so—he in whose district the session was held.[8]

The coroner's attendance at other local courts was at most spas-
modic. Just as he did not normally fulfil his theoretical obligation to
attend franchisal courts when they exercised the liberty of *infangenetheof* in order to enrol,[9] so it is very doubtful whether there was

---

[1] Above, pp. 86–7. One Sussex coroner, however, was able to impose amercements in the county court (*Sx. Arch. Colls.* XCVIII, 51).

[2] *Cal. Close Rolls, 1435–1441*, p. 416. Until 1337 the Sussex county court was
held at Chichester, Lewes, Shoreham and, less frequently, Horsham, with a
different venue nearly every month—an inconvenience for the sheriff and his
staff, but involving a fair distribution of the burden of travelling among the
county coroners. In 1337, however, it became permanently established at
Chichester, which meant that a coroner living in the extreme east of the county
might have to travel nearly seventy miles to the county court each month. Not
until 1504 was it enacted that the county court should be held alternately at
Chichester and Lewes, when the burden was spread once more (*Victoria County
History: Sussex*, I, 504; III, 95–6; VII, 15).

[3] See above, pp. 93–4.

[4] E.g. *The English Government at Work*, II, 66.

[5] E.g. *Sx. Arch. Colls.* XCVI, 28–9. There was no need for them to attend to
deal with exactions and outlawries, as maintained in *Yorkshire Sessions of the
Peace, 1361–1364*, ed. B. H. Putnam (Yorks. Arch. Soc., Rec. Ser. c), p. xxiv.
These were not promulgated in quarter sessions but in the county court (see
above, p. 61).

[6] See below, pp. 120, 198–9.

[7] *Proceedings before the Justices of the Peace in the Fourteenth and Fifteenth
Centuries*, p. xcvii.

[8] E.g. *Sx. Arch. Colls.* XCVI, 28–9. For coroners' districts see below, pp. 135–7.

[9] See above, p. 6.

H

ever a time when he attended every tourn, except in the liberty of the abbot of Furness where it was the duty of the bailiff and coroner to take inquests in all matters relating to the crown.[1] There is certainly no confirmation of the statement that the coroners should have kept a counter-roll of the pleas of the crown presented at the tourn,[2] and it seems that, at least after 1300, they only attended the tourn when there was a special reason, as in 1342 when the Buckinghamshire sheriff and coroners found it convenient to inquire into the lands and chattels of outlaws there.[3] Similarly, in the early thirteenth century they only attended hundred and wapentake courts at which appeals were made, and in the fifteenth century the Chichester coroners only attended the city view of frankpledge, which involved no travelling, when specially summoned to record approvers' appeals.[4]

Coroners had to bring their rolls and other records to many other courts for the determination of the cases. In the thirteenth century many special commissions were appointed to determine individual appeals[5] and there can be no doubt that the county coroners had to attend their sessions with their record of the original appeals. They were also always summoned to the delivery of gaols normally holding prisoners from their county.[6] General gaol deliveries were not as frequent in the thirteenth century as they became later, but the closing years of the century saw a great increase in the number of special deliveries for individual prisoners, especially from gaols which did not have general deliveries;[7] and when the prisoner had been indicted of homicide, the coroner who had held the inquest had to attend.[8]

In the late twelfth century and the first third of the thirteenth coroners were frequently summoned before the *Curia Regis* at Westminster or elsewhere. Although non-official knights of the shire were sometimes summoned to 'bear the record' of appeals and outlawries as well as of other matters,[9] they were more often accompanied or replaced by one or more of the coroners. The first duty known to have been performed by any coroners was the personal

---

[1] E.g. *Placita de Quo Warranto*, p. 371. In this liberty the coroner took his rolls to the tourn.
[2] *The English Government at Work*, III, 164.
[3] E.163/4/33.   [4] See above, pp. 56–8.
[5] E.g. *Cal. Pat. Rolls, 1272–1281*, pp. 117–18, 412; *1281–1292*, pp. 103, 145.
[6] E.g. *Rotuli Litterarum Clausarum*, I, 437; *Pat. Rolls, 1225–1232*, p. 183.
[7] E.g. *Cal. Pat. Rolls, 1272–1281*, pp. 339, 407.
[8] *Registrum Omnium Brevium: Judicialium*, ff. 74v, 76.
[9] E.g. *Curia Regis Rolls*, I, 166.

recording of an appeal of homicide by the Lincolnshire coroners in the *Curia Regis* in November 1194,[1] and the only recorded official act of the first known Sussex coroner is his journey in 1221 with the sheriff and ten knights to Westminster, where they personally recorded an outlawry.[2] Although in such cases the coroners may well have given oral testimony in court, it would have been natural for them to have taken a written record of the cases with them, and oral testimony came gradually to be dispensed with and the inconvenience of summoning coroners and others to Westminster was obviated by the almost exclusive use of the written record. As early as 1214 the sheriff was sometimes ordered to make a record of an appeal in writing and to send it under his seal either with some knights of the shire or by a coroner and knights.[3] By the 1220's the sheriff was often required to make a record of an appeal in the county court and send it to Westminster under his seal and those of the coroners, either with knights or without. This was the system described by Bracton,[4] but it was soon to be replaced in its turn. As early as 1229 the sheriff of Hampshire was ordered to send the record of an appeal from the coroners' rolls.[5] This was unusual at that date, but by the last quarter of the century it was normal for a *certiorari* from a central court to demand the record of a case as contained in the coroners' and sheriff's rolls. Only in exceptional cases was a special inquisition held in the county court, as in 1282 when the sheriff and coroners of Leicestershire held one into an abjuration, which had occurred twelve years before, because the coroners of that time were both dead and the sheriff could not certify the abjuration from their rolls.[6] From the late thirteenth century onwards coroners had only to attend King's Bench at Westminster when they were personally involved in a case or had defaulted,[7] or in

---

[1] *Trans. R. Hist. Soc.* 5th ser. VIII, 87–8.

[2] *Curia Regis Rolls*, X, 121. The outlaw was therefore hanged. In 1210 the Rutland coroners and knights attended the *Curia Regis* and reported a homicide's confession (*ibid.* VI, 10).

[3] E.g. *ibid.* VII, 110 (coroner and one knight), 169 (four knights). In the second case only two knights accompanied the written record, and later the sheriff and twelve knights had to attend personally (*ibid.* pp. 169, 172).

[4] II, 423, 434.

[5] *de rotulis coronatorum de interogacionibus responsionibus et confessionibus et omnibus aliis coram eis factis* (*Curia Regis Rolls*, XIII, 1905).

[6] *Cal. Inqs. Misc.* I, 2254. In 1274 the sheriff of Kent was ordered to discover details of an outlawry by inquisition in full county court and by the coroners' rolls (*ibid.* no. 2186).

[7] E.g. K.B.27/612, Rex m. 2.

very unusual circumstances, as when the sheriff and coroners of Sussex had to receive abjurors whom they were to conduct back to the highway from which they had been forcibly removed.[1]

During the thirteenth century, individual cases sometimes required the attendance of coroners in King's Bench or before special commissioners, and a number of coroners' cases might be dealt with by gaol delivery justices, but every case with which every coroner was concerned was heard during the general eyre. Held every few years at first, general eyres became more infrequent but also more lengthy as the century wore on,[2] and the coroners had to attend throughout the session. Although held within the county, the general eyre must have meant for many coroners a long journey, followed by a prolonged and expensive spell away from home. Few, and those mainly borough coroners, can have been so fortunate as to find that the session was to be held in their home town, while only coroners of highly privileged franchises, such as that of the abbot of Battle, found the justices coming to them to hold a special eyre instead of demanding their presence elsewhere.[3]

The coroner was originally established to minister to the general eyre, to keep the pleas of the crown until the eyre justices determined them, and at every eyre after 1194 the coroners were required to answer for all pleas with which they had been concerned since the previous eyre.[4] The sheriff was ordered to summon all who had been sheriffs and coroners to appear before the justices to answer for their periods of office.[5] In the early fourteenth century, when the general eyre was a very complicated affair, and the preliminary proceedings took several days, it was the practice for proclamation to be made on the first day that the coroners' rolls should be produced on a subsequent day—the third in the case of the Kent eyre of 1313–14.[6] The rolls of those coroners who had died before the eyre had also to be brought. For much of the thirteenth century the dead coroner's heir was nearly always responsible for producing his rolls. The eyres were fairly frequent, and so the proportion of dead to living coroners at each eyre was small and the heirs who acted for the deceased were normally the coroners' sons.[7] As eyres

[1] *Sx. Arch. Colls.* XCVI, 24.
[2] H. M. Cam, 'Studies in the Hundred Rolls', *Oxon. Studies in Soc. & Leg. Hist.* VI, 92–113.
[3] E.g. Selden Soc. vol. 24, p. 28.   [4] E.g. Linc. Rec. Soc. XXII, xliv–xlv.
[5] E.g. *Close Rolls, 1227–1231*, p. 379.   [6] Selden Soc. vol. 24, p. 92.
[7] E.g. J.I.1/40, m. 28d; 569A, m. 36; 701, m. 19; 954, m. 48.

grew less frequent, although deceased coroners' sons still produced the rolls most often,[1] the liability gradually extended to others. If the son had also died, his widow or son (the coroner's daughter-in-law and grandson) might be made accountable.[2] There might never have been a son, in which case the coroner's daughters and co-heiresses were jointly responsible; on one occasion there were five of them.[3] The heir did not need to be a direct descendant, and there are many instances of more remote 'kinsmen' bringing the rolls;[4] sometimes as many as four or six attended.[5] If the heir were a minor and in wardship at the time of the eyre, the responsibility devolved upon his guardian.[6]

Britton mentions only coroners and their heirs as responsible for producing the rolls at eyres,[7] but the justices had been confronted with the problem of the heirless coroner much earlier.[8] As general eyres grew less frequent, the theory gained ground that coroners' rolls descended with their lands and general orders were given to the sheriff to summon the heirs, executors or holders of the lands of dead coroners.[9] Coroners' widows often brought their husbands' rolls as sole or joint executrix,[10] although many executors of dead coroners were unrelated to them and they still had to bring the rolls.[11] In one case the heir and executors jointly answered for a deceased coroner and in another the son and heir and the coroner's widow jointly did so;[12] possibly the heirs had inherited only a part of the coroners' lands. The heir was normally the holder of the lands,[13] but obviously not of all of them in such cases as when the rolls were brought by the coroner's son and heir and two holders of his lands or by his brother and heir and by a man and woman who held his lands.[14] When a dead coroner had neither heirs nor executors, the holder of his lands had to bring his rolls.[15] If the lands had been

---

[1] E.g. J.I.1/806, m. 1; 1011, mm. 42, 59d.

[2] E.g. J.I.1/547A, m. 2; 635, m. 78.   [3] J.I.1/883, m. 1.

[4] E.g. J.I.1/169, m. 1d.   [5] E.g. J.I.1/383, m. 4; 384A, m. 8.

[6] E.g. J.I.1/66, m. 1; 1028, m. 1.   [7] i.3.8.

[8] E.g. J.I.1/238, m. 46.   [9] E.g. J.I.1/635, m. 78.

[10] E.g. J.I.1/549, m. 8d. After sons, widows most frequently brought dead coroners' rolls, but it is sometimes not known in what capacity they acted.

[11] E.g. J.I.1/369, m. 1; 544, m. 49.   [12] J.I.1/1078, m. 1; 635, m. 76d.

[13] E.g. J.I.1/169, m. 1d.   [14] J.I.1/635, m. 76d.

[15] E.g. J.I.1/169, m. 1d; 653, m. 31. There is one example of a father and son who had both been coroners and had both died before the Bedfordshire eyre of 1330, when the holder of their lands answered for both (J.I.1/26, m. 1). There are several cases of sons of dead coroners being coroners themselves and bringing their fathers' and their own rolls (e.g. J.I.1/247, m. 38), while Thomas de Bukton

divided, the holders of every part of them had to attend the eyre,[1] and when the lands were divided among the coroner's co-heiresses, both they and their husbands had often to attend, although the husbands sometimes came alone.[2]

There are only two exceptions to the rule that the rolls of dead coroners had to be produced before the eyre justices by their heirs, executors or the holders of their lands. When contemporary borough coroners kept one joint roll, the survivor had often to answer for both himself and his dead colleague, while in some other boroughs those coroners who were in office at the time of the eyre had to answer for those ex-coroners who were dead.[3] Secondly, but much less frequently, dead coroners' clerks might answer for them. One clerk attended the Hampshire eyre of 1256 in place of two deceased Winchester coroners,[4] but throughout the whole period of the general eyre there is only one other recorded instance of a clerk so acting and one of a clerk's widow doing so.[5] By contrast, there are many instances of clerks bringing, or being punished for failing to bring, the rolls of living coroners, and others which suggest that they could represent living coroners before the justices.[6]

The sheriff gave the justices the names of all who had been coroners since the previous eyre, whether county, borough or franchisal, and on the appointed day each coroner, or his representative if he were dead, handed in his rolls in a bag. Each bag was then sealed with the chief justice's seal and the name of the coroner to whom it belonged was written upon it. The bag was then redelivered to the coroner or his clerk, who was warned to have it ready when it was needed. The coroner had to bring the sealed bag on every subsequent day during the eyre.[7] In very exceptional circumstances

answered for three dead Northamptonshire coroners, his father John, Gregory de Lullyngton, part of whose lands he held, and Ralph Dyne (J.I.1/635, m.1).

[1] E.g. J.I.1/169, m. 1d; 207, m. 34; 635, m. 76d; 686, m. 1d.

[2] E.g. J.I.1/383, m. 61d.

[3] E.g. J.I.1/10, m. 40d; 361, m. 60(1); 579, mm. 66, 70; 686, m. 1d.

[4] J.I.1/778, m. 58d.   [5] J.I.1/686, m. 1d; 169, m. 1d.

[6] E.g. J.I.1/303, m. 52; 320, m. 30.

[7] *Britton*, i.3.8; Selden Soc. vol. 24, pp. 5, 14, 23, 47–9, 54–5; L. W. V. Harcourt, 'The Baga de Secretis', *Eng. Hist. Rev.* XXIII, 510; *Year Books 30 & 31 Edward I*, p. 74. There were minor variations from eyre to eyre. The bags were sometimes sealed with the chief clerk's seal (e.g. *ibid.*), at the 1329 Nottinghamshire eyre the coroner's name had to be written on each bag before it was delivered to the justices and at Northampton in the same year the justices proclaimed that the coroners' rolls had to be handed in in white bags on which were to be written the years covered by the rolls (*Eng. Hist. Rev.* XXIII, 510, n. 16).

coroners could attend by attorney. Thus Lawrence de Chaworth, a former coroner, who was probably very old, brought his rolls to the Nottinghamshire eyre of 1329 but was allowed to be represented by John de Chartres on subsequent days,[1] and when the holder of a dead coroner's lands was a notable person he usually attended by attorney.[2]

Whether the coroner attended personally or by proxy the procedure at the eyre was the same. When the hundred jurors' presentments of crown pleas began, he and his clerk had to swear that they would read the entries as they appeared in the rolls, adding nothing to them, that they would keep secret the king's and justices' counsel and that they would answer every question truthfully. They were then asked on their oath whether they had given anyone a copy of their rolls since they were summoned to the eyre; those confessing that they had were amerced. The justices next called for the bags and inspected the seals to see that they were unbroken. Only then were the coroners allowed to remove their rolls, and at the end of each day's sitting the bags were resealed, the seals being examined every morning.[3]

The extreme care taken with the coroners' rolls had a financial cause. These rolls were 'of record', and whenever the hundred jurors' presentments varied from them, however slightly, the jurors were amerced. It is arguable that there was no point in sealing the rolls. As soon as the first notice of the eyre had been given the hundred jurors knew that they would have to present all crown pleas which had arisen since the last eyre. If they did not possess full notes of all relevant coroners' inquests and abjurations, compiled at the time by other representatives of the hundred,[4] they could have approached the coroners for information at once. Even if they had waited until the eyre had begun, they could probably have had access to the coroners' files upon which the rolls were based, since only the rolls were sealed. Any coroner or jurors who wished to do trade of this kind would therefore have experienced no difficulty.

---

[1] J.I.1/686, m. 1. Chaworth had been coroner long before (see J.I.1/690, mm. 14–17, 19).

[2] E.g. J.I.1/653, m. 31 (the prior of Tynemouth). At the Bedfordshire eyre of 1330 one Dunstable coroner and the widow of a dead coroner's heir both appointed the same attorney (J.I.1/26, m. 51).

[3] Selden Soc. vol. 24, p. 21.

[4] As reasonably suggested in Wilts. Arch. & Nat. Hist. Soc., Rec. Branch, XII, 58, 63.

The fact that many differences were always found between the coroners' rolls and the jurors' presentments proves that the jurors rarely made any effort to gain access to the coroners' records, probably because they recognized the inevitable: that the eyre was primarily a taxing machine and that each locality would have to pay what it could reasonably afford whether the total number of its amercements was great or small.[1]

It is probably true that the general eyre would have been radically different if the coroner had been established before the first eyre.[2] Crown pleas were presented by the hundred jurors because originally they were the justices' main source of information. It must soon have become obvious that some check upon the presenting jurors was needed to ensure that they presented every case, even those which were certain to result in their financial loss, as through the *murdrum* fine. Such a check was provided by the coroner for all cases with which he was concerned—practically all the cases presented during the early thirteenth century, but an increasingly smaller proportion as the century wore on, although unnatural deaths always remained by far the largest single item.[3] For these cases the coroners' rolls made the hundred jurors' presentments 'an otiose ritual, productive merely of amercements'.[4] The justices imposed amercements whenever possible, whereas the long gaps between eyres rendered the arrest and trial of felons as a result of the presentments most unlikely.

There were many additional checks upon the presentments at eyres during the first quarter of the thirteenth century. At the 1218–19 Yorkshire eyre, for example, there were two cases of jurors presenting an outlawry and the coroners saying that they knew nothing about one and that there had been no outlawry in the second case. On each occasion the justices turned to 'the county' for information.[5] It was 'the county', in the person of twelve knights,[6] whose testimony was most frequently required after that of the coroners' rolls, but beadles, serjeants of hundreds, wapentakes and ridings, the four townships and the sheriffs' rolls were all called upon at times, while there were always the four neighbours and the 'first finder' or witnesses who might be questioned about unnatural

[1] Cf. above, p. 28.   [2] *Columbia Law Rev.* XXXIII, 1339–40.
[3] See above, p. 4.   [4] *Columbia Law Rev.* XXXIII, 1331, 1339–40.
[5] Selden Soc. vol. 56, nos. 817, 858.
[6] E.g. Linc. Rec. Soc. XXII, 629.

deaths. Sometimes several of these gave unanimous testimony about a case. Thus at the 1221 Gloucestershire eyre the sheriff, bailiffs, coroners and knights of the county all witnessed to an approver's appeal before the coroners.[1] In the same year two sureties denied their responsibility for producing a homicide's wife and chattels, the coroners and bailiffs thereupon declaring that they were responsible; and in 1225 the county and coroners of Somerset agreed that a homicide had occurred in wartime.[2] Finally, the county and coroners sometimes attested to having seen, or not seen, the wounds in an appeal of wounds, mayhem or rape,[3] but so might any one or more or all of the county, coroners, sheriff, beadle and hundred serjeant,[4] and there are examples of the same combinations testifying to the due prosecution of, or variations in, appeals.[5]

The fact that in these early years so many officials and bodies of men were called upon to bear witness to the same matter, even when there was no dissident, suggests that the justices often sought as much different testimony as possible in the hope of getting some disagreement and consequent amercements. If so, they were often successful. At the 1202 Lincolnshire eyre, for example, the county paid a fine for recording an appeal otherwise than as it was recorded by the coroners' rolls and the jurors' *veredictum*, 'because the county could not contradict the coroners and jurors'.[6] During the 1203 Staffordshire eyre the hundred jurors presented both orally and in their written *veredictum* that a homicide had not been outlawed and the county and coroners made a similar statement, but the coroners' rolls and sheriff's roll contained the outlawry and judgment was therefore passed against the jurors, county and coroners.[7] With very few exceptions, whatever was written in the coroners' rolls was

[1] *Pleas of the Crown for Gloucester, 1221*, no. 466.

[2] *Ibid.* no. 497; Somerset Rec. Soc. XI, 153. For other identical presentments by coroners and county about appeals and outlawries see *Pleas of the Crown for Gloucester, 1221*, nos. 87, 111; Selden Soc. vol. 56, no. 876.

[3] E.g. *Pleas of the Crown for Gloucester, 1221*, no. 87; Linc. Rec. Soc. XXII, 899.

[4] E.g. *ibid.* nos. 644 (county alone), 647 (sheriff and coroners), 851 (serjeant and coroners), 916 (serjeant and county), 625 (serjeant, coroners, sheriff and county), 629 (beadle, serjeant of the riding, coroners and twelve knights).

[5] E.g. *ibid.* nos. 773 (county alone), 916 (serjeant and county), 765 (sheriff and coroners); Selden Soc. vol. 59, no. 976 (sheriff, coroners, jurors and county).

[6] Linc. Rec. Soc. XXII, 811. Cf. *Select Pleas of the Crown*, ed. F. W. Maitland (Selden Soc. I), no. 75 (amercement of Shropshire hundred jurors in 1203 because they 'cannot contradict the county and the coroners').

[7] *Ibid.* no. 62.

regarded as true and any divergences from them, even by the coroners themselves, brought amercements. In 1221, however, judgment went against some Worcestershire jurors for concealing a plea found in the sheriff's roll.[1] There must have been some special reason for not preferring the coroners' rolls in this case.

After the 1220's the procedure in crown pleas at general eyres changed. Serjeants naturally ceased to give testimony as they sank to the level of subordinates,[2] and the county was also rarely called upon.[3] In most cases it is specifically stated to be the coroners' rolls alone which were used to check the hundred jurors' presentments, and in the rest, where the jurors are merely said to have concealed something, it may reasonably be assumed that the concealment had been revealed by the coroners' rolls. The sheriffs had always to hand in their crown plea rolls,[4] but they do not seem to have been used to check the presentments even with the coroners' rolls, as had often been done until the 1220's.[5] In 1262, when an appeal of theft was not found in the Sussex coroners' rolls, recourse would have been had to the sheriff's roll, but it was found that no sheriff had kept a crown plea roll since the previous eyre; judgment was therefore passed against all those who had been sheriff.[6] This case merely serves to show how unimportant the sheriffs considered their rolls to be and what little use the justices normally made of them even in appeals which they must have attended. By 1300, if the jurors presented an abjuration and it was not found in the coroners' rolls, it was assumed that there had been no abjuration and some group was amerced for an escape, even if the reason for the abjuration not being found was that the relevant coroner's rolls had not been handed in to the justices.[7]

This more summary procedure used in crown pleas was undoubtedly caused by the great increase in the number of crown pleas presented by reason of the increasing number of eyre articles and

---

[1] Selden Soc. vol. 53, no. 1105.   [2] See above, p. 3.

[3] In the 1248 Sussex eyre judgment was passed against the presenting jurors and coroners of the city of Chichester for saying that one man had been outlawed, whereas the coroners' rolls and the county recorded that it was another (J.I.1/909A, m. 21d), but the county was probably called upon to arbitrate between conflicting city and county coroners' rolls; this is the only example of the use of the county in coroners' cases in that or any of the later Sussex eyres.

[4] E.g. Selden Soc. vol. 24, pp. 22–3.

[5] E.g. Selden Soc. vol. 59, no. 809.   [6] J.I.1/912A, m. 36d.

[7] E.g. *Year Books 30 & 31 Edward I*, p. 514; Selden Soc. vol. 24, pp. 88, 91–2, 94, 109, 129–30.

the greater infrequency of eyres. Nevertheless, despite the smaller amount of testimony, there were still four important elements in each case: the oral presentments of the jurors and their written *veredicta*, and the coroners' rolls, which were both read by the coroners and inspected by the justices. This still allowed considerable scope for amercements for variations. It seems that after each oral presentment of a case the coroner read his record of it from his rolls and the jurors were amerced for any variation,[1] as they were for any variation between their written *veredictum* and the coroners' rolls which were compared later.[2] Defects in the written *veredicta* were punished even if the oral presentments had been flawless,[3] while judgment was also passed against those coroners who contradicted their rolls.[4]

The coroners' rolls served many purposes, financial and judicial. At general eyres the financial ones were most in evidence. Although the coroners' rolls alone were 'of record', the check could work both ways. Thus coroners were sometimes forced to admit that their rolls were deficient, not containing a genuine case or some details of a case presented by the hundred jurors.[5] Similarly, when the jurors' presentments and coroners' rolls differed as to the value of forfeited chattels, theory gave way to financial advantage and the higher value was usually assumed to be correct; either the coroner(s) or jurors, whichever presented the lesser price, were amerced, although the coroners could avoid amercement in such a case by having the names of the appraisers in their rolls.[6] In all other circumstances the jurors were automatically amerced if their presentments differed from the coroners' rolls. Their most frequent offence was termed 'concealment', which ranged from failure to present a case[7] or some detail of

---

[1] E.g. Selden Soc. vol. 24, p. 21.   [2] E.g. *ibid.* p. 57.

[3] E.g. J.I.1/921, mm. 10d, 12d.

[4] E.g. Selden Soc. vol. 59, no. 783. Such cases refute the statement that 'it is improbable that the coroner could have borne oral record at the eyre' (*Columbia Law Rev.* XXXIII, 1363). On Chester eyre rolls many crown pleas are entered in the form of presentments by the coroner and townships (e.g. Chester 17/13, mm. 18–19). There are even two fairly early examples of coroners stating how Englishry should be presented, although the county normally did that (J.I.1/37, mm. 28, 34; 318, m. 18. Cf. above, p. 29, n.1).

[5] E.g. J.I.1/912A, mm. 36d, 43; *Pleas of the Crown for Gloucester, 1221*, no. 257.

[6] Selden Soc. vol. 24, pp. 92–3.

[7] E.g. J.I.1/912A, m. 47; 921, m. 12d. At one Kent eyre judgment was passed against the presenting jurors of Canterbury for presenting no homicides and misadventures whereas the city coroner's rolls showed that there had been many since the last eyre (J.I.1/369, m. 36).

a case[1] enrolled by the coroners to presenting information which was at variance with the coroners' rolls.[2] Many of the variations were the result of attempts by the jurors to reduce some financial obligations. Into this category fall their 'false appraisals' of forfeited chattels,[3] while some Gloucestershire jurors were amerced in 1221 for presenting that a man had been drowned by falling into the Severn from a cliff, whereas the coroners' rolls disclosed that he had fallen from a boat which was therefore deodand.[4] The most important variation, however, was at the 1218–19 Yorkshire eyre, when the jurors tried to protect the sheriff, who had secured the conviction and hanging in the county court of a man appealed of homicide, by presenting this as a case of hanging after capture with the mainour; but the coroners' rolls disclosed the truth.[5]

It was not only the hundred jurors who suffered from the coroners' rolls. These rolls brought to light many facts which led to the amercement or more severe punishment of others: the names of neighbours, 'first finders' and presenters of Englishry who failed to attend the eyre,[6] the fact that townships or individuals had not attended inquests[7] or had made false appraisals or not made presentments there,[8] the omission of the hundred or townships to present inquests at the first county court after they had been held,[9] the removal or burial of bodies before the view,[10] undue delay in summoning the coroner,[11] obstruction of him,[12] and many other matters. When the rolls showed that any had fled on account of homicide their chattels were confiscated, and if they were also suspected of the

[1] E.g. J.I.1/912A, m. 36 (forfeited chattels); 921, mm. 10d (neighbours), 12 (suspects); 930, mm. 1d ('first finders' and neighbours), 3d (witnesses of deaths), 7 (sureties of neighbours and 'first finder'). Occasionally they were even amerced for not giving the name of the officiating coroner (e.g. Surtees Soc. LXXXVIII, 328).

[2] E.g. Somerset Rec. Soc. XI, 1022 (wrong coroner); Selden Soc. vol. 56, no. 506 (wrong 'first finder').

[3] E.g. ibid. no. 512; J.I.1/912A, m. 37.

[4] Pleas of the Crown for Gloucester, 1221, no. 231.

[5] The coroners had tried to prevent the sheriff's illegal action but had been overruled (Selden Soc. vol. 56, no. 744).

[6] See above, pp. 25–8.

[7] E.g. J.I.1/930, mm. 1, 3d, 4d, 6d, 19d.

[8] E.g. Selden Soc. vol. 56, no. 725.

[9] E.g. Selden Soc. vol. 24, pp. 75, 140.

[10] E.g. J.I.1/930, mm. 1, 16.   [11] E.g. ibid. m. 3d.

[12] E.g. J.I.1/912A, mm. 41d (preventing appraisal of deodand), 47d (preventing coroner from receiving abjuration); Somerset Rec. Soc. XI, 164 (preventing inquests).

felony by the jurors the justices placed them in the exigent.[1] Unnecessary orders or investigations were sometimes saved by the coroners' rolls testifying to the arrest, conviction and hanging of a homicide before the eyre.[2]

The coroners' rolls were very important in appeals. They were used to check them as they were made before the justices, in order to ensure that they were verbatim the same as they had been made in the county court. If they were not, the rolls would be used to support the appellee's plea of variation, however minute, the appeal would be quashed, the appellor arrested for a 'false appeal', the pledges for the prosecution amerced and the appellee tried at the king's suit.[3] Bracton emphasised that the appellor should make his appeal at the eyre before the coroners' enrolment was read, lest he should base his appeal on the enrolment.[4] The appellee might alternatively plead that suit had not been adequately made: the hue had not been raised, wounds had not been shown, there had been delay in prosecuting the appeal in the county court or it had not been prosecuted up to the fifth county court. In that event the appeal would again be quashed if the coroners' rolls supported the appellee.[5] Occasionally, the appellee denied that he had been appealed at all, only for the appeal to be found in the coroners' rolls.[6] The rolls often revealed the names of the sureties who guaranteed at the fourth county court to produce the appellee at the fifth and who were amerced for failing to do so;[7] and, when an appeal ceased, the rolls either disclosed the names of the pledges for its prosecution or the fact that the appellor was poor and had pledged his faith instead.[8] The date of the appeal could be very important. At the 1218–19 Yorkshire eyre, for example, the coroners testified that a woman, who was bringing an appeal of rape, had not prosecuted it before on account of the war, and because of this the appeal was not quashed for insufficient prosecution.[9] Similarly, after an appeal of rape had been adjudged to have been maliciously procured at the 1288 Sussex eyre, the justices wished to sentence the procuror, but he pleaded that the appeal had been made before the

---

[1] E.g. J.I.1/921, m. 1.
[2] E.g. *ibid.* m. 10. Cf. *ibid.* m. 8 (capture and imprisonment); J.I.1/930, m. 3d (harbouring).
[3] Bracton, II, 395–6; *Britton*, i.26.2; J.I.1/926, m. 26d. This was the practice as early as 1202 (e.g. Linc. Rec. Soc. XXII, 979).
[4] II, 415.   [5] *Ibid.* pp. 396, 406–7; Selden Soc. vol. 56, no. 581.
[6] E.g. *Pleas of the Crown for Gloucester, 1221*, no. 432.
[7] E.g. J.I.1/912A, mm. 43, 45d.
[8] E.g. Selden Soc. vol. 56, no. 510.   [9] *Ibid.* no. 740.

statute giving the king suit in such cases and the coroners' rolls upheld his plea.[1]

Coroners' rolls were the sole 'record' of abjurations, in that only
on their testimony could abjurors found at large in the country be
hanged.[2] The coroners' record usually meant hanging for such abjurors, unless it mentioned that the abjuration had been made
through fear and not as a result of a felony, in which case the justices
declared it void.[3] The coroners' rolls were equally important in confessions and appeals of approvers. The approver or confessed felon
could not deny his confession and, if his appeals failed, he was hanged on the testimony of the coroner's record.[4] Similarly, captured
outlaws could be summarily hanged on the production of the coroners' record of their outlawry.[5] In theory the coroners' rolls had the
same authority in cases of prison breach, but in practice coroners
enrolled neither prison breach nor cases of treasure trove or
wreck.[6]

The coroners' rolls sometimes produced unexpected punishments. They occasionally brought amercements upon the coroners
themselves, when they disclosed some irregularity in the execution
of their duties. A Sussex coroner was so misguided as to enter in his
roll that he had delivered four men, who had been arrested for homicide at his inquest, to four other men who had to produce them at the
next county court; and when they, rather surprisingly, attended, he
allowed them to go free. The hundred jurors said that the coroner
had taken nothing from the accused in return, but judgment was
passed against him for allowing unbailable men to go free without
warrant.[7] Coroners' rolls could also bring amercements upon
sheriffs,[8] and the Bedford and Northampton town coroners' rolls incidentally revealed that the borough courts had illegally exceeded
the bounds of their jurisdiction by extending their liberty of *infangenetheof*, for which offence many of the towns' liberties were
taken into the king's hand.[9]

The process of exigent arising from appeals often involved the

---

[1] J.I.1/930, m. 14d. The statute was 13 Edw. I, c. 34.
[2] Selden Soc. vol. 24, pp. 129–30; J.I.3/163, m. 10d. Hence, according to
Britton (i.17.1), it was essential for the coroner to enrol the abjuror's admission
that he was unwilling to surrender to the peace.
[3] E.g. J.I.1/921, m. 14.   [4] See above, p. 69.
[5] *Ibid.* pp. 67–8.   [6] *Bull. Inst. Hist. Research*, XXXII, 118–20, 131–6.
[7] J.I.1/921, m. 19. See also *ibid.* m. 26; 930, m. 10.
[8] E.g. J.I.1/921, m. 5.
[9] *Placita de Quo Warranto*, p. 18; J.I.1/635, m. 78.

county court in arithmetical error and consequent amercement. It was always the coroners' rolls which revealed such errors, although incidentally, and it is strange that the coroners did not exercise greater care and warn the suitors, especially as they often suffered themselves. Thus at the 1262 Sussex eyre the coroners' rolls revealed that one man had been outlawed on an appeal of homicide at the third county court, while the other three appellees found sureties to appear at the next, when, however, the appeal ceased. For this premature outlawry the whole county, the sheriff and the coroners were amerced.[1] This error is understandable, the suitors probably having forgotten that the first exaction did not coincide with the first day of the appeal in the county court.[2] It was against premature outlawries that *Britton* gave warning.[3] At the 1279 eyre, however, the coroners' rolls proved that the Sussex arithmetic had erred in the other direction, and the county was amerced for not outlawing those against whom an appeal had been prosecuted at five county courts.[4] The eyre of 1248 provides an even more unusual case. An appeal of homicide was made against five men at four successive county courts, not counting the first, and at the fourth one man undertook to have all five at the sixth county court. Why the sixth and not the fifth is not explained, but there must have been some special circumstances to account for this latitude, for the justices, instead of querying it, passed judgment against the whole county for not outlawing the appellees at the sixth or seventh county courts.[5] One final illegal practice, which the coroners' records of appeals and consequent exactions exposed, was irregularity in holding the county court. In common with most counties, Sussex should have held its county court at four-weekly intervals, but at both the 1279 and 1288 eyres judgment was passed against the whole county when the record of appeals in the coroners' rolls disclosed an interval of five weeks between two courts.[6] Similarly, the Northumberland coroners' record of an appeal incidentally informed the eyre justices that there had been an interval of seven weeks between two courts instead of the customary six.[7]

By the year 1300 most counties had experienced their last general eyre, the machinery of which had grown too cumbersome. A num-

[1] J.I.1/912A, m. 42. [2] See above, pp. 62–3.
[3] i.14.6. [4] J.I.1/921, m. 15d.
[5] J.I.1/909A, m. 22. [6] J.I.1/921, m. 8d; 926, m. 8d.
[7] Surtees Soc. LXXXVIII, 314–15.

ber of alternatives were introduced in its place. General deliveries of county, borough and franchisal gaols took on an increased importance and became much more frequent; there were at least three a year after 1330.[1] On receiving their commission, the justices sent a writ to the sheriff ordering him to warn all the coroners of the county and many other officials to attend,[2] but the sheriff seems generally to have used his discretion and summoned only those before whom the prisoners had been indicted or appealed. Even this meant that the Sussex county coroners had to attend every delivery of Guildford, the county gaol, and the borough and franchisal coroners some of them.[3] Occasionally, the Sussex prisoners were delivered from Horsham[4] but normally the Sussex coroners had to travel to Guildford in Surrey. The county coroners were also required to attend deliveries of the city gaol at Chichester, which the city coroners naturally attended regularly,[5] and the abbot's gaol at Battle, which the abbot's coroner always attended,[6] while the county coroner who officiated in the archbishop of Canterbury's Sussex lands had to attend many deliveries of the archbishop's gaol at Maidstone in Kent as well.[7] Not all counties had such great complications, but gaol deliveries must everywhere have been a burden on the coroner.

Fairly general commissions of oyer and terminer were appointed from time to time for most counties, beginning with the trailbaston commissions of the closing years of Edward I's reign. Coroners certainly attended the trailbaston sessions and the subsidiary inquiries which preceded them[8] and must often have attended other general sessions of oyer and terminer when their cases were determined. But compared with the eyre justices, who were justices *ad omnia placita*, their immediate successors had very limited commissions. Gaol delivery justices could only try felons who were in gaol, while the others, however wide the terms of their commissions might be, never dealt with cases of death by misadventure and abjurations. Misadventures and abjurations often resulted in forfeitures to the king of deodands and abjurors' chattels, and with the discontinuance of

---

[1] 4 Edw. III, c. 2.
[2] *Registrum Omnium Brevium: Judicialium*, f. 30. E.g. J.I.3/216A/4, mm. 39, 104, 151, 199, 206.
[3] E.g. *ibid.* mm. 40, 84, 151d, 199d, 205.
[4] E.g. *Sx. Arch. Colls.* XCVI, 29.   [5] E.g. J.I.3/123, m. 2.
[6] E.g. J.I.3/129, mm. 70–1; 163, m. 12; 216A/4, m. 104d.
[7] E.g. *Sx. Arch. Colls.* XCVI, 24; J.I.3/27, m. 35.
[8] E.g. J.I.1/933, m. 4; 934, m. 3d.

the general eyre these accrued in the hands of townships and individuals. It had been unprofitable to collect them by means of the general eyre, but the Hundred Years' War made it impossible for the king to surrender any source of revenue. Several other experiments were therefore tried in an attempt to fill the gap left by the general eyre.[1]

On 6 October 1337 the treasurer and barons of the Exchequer were ordered to summon before them all those who had been coroners in Yorkshire, Lincolnshire and Lancashire since the last eyres in those counties and the executors, heirs or others who might possess the rolls of dead coroners. They were to bring all their rolls and memoranda, as were those who had been justices of gaol delivery there, in order that the chattels of felons and fugitives and other issues might be levied after deliberation in the Exchequer between the treasurer and barons and two or three justices of the court of Common Pleas. This experiment was not a success, because a very large number of those who appeared pleaded that their rolls had been destroyed by the Scots. It would have been very difficult to have enforced the regular attendance at the Exchequer of large bodies of coroners, ex-coroners and representatives of those who had died from all the counties of England, even if the Exchequer officials had had the time to determine any outstanding pleas involved. The experiment was therefore not repeated.

Preference was given instead to another which had been introduced on the same day, when the justices of King's Bench were ordered to summon before them all those who had been coroners in Kent and other counties that they might visit since the last eyres there, and the heirs, executors or possessors of the rolls of those who had died. They were to bring their rolls and memoranda, as were those justices who had held gaol deliveries there. Once again the chief motive was to gain the forfeited chattels and deodands. This experiment may have been occasionally anticipated during the previous twenty years, but it was considerably developed after 1337.

---

[1] For an elaboration of the points made in the next six paragraphs see *Am. Journ. Leg. Hist.* III, 205–21. Detailed lists of all surviving medieval coroners' rolls with the occasions leading to their preservation will be found *ibid.* pp. 324–59, and a detailed analysis of the various kinds of rolls *ibid.* pp. 95–124. The majority of the coroners' rolls are sewn in Exchequer fashion, with a substantial minority sewn in Chancery fashion and a few showing a combination of the two methods. Many of the membranes have small pieces of parchment sewn to their sides (*ibid.* pp. 98–100).

King's Bench became increasingly peripatetic, and on its tours it held what Professor Putnam has called 'superior eyres' with augmenting frequency. When it did so, it called in all the rolls of the coroners, keepers and justices of the peace and other local officials of the county, and dealt with all the cases upon them. In the last years of Edward III's reign and throughout that of Richard II 'superior eyres' were constantly being held. The reign of Richard II, however, stands in the same relation to the 'superior eyre' as does that of Edward I to the general eyre. Just as there were very few general eyres after 1300, so only four counties experienced 'superior eyres' after 1400. One reason for this is the extreme unpopularity of all judicial visitations, but especially eyres, coupled with the weakness of the Lancastrian monarchy and its need to gain widespread support. Secondly, the Lancastrians probably jettisoned the 'superior eyre' the more willingly because the revenue thereby obtained must have been more than offset by the difficulties which it occasioned the court. Again, when King's Bench was most peripatetic, it could not keep a regular control over all counties and there were many that it never visited and others that it only visited once. Even in the fourteenth century it had been found more profitable to pardon all forfeited chattels periodically in return for a Parliamentary grant. Concurrently, the powers of the J.P.'s were continually augmented, until, by the fifteenth century, 'superior eyres' had been made largely unnecessary. Instead of concentrating unduly on a few counties, King's Bench in future remained at Westminster and exercised a more general control over them all. For those coroners who had to attend them, however, 'superior eyres' must have been a long and gruelling ordeal.

All coroners should have kept formal rolls, but there is ample proof that, with very few exceptions, they only had such rolls compiled when they were specifically summoned into a court. The basic coroners' records were not rolls but files of small pieces of parchment, each containing the record of a single case in note form. The general eyre justices, however, were adamant in demanding the rolls, and only the rolls, of all coroners and ex-coroners. When a Kent coroner's heir gave up the coroner's file instead of rolls, he was imprisoned and his lands were seized because the justices suspected that the records were forged. This case was unusual. Few coroners dared to present anything but formal rolls at general eyres, with the result that rolls were compiled for almost every thirteenth-century coroner, although this was not usually done until after the eyre had been announced. A few of these rolls have survived with the eyre rolls and a few others have survived from the small number of general eyres of the early fourteenth century; they are all now among the Public Records.

After the period of the general eyre formal rolls were only compiled on rare occasions. A few, mainly borough, coroners continued to compile them for some years after 1300 and some of these are still preserved among borough archives, but, with very few exceptions, they ceased doing so as both the memory of the last eyre and the possibility of another receded. Gaol delivery justices and justices of oyer and terminer were normally satisfied with fair copies of those inquests and other cases with which they were concerned and did not insist that the coroners produce formal rolls. In 1337, however, the rolls of the Yorkshire, Lincolnshire and Lancashire coroners were summoned into the Exchequer. None of these now survives, and the regularity with which the Yorkshire coroners or their representatives pleaded that their rolls had been destroyed by the Scots suggests that fifty years of freedom from general eyres had lured them into a sense of false security. Thereafter the occasional 'superior eyres', which did not affect every county, were the only occasions when any justices required a record of every case dealt with by every coroner. They did not demand formal rolls, but the announcement of a 'superior eyre' nevertheless produced a considerable flurry of hasty enrolment and most of the resulting rolls have been preserved among the records of the court of King's Bench and form the bulk of the surviving medieval coroners' rolls.

No 'superior eyre' was held after 1421 and the only coroners' rolls to survive from a later date are a few Middlesex and Surrey ones, which were required at Westminster by King's Bench, and one Monmouth borough roll. Other coroners had occasionally to certify particular cases into King's Bench and Chancery and send those concerning prisoners to the justices of gaol delivery, but the vast majority of their cases remained on their files and were never dealt with. The coroners of those counties which escaped 'superior eyres' and the 1337 Exchequer summons were therefore almost completely unsupervised for some two centuries—from the date of their last general eyre until 1487. The position was radically changed by statute in 1487. Thereafter every coroner was obliged to deliver regularly to the justices of gaol delivery all his indictments of homicide. These justices tried all the suspects who were in gaol and passed all the other indictments on to King's Bench. By 1500 most coroners were surrendering copies, in the form of individual indentures, of all their inquests, into cases of homicide, suicide, death by misadventure and natural death, and of their abjurations to the gaol delivery justices. Thus after 1500 coroners kept no crown plea for more than a few months and were neither able nor expected to compile formal rolls. But whereas there survive records of only a small proportion of the total number of the cases heard by medieval coroners, even for those counties from which some coroners' rolls are extant, for two and a half centuries after 1500 the records of King's Bench contain copies of almost every case of every coroner.

The history of the medieval coroner as a record keeper throws some light on the coroners' clerks. The eyre article of 1194, which created the office of coroner, possibly visualised the three knights always acting together, holding the inquests and abjurations and performing the other duties, while the clerk kept the written record of these events. If so, this did not last for long. By 1198 four knights were coroners in Cambridgeshire and only two clerks are certainly known to have been coroners in the whole of the Middle Ages.[1] There was far more work than the coroners could cope with jointly, and by the early thirteenth century, if not earlier, only one county coroner normally officiated at inquests and abjurations with the result that every coroner soon came to have his own clerk, who kept his files, sent fair copies of particular cases to superior courts when they were required and compiled formal rolls on the eve of the general eyres. The Worcestershire coroners had one clerk each by 1221,[2] and this soon became general.

Unfortunately, little is known about these clerks and very few are known by name.[3] Some seem to have been the private servants of the coroners and continued to serve them in another capacity when their period of office had ended. Thus Simon de Sherington was Robert Lyvet's clerk when Lyvet was sub-escheator in Sussex and also later when he was a Sussex coroner.[4] Others may have been permanent coroners' clerks, passing from the employment of one coroner to the

[1] J.I.1/497, m. 46 (Grimsby); *Hist. MSS. Comm., 9th Report*, App. Pt. 1, p. 226 (Ipswich).
[2] Selden Soc. vol. 53, no. 1231.
[3] For a list of the few Sussex coroners' clerks known by name see *Sx. Arch. Colls.* xcviii, 70.
[4] *Ibid.*

next. Others again, especially if, like two Sussex clerks, they came from landed families, may have served as coroners' clerks for a short time preparatory to taking up higher employment elsewhere. However that may be, while they were in office coroners' clerks were regarded as ministers of the king, and a king's attorney therefore pleaded that it was contempt of the king to take away writs and panels which were being carried by a coroner's clerk.[1]

Even less is known of fourteenth- than of thirteenth-century coroners' clerks, and only one is known by name after the end of the general eyre. The extant coroners' rolls of the late fourteenth century prove that one clerk, or a group of clerks acting together, often compiled the rolls of all the contemporary county coroners and sometimes those of borough and franchisal coroners as well. It would have been extravagant for a coroner to employ a clerk merely to keep his files, and it is therefore possible that the extension of literacy and cessation of eyres led many coroners to keep their own files and to employ local clerks, perhaps clerks on the sheriff's staff, when more formal documents were needed by a superior court.[2]

---

[1] *Placitorum Abbreviatio,* p. 284.   [2] *Am. Journ. Leg. Hist.* III, 215–17.

CHAPTER VII

CHARACTER AND EFFICIENCY

THE medieval coroner is thought to have been of a far higher character, less oppressive and less extortionate than the sheriff.[1] He may have been, but he nevertheless practised extortion regularly, if moderately. This was the inevitable result of his office being unpaid and, with very few exceptions, having no legitimate perquisites attached to it.[2] Before 1274 there was no deliberate campaign against extortion, although cases of it were occasionally presented to and punished by justices in eyre.[3] The Hundred Roll inquiry of 1274–5, however, was specially aimed at the misdeeds of local officials, including coroners and their clerks, and several articles were concerned with their receiving bribes to perform or not to perform their duties, concealing felonies and forfeitable chattels and amercing men summoned to inquests.[4] As far as coroners were concerned, this inquiry had three results. The first was contained in the 1275 Statute of Westminster, which decreed that any sheriff, coroner or other official found guilty of concealing felonies, not attaching or arresting felons or otherwise performing his duties out of favour for the felons, because of reward, fear or affinity, should have a year's imprison-

---

[1] E.g. *Select Coroners' Rolls*, p. xxvii; *The English Government at Work*, III, 165.

[2] By 23 Hen. VI, c. 9, he was allowed fourpence for making copies and returns of panels. Before that most coroners were merely paid a penny by each district when they attended the eyre as a contribution towards their expenses (E. Coke, *The Second Part of the Institutes of the Laws of England* (1797 ed.), p. 176), but even if this was paid at every eyre it would have been grossly inadequate. Lawful payments are otherwise only known to have been made to special coroners, such as the coroner of the verge, who seems to have been paid half a mark by the locality for holding inquests as well as other sums for his other duties (e.g. *Records of the Borough of Leicester*, ed. M. Bateson, II (1901), 10, 25, 65); the Durham coroners, who received sheaves of corn levied on the townships (Lapsley, *The County Palatine of Durham*, p. 87), but they were very exceptional (see above, p. 95); those of Shrewsbury, who after 1389 received sixpence a week, but for superintending the town works and not for their duties as coroners (Owen and Blakeway, *A History of Shrewsbury*, I, 173); and Roger Rolleston, who was appointed escheator and coroner of Holderness in 1438 and was permitted to take the 'due and customary wages and fees', which probably belonged to the office of escheator (*Cal. Fine Rolls*, XVII, 62).

[3] E.g. J.I.1/912A, m. 40.

[4] L. F. Salzman, 'The Hundred Roll for Sussex', *Sx. Arch. Colls.* LXXXII, 21–4.

ment, and then make a 'grievous fine' or, if he had nothing with which to fine, three years' imprisonment. The statute also insisted upon knighthood qualification for coroners and that sheriffs should keep 'counter-rolls' of crown pleas, and ordered 'that no coroner demand nor take any thing of any man to do his office, upon pain of great forfeiture to the king'.[1] Secondly, most of the Hundred Roll articles were incorporated among the articles of every general eyre after 1275 as part of the *nova capitula*.[2] Thirdly, the Hundred Roll inquiry inaugurated a series of special inquiries concerned solely or largely with the misdeeds of local officials.

The first of these special inquiries, held in Bedfordshire and Buckinghamshire and perhaps elsewhere in 1278, is only known to have dealt with the misdeeds of coroners and their clerks.[3] Next came 'Kirkby's quest' of 1284-5, which inquired concerning the misdeeds of many local officials,[4] but contained only one article concerning coroners: *Item de officio coronatorum qualiter officia sua secuntur.* The juries must have considered this very vague and must often have wondered exactly what coroners were expected to do and what was forbidden. Because of this and because the articles of the Hundred Roll inquiry touching coroners were also vague, it was eventually realised that such articles needed elaboration. That elaboration is now known as the Statute of Exeter and was promulgated at the end of 1285.[5] It consists of a long series of articles, which demanded detailed information of all duties performed by coroners and their clerks and inquired of almost every possible oppression and extortion. No special inquiry was intended immediately: indeed, a comprehensive one had only just been completed. The Statute of Exeter seems rather to have been intended as the basis of all future inquiries into coroners' offences. *Britton*, for example, in the section on the general eyre, said that inquiry was to be made concerning coroners' offences according to the Statute of Exeter.[6] Between 1289 and 1293 another special commission sat in London to hear complaints of misdeeds of officials during the king's absence overseas from 1286 to 1289, and complaints were made against fifteen coroners of various counties.[7]

---

[1] 3 Edw. I, cc. 9, 10.   [2] *Oxon. Studies in Soc. & Leg. Hist.* VI, 94-9.
[3] J.I.2/255/1B.   [4] *Feudal Aids, 1284-1431*, I, xii-xiii.
[5] *Statutes of the Realm*, I, 210-12.
[6] i.22.3. It was not, however, incorporated into the eyre articles.
[7] *State Trials of the Reign of Edward I, 1289-1293*, ed. T. F. Tout and H. Johnstone (Camden 3rd ser. IX), p. xxix.

Coroners' offences were later investigated by trailbaston justices and justices of general oyer and terminer,[1] and in 1330 oyer and terminer commissions were ordered for all counties to deal solely with local officials, including coroners.[2] When King's Bench toured under Edward II in the guise of a very general commission of oyer and terminer, one of its articles of inquiry concerned the taking of money by local officials,[3] and presentments of coroners' extortions continued to be made to King's Bench whenever it was itinerant.[4] Finally, J.P.'s were also empowered to deal with extortions by coroners and other local officials in 1380[5] and had been dealing with them in practice since 1361, if not before.[6]

These numerous attempts at prevention merely show how widespread extortion by coroners was, as do the resulting presentments. The returns to the Hundred Roll inquiry make it plain that coroners almost invariably refused to hold inquests on dead bodies until they had been bribed to do so. The bribes normally varied from a shilling to half a mark, sometimes paid by the tithing or township and sometimes by an individual, undoubtedly depending upon whether one or all were suffering inconvenience.[7] The worst Sussex case was that of a woman drowned in the Cuckmere, who lay there for nine weeks and three days before the coroner was paid and held his inquest.[8] In Lewes the same coroner not only took money for holding inquests but also an extra two shillings for producing his rolls before the justices at Chichester.[9] Coroners' clerks were mentioned less frequently, but still quite often. They usually took one or two shillings a time, but occasionally as much as five shillings, presumably before they would record the inquests.[10] It is strange to find townships paying for this and also for the coroner to produce his rolls before the justices, since both could prove to be against their financial interests. All such payments must have been extorted before and in return for the inquest and burial.

---

[1] E.g. J.I.1/934, m. 11; 941A, m. 51d.
[2] *Rotuli Parliamentorum*, II, 60.
[3] *South Lancashire in the Reign of Edward II*, ed. G. H. Tupling (Chetham Soc. 3rd ser. I), pp. 5, 128–9.
[4] E.g. J.I.2/36, m. 9.
[5] *Proceedings before the Justices of the Peace*, pp. 14–15.
[6] E.g. Yorks. Arch. Soc., Rec. Ser. c, 93–4, 108.
[7] *Rotuli Hundredorum, passim*. For the Sussex examples see *Sx. Arch. Colls.* LXXXII, 27, 29, 32; LXXXIII, 37–8, 40–2, 44, 46, 49–52; LXXXIV, 67, 70, 72.
[8] *Ibid.* LXXXIII, 38.   [9] *Ibid.* p. 50.
[10] E.g. *Sx. Arch. Colls.* LXXXII, 26, 29, 32; LXXXIII, 52; LXXXIV, 64, 66, 76.

There are many similar examples on all subsequent eyre rolls,[1] proving that the first Statute of Westminster had little deterrent effect. *Fleta*, paraphrasing the statute, described the penalty for taking bribes as 'heavy forfeiture of their goods',[2] but in practice it was rarely heavy.[3] The justices may well have sympathised with the coroner, who, unpaid, could not even extort very much, for there was naturally a limit to the amount that men would pay to rid themselves of the nuisance of an unburied body: in the late fourteenth century half a mark still seems to have been the limit.[4] Early in the century it was laid down as a rule that when a coroner took money for performing or omitting to perform his duties, he should restore what he had taken as well as pay his amercement.[5] A Kent coroner, who was convicted of taking half a mark from a woman before he would allow her slain husband to be buried, had to pay the woman the half mark and damages and also was imprisoned until he paid a fine,[6] but this was abnormally severe. By contrast, a Yorkshire coroner, who was indicted before the J.P.'s in 1361 of taking half a mark for viewing every dead body 'as the other coroners did', paid a fine of only half a mark for his trespass and is not known to have restored his takings.[7]

With the end of the general eyre there was no longer any regular check upon the coroners and such bribes had become an established and invariable fee before the J.P.'s were empowered to deal with them. The result was that the J.P.'s rarely attempted to get to grips with the problem. If the bribe was not paid, no inquest was held. It therefore reflects no credit upon the coroners that they continued to hold inquests after regular supervision had ceased. It was to legalise existing practice as well as to ensure that inquests were always held and action was taken against felons that in 1487 coroners were authorised to take a fee of a mark for every inquest occasioned by homicide from the goods of the felon if he had any or, if he had not, from the amercements imposed on any township for the felon's escape. The same statute ordered that every time a coroner failed to

---

[1] E.g. J.I.1/930, mm. 1d, 4, 12d.

[2] i. 18 (Selden Soc. vol. 72, p. 41).

[3] No punishments compared in severity with the £10, £20 and £40 fines laid upon them by fifteenth-century statutes for their defaults in rarely performed duties (2 Hen. V, stat. 1, c. 8; 15 Hen. VI, c. 5; 23 Hen. VI, c. 9).

[4] E.g. J.I.2/36, m. 9. A Devon coroner of the late thirteenth century on one occasion took an ox worth half a mark instead of money (J.I.1/186, m. 15d).

[5] Selden Soc. vol. 24, p. 143.   [6] *Ibid.* pp. 94–5.

[7] Yorks. Arch. Soc., Rec. Ser. c, 93–4, 108.

hold an inquest or to deliver it to the gaol delivery justices he should forfeit five pounds.[1] Naturally, coroners then refused to hold inquests in cases of death by misadventure until they had received a mark. Therefore in 1510 they were ordered to hold them without taking anything under pain of forty shillings a time for disobedience, justices of assize and J.P.'s being given the power to hear and determine such cases.[2]

Money was most frequently extorted by medieval coroners as an inducement for them to hold their inquests,[3] but inquests provided other opportunities for extortion. The taking of the upper garment from the dead body possibly came second in frequency, and in 1323 the Leyland hundred jurors presented in King's Bench at Wigan that it was the custom in that hundred for the coroner to have the upper garment.[4] This offence was normally punished by amercement,[5] but when a Lancashire coroner admitted that he had habitually taken the best garment, had often sent his man to view and bury bodies, had often delayed holding inquests, sometimes adjourning them to other places, until the four neighbouring townships had each paid him a shilling, and that he had often neglected to appraise felons' chattels and to commit them to safe custody, he was committed to the marshal, later paying a fine of five pounds and finding two sureties for his future good behaviour.[6] Another fairly common offence was for coroners to cause felons' chattels to be appraised at less than their true value, retaining the difference for themselves,[7] and a Sussex coroner's clerk took two shillings from a juror who arrived late for an inquest.[8]

Abjurations of the realm gave less scope for extortion. A Norfolk coroner did well to extract ten shillings from the township of Hingham: 3s. 6d. for taking an abjuration and 6s. 6d. for concealing an escape.[9] It paid the second in an attempt to escape a later amercement and the first possibly in order to avoid having to keep a lengthy watch on the church. Some Year Books note that abjurors' clothes, apart from the garments allowed for their journey, were forfeitable and that neither the coroner nor his man should take any of them for

[1] 3 Hen. VII, c. 2.   [2] 1 Hen. VIII, c. 7.
[3] E.g. J.I.1/194; J.I.2/255/1B, m. 2.
[4] Chetham Soc. 3rd ser. I, 128–9.
[5] E.g. Selden Soc. vol. 24, pp. 147, 150, 155–6.
[6] Chetham Soc. 3rd ser. I, 128–9.
[7] E.g. J.I.1/710, m. 36d; J.I.2/255/1B, mm. 1, 2.
[8] J.I.1/930, m. 13d.   [9] J.I.1/579, m. 11.

his fee on pain of amercement and restitution to the king.[1] This suggests that the offence must have been quite common. Devon coroners also lost the king much money by refusing to view wrecks or by causing them to be grossly undervalued.[2]

All these cases are venial compared with the deliberate perversion of justice practised by some coroners. Thus one Devon coroner refused to hold an inquest upon a baby, alleged to have been stillborn as a result of a quarrel, because one of the principals was in his service; and another was alleged to have delivered men arrested for homicide from gaol in return for gifts to him and the sheriff, and he and his clerk to have taken a pound each from an appellee to deliver him from the appeal.[3] The justices were always looking for this type of offence. When a Sussex coroner was found to have attached by sureties, instead of committing to gaol, four men indicted of homicide, the jurors were specifically asked whether he had taken anything from them as a bribe but they confirmed that he had not.[4] Coroners were also often suspected of empanelling partial juries,[5] and, in order to prevent this and also the empanelling of jurors who knew nothing of the matter, a statute of 1360 ordered that coroners and other local officials should empanel those men who lived nearest to the matter to be inquired into and who were impartial.[6]

Falsification of coroners' rolls was also frequently suspected.[7] Thus the heir who gave in a coroner's records in file form at the 1313–14 Kent eyre was committed to prison and his lands were seized because the justices suspected forgery, and two Buckinghamshire coroners were accused in 1278 of altering or suppressing entries in their rolls between the time of the inquests and the following

---

[1] E.g. Selden Soc. vol. 24, p. 94; Harleian MS. 5145, f. 32b.
[2] E.g. J.I.1/194.
[3] *Ibid.* Similarly at the 1241 Berkshire eyre a coroner's clerk was punished for accepting five shillings from a man appealed of theft in the hundred court, who also restored the stolen sheep, paid the appellor's servant a mark as compensation and two other men lesser sums. The coroner's clerk was presumably paid for deleting the appeal from his roll, for he took two shillings from the presenting hundred jurors for amending their *veredictum* to accord with his roll (J.I.1/37, m. 31). All this bribery was not only unsuccessful; it was also pointless, since appeals could be agreed without serious consequences (e.g. J.I.1/874A, m. 26d: a Surrey case of 1263 in which a coroner and his clerk were amerced for 'concealing' such an agreement). I am indebted to Mr C. A. F. Meekings for drawing my attention to these two cases.
[4] J.I.1/921, m. 19.   [5] E.g. *Britton*, i.2.11. Cf. J.I.2/255/1B, m. 2.
[6] 34 Edw. III, c. 4.
[7] E.g. Statute of Exeter (*Statutes of the Realm*, I, 210, 211a).

county courts at which the deaths were presented, because of bribes and affinity.[1] It was found during the 1272 Staffordshire eyre that the promulgation of an outlawry, resulting from an appeal, appeared in the rolls of two county coroners but that it had been erased from the roll of a third. Both the coroner and his clerk were imprisoned until the coroner paid a fine of ten marks for their release. The king gained the year and waste of the coroner's lands and tenements and the whole of his chattels; the clerk's chattels would presumably have been forfeited also, but it was found that he had none.[2] Even as late as the early fifteenth century the Exchequer treated a Suffolk coroner's roll with grave suspicion because of the inconsistency of hand displayed in its marginal notes,[3] which is remarkable in view of the condition of the average coroner's roll of that period and the large number of additions which were made to them.[4] To prevent the 'embezzlement' of indictments, all officials were ordered by statute in 1327 to take them by 'roll indented', one part remaining with the indictors and the other with the official,[5] and in 1429 royal justices were empowered at their discretion to amend the records of coroners and other officials if a letter or syllable too many or too few had been written, except in records of outlawries in felonies or treason, a similar petition having been rejected eight years earlier.[6] All these examples confirm the law-book teaching that tampering with records was forbidden to coroners and their clerks,[7] although in the early thirteenth century a much laxer rule obtained, a Gloucestershire coroner being amerced in 1221 not for amending his rolls but for doing so without his colleagues.[8]

Deliberate perversion of justice, with the oppression of innocent people or the escape of the guilty, was rightly punished more severely than mere extortion. Thus a Cornish coroner, who not only held an inquisition to discover if two men who had taken sanctuary

---

[1] Selden Soc. vol. 24, p. 24; J.I.2/255/1B, m. 2.

[2] 'Plea Rolls of the reign of Henry III', ed. G. Wrottesley, *Wm Salt Arch. Soc.* IV, 215.

[3] E.159/186, *Communia*, Mich. ro. 33.

[4] *Am. Journ. Leg. Hist.* III, 98–100, 111–17.

[5] 1 Edw. III, stat. 2, c. 17. The author of *The Mirror of Justices* had advocated that coroners should present their records under the seals of the jurors as being more effective than the keeping of 'counter-rolls' by the sheriffs (v. 4: Selden Soc. vol. 7, p. 185).

[6] 8 Hen. VI, c. 15; *Rotuli Parliamentorum*, IV, 155.

[7] E.g. *Britton*, i.2.5, 11; *Fleta*, i. 25 (Selden Soc. vol. 72, p. 64).

[8] Selden Soc. vol. 59, no. 67.

after an alleged death by misadventure were guilty but also let them go free when they were found guilty, was imprisoned.[1] Similarly, a Sussex coroner, who fraudently procured the delivery from gaol of a man indicted of robberies who had bribed him with eight acres of meadow, was sent to gaol under the terms of the first Statute of Westminster and remained there for fifteen months until he produced six sureties and paid a fine of twenty pounds.[2] The worst oppressions, however, were practised in connection with appeals of approvers, and some coroners proved themselves just as extortionate as sheriffs and gaolers, procuring false appeals and then taking money from the appellees in return for a promise to arrange for their delivery from the appeals.[3]

It is clearly impossible to give the medieval coroner an unblemished character. Those were exceptional who did not use their chances of extortion, and no useful comparison can be made with other local officials who had different duties. The real causes of the trouble were that the office was unpaid, punishments were not severe enough and, especially during the fourteenth and fifteenth centuries, supervision was completely inadequate. Suggestions were constantly made to help reduce oppression. In 1351 the Commons tried to get sheriffs, escheators and coroners changed annually, alleging, incorrectly in the case of coroners, that statutes had ordered this. The reply, that there had been a previous petition on this subject resulting in a statute which should be enforced, is true of only the second part of the petition, which urged that these officials be chosen from those who had sufficient possessions in the county wherewith to answer the king and his people.[4] Even if this petition had been granted, there would still have been the problem of enforcement. In 1376 the Commons petitioned that justices of gaol delivery or other justices should inquire about false indictments

[1] *Year Books 30 & 31 Edward I*, p. 524.

[2] *Sx. Arch. Colls.* xcviii, 51. For the allegation that another Sussex coroner, after an agreement with the farmer of amercements in Bramber rape, imposed amercements to the sum of £10 upon two hundred men in the county court, see *ibid.*

[3] E.g. *ibid.* pp. 50–1; *Rotuli Hundredorum*, ii, 21. Cf. above, p. 72.

[4] *Rotuli Parliamentorum*, ii, 229. Cf. below, p. 174. Both king and Commons were probably deceived by 14 Edw. III, stat. 1, cc. 7 and 8, which ordered the annual appointment of sheriffs and escheators in the Exchequer, for c. 8, after dealing with the appointment of escheators, suddenly changes subject and ends by saying that coroners should have sufficient lands in fee in their county. It could therefore easily have been assumed that annual elections had been ordered for them.

before coroners, some coroners having caused men to be falsely indicted, so that their goods were forfeited, but the reply was merely
that petitions should be made in particular cases.[1] They sometimes
were, but, however heinous the offences, they very seldom resulted
in the removal of the coroner from office.[2]

The strictest precautions were taken to ensure against mal-
practices in connection with approvers.[3] *Britton* maintained that
coroners ought only to hear their appeals in the presence of the
sheriff, their controller.[4] Sheriffs sometimes attended, but many
appeals were made in their absence,[5] probably because of the pressure of their other duties. Another safeguard, requested by the Commons in the early fourteenth century, was that two coroners should
always hear and enrol appeals of approvers in order to prevent co-
ercion and false enrolment.[6] This was an ideal, and the number of
coroners who heard approvers' appeals remained completely arbi-
trary. When felons turned approver in gaol and there was no coroner
on the spot, only one normally came;[7] but when the gaol was in a
borough which had two coroners, they normally, although not invariably, acted together.[8] When felons turned approver before
J.P.'s, they assigned either one or more coroners to them according
to the number present in court.[9] Similarly, if two coroners were present at a gaol delivery, they were both normally assigned to anyone
turning approver there, although when two Sussex coroners had
heard the appeals of an approver at a delivery of Guildford gaol in
1481 and were again assigned to hear his further appeals at a later
date, only one of them then attended and the appeals were not thereby invalidated.[10] In short, coroners neither acted as effective checks
on the rapacity of other officials nor had difficulty in practising their
own extortions.

Poor character did not necessarily mean inefficiency. Indeed,
the virtual certainty of being able to extort with impunity meant
that coroners continued to hold a large number of inquests when
they were no longer regularly supervised and that they wasted little
time in going to hold them.[11] When they did not act speedily it was

---

[1] *Rotuli Parliamentorum*, II, 334.
[2] See below, pp. 178–9; *Sx. Arch. Colls.* XCVIII, 50–1.   [3] See above, p. 73.
[4] i.2.16.   [5] E.g. *Sx. Arch. Colls.* XCVI, 26–32.
[6] *Rotuli Parliamentorum*, II, 9; Camden 3rd ser. LI, 124.
[7] E.g. J.I.2/179A, mm. 2–3.   [8] E.g. J.I.1/934, mm. 9, 9d; J.I.3/123, m. 2.
[9] E.g. *Sx. Arch. Colls.* XCVI, 28–9.   [10] *Ibid.* pp. 29–32.
[11] See above, p. 13.

not always their fault. It is true that there were complaints of corpses decaying because the coroner refused to view them or because he refused to do so until paid an adequate bribe,[1] but delays were also caused by others. The 'first finder', townships or bailiff sometimes neglected the hue and cry, while some coroners had difficulty in assembling enough jurors.[2] More important, coroners were sometimes physically prevented from acting, especially by lords or officials of liberties which did not have coroners of their own. At the 1248 Sussex eyre the lands of the Hospitallers in Eastbourne hundred were taken into the king's hand because all county officials had been refused entry into these lands to hold an inquest when two women were slain.[3] There was an almost identical case involving the abbot of Athelney's bailiff, who was amerced in 1225, while at the 1285 Oxfordshire eyre the bailiff of Holywell manor was arrested for preventing a town coroner from holding an inquest on the body of a man who had been drowned by misadventure in the Cherwell and then removed to St Cross church.[4] Other common offences were the prevention of the coroner and his jury from entering the house of a homicide to view and appraise his chattels[5] and the seizure of such chattels before the coroner's view and appraisal.[6] The second of these offences was most frequently committed by lords of liberties who claimed the right to forfeited chattels,[7] just as they also prevented the coroner from appraising deodands on their lands and took possession of them before he had viewed them.[8] The steward of an Essex manor ordered the body of a man, who had died by misadventure, to be buried before the coroner could hold his view in order that his lord and not the king might get the deodand.[9] On occasions, unauthorized persons also took possession of the chattels of abjurors. A man who abjured the realm from St Mary's church, Shrewsbury, was found to have a cart-horse worth half a mark, a sword worth a shilling and a knife worth a halfpenny. He must

[1] E.g. J.I.1/194; J.I.2/255/1B, m. 2; *Close Rolls, 1251–1253*, pp. 433, 496; above, pp. 120–2.
[2] *Ibid.* pp. 10–13, 17–19.   [3] J.I 1/909A, m. 28d.
[4] Selden Soc. vol. 1, no. 181; Oxon. Hist. Soc. XVIII, 201.
[5] Selden Soc. vol. 24, p. 97.
[6] E.g. Beds. Hist. Rec. Soc. III, p. 158; XXI, no. 148.
[7] E.g. *Pipe Roll 14 Henry III*, p. 238; *Placita de Quo Warranto*, pp. 333, 364–5.
[8] E.g. *Sx. Arch. Colls.* XCVIII, 47; Selden Soc. vol. 53, no. 1112; Oxon. Hist. Soc. XVIII, 200–1.
[9] *Cal. Pat. Rolls, 1364–1367*, pp. 55–6.

have had the sword and knife with him in the church, because the proctor of the dean of St Mary's refused to give them up to the coroners.[1]

It was not only lords of liberties and officials who obstructed coroners. John atte Bokholte, who terrorised the people of East Sussex and was known as 'the king of the countryside' in the mid-fourteenth century, committed many murders, but no coroner dared to hold an inquest on the bodies for fear of him.[2] In 1264 certain citizens of Norwich threatened to cut the city coroners into small pieces unless they gave them their copy of an inquest, and later seized one coroner, took him to his home, made him take the inquest from a chest, took it from him and cut it up. Thereafter the city coroners did not dare to hold inquests 'on account of the threatening war and the large number of foolish people'.[3] In 1303 Roger de Hales, a Norfolk coroner, was assaulted by the men of Norwich, who prevented him from holding an inquest on land within the city belonging to the body of the county, took his rolls from his hands, tore them and stamped upon them.[4] Another Norfolk coroner was prevented from taking an abjuration in 1311 by men who beat the guards and rescued the sanctuary seeker.[5] One commission of oyer and terminer was appointed in 1319 on the petition of John de Cotes, a Lincolnshire coroner, that a man had assaulted him and prevented him from holding an inquest, and another in 1349 on the complaint of Roger le Longe, an Oxfordshire coroner, that a number of men had broken his close at Tetsworth, assaulted him and carried away his goods, thereby preventing him from holding an inquest, while in 1390 six members of the Jay family were bound over to keep the peace towards John Tye, a Lincolnshire coroner, who had complained that they had threatened his life and limbs.[6] The fact that these coroners initiated the proceedings proves that the assaults and threats were made. Similarly, the pardon issued to Thomas de Berkele in 1320 shows that he was guilty of arresting the four Gloucestershire coroners, thereby preventing them from performing their duties.[7] Walter Pateshull, mayor and coroner of North-

---

[1] *Hist. MSS. Comm., 15th Report*, App. x, p. 26. For another example of the unlawful retention of an abjuror's chattels, see J.I.2/266, m. 12d.

[2] J.I.1/941A, m. 51.   [3] *The Records of the City of Norwich*, I, 205-6.

[4] *Cal. Close Rolls, 1302-1307*, p. 45.   [5] Above, p. 40, n. 4.

[6] *Cal. Pat. Rolls, 1317-1321*, p. 468; *1348-1350*, p. 311; C.47/108/11, mm. 43-4.

[7] *Cal. Pat. Rolls, 1317-1321*, p. 451. For other examples of the use of threats

ampton, was dragged by his hair from his house and made to for-
swear the office of coroner in the borough court; Nicholas Turpin, a
Northumberland coroner, alleged that, having held an inquest on a
dead body, he found that one of his colleagues had secretly held another and had caused him to be indicted and the escheator to seize
his goods and chattels; and one Lancashire coroner was even mur-
dered, but whether on personal grounds or for his acts as coroner is
unknown.[1]

Another source of inefficiency for which the coroners were not
responsible was the thirteenth-century failure to elect coroners regularly and the consequent necessity for individuals to be specially
commissioned to hold inquests in particular cases, while in 1276 a
non-coroner was commissioned to hold one at Stonor because the
Kent coroner was 'in remote parts'.[2] Thereafter the situation was
never quite so bad, although between 1392 and 1396 individuals
were commissioned to hold inquests on five bodies in Surrey, which
had long lain unburied because the coroners dwelt in distant parts
of the county, and another was similarly commissioned in 1403 in
Rochester, whose coroner was too sick and infirm to view the body.[3]
Finally, in 1496 there was no Salisbury coroner, 'a thyng that was
never seyn in tymes past', and a body lay unburied 'to the lothsome
and noyous syght of the peple'; the mayor and citizens therefore
petitioned the bishop to order the election of two coroners.[4]

It is strange that more special commissions were not issued. The
writ replacing John Fermer, an Essex coroner, announced that he
had been unable, on account of other duties, to exercise his office for
a long time,[5] and there was often a long delay in the issue of writs.
Gervase de Leem, a Sussex coroner, was dead before 27 November
1337, but the writ to replace him did not issue until 26 January 1338.[6]
In this case the information may not have been given to Chancery
until long after his death, although the justices of King's Bench
knew in November, but the warrant for the issue of the writ to

and force to prevent coroners from performing their duties, see *Cal. Inqs. Misc.*
IV, 307; *Rotuli Parliamentorum*, v, 211–12; *Some Sessions of the Peace in Lincoln-
shire· 1360–1375*, ed. R. Sillem (Linc. Rec. Soc. xxx), pp. 75–6.
[1] *Victoria County History: Northamptonshire*, III, 8; *Cal. Close Rolls, 1419–
1422*, p. 152; *Cal. Pat. Rolls, 1377–1381*, p. 313.
[2] See below, pp. 154–5; *Cal. Pat. Rolls, 1272–1281*, p. 144.
[3] *Cal. Close Rolls, 1389–1392*, p. 445; *1392–1396*, pp. 56, 349, 464; *1402–1405*,
p. 220.
[4] *Hist. MSS. Comm., Reports on Various Collections*, IV, 211–12.
[5] *Cal. Close Rolls, 1339–1341*, p. 195. [6] *Sx. Arch. Colls.* XCVIII, 59.

K

replace William de Bulsham is dated 4 November 1301 and the writ did not issue until 16 February 1302.[1] Sussex was therefore probably reduced to one active coroner for about four months, and the coroner's duties must often have been neglected at such times. When a serious emergency arose, however, inquests were dispensed with. In 1258, for example, so many men died of famine in Lincolnshire, Norfolk, Suffolk and Essex that the townships were allowed to view and bury them without the coroner, provided that the bodies had no wounds and nobody was suspected and that the deaths were entered in the coroners' rolls.[2] Similarly, the king often ordered the burial of bodies, noticed during his tours, without the coroner's view.[3]

When there were not enough coroners it was inquests and abjurations that were neglected, and it was inquests and abjurations which suffered most from obstructions offered to coroners. On the other hand, inquests, abjurations and appeals of approvers were otherwise dealt with expeditiously by the coroners because they offered the greatest chances of extortion. They performed their other duties much less efficiently. Their dislike of keeping formal rolls has already been discussed.[4] Even when they kept them, they often failed to see that every case was entered. When an abjuration was presented by the hundred jurors but was not found in the coroners' rolls, the justices adjudged that there had been no abjuration but only an escape, for which a local official or the locality was amerced, although there is no doubt that in some cases the coroners had failed to enrol a genuine abjuration.[5] This type of default thus brought an unfair punishment on guiltless people, as did the frequent failure of coroners to take or send indictments of prisoners to gaol deliveries. The majority of medieval prisoners were, rightly or wrongly, acquitted. It was therefore extremely culpable of coroners to withhold their indictments, without which there could be no trial, but the gaol delivery rolls teem with cases adjourned for this reason. The younger Thomas de Pelham, the Sussex coroner, heard an indictment of a woman of killing her husband with an axe at his inquest upon the body in 1369. When the woman was arrested is unknown, but she was in Guildford gaol in 1374, when the case was adjourned

[1] *Sx. Arch. Colls.* xcviii, 56–7.   [2] *Close Rolls, 1256–1259,* p. 212.
[3] E.g. *Close Rolls, 1234–1237,* p. 38; *1251–1253,* p. 301; *Cal. Pat. Rolls, 1358–1361,* p. 298.
[4] Above, pp. 114–15.   [5] *Ibid.* p. 106.

and order was given for the indictment, which was still with Pelham who was by then no longer a coroner, to be sued for. After many subsequent gaol deliveries, at each of which the woman was returned to gaol for lack of the indictment, it was discovered in 1378 that Pelham had died. By 1383, although the woman was still being kept in gaol, writs had begun to issue after each delivery to Pelham's heirs and executors, ordering them to send the indictment. The last known mention of the case comes from 1394, when the hardy woman, who must long since have amply atoned for the felony, even if she was guilty, was once again sent back to gaol, but by this time the justices seem to have forgotten that Pelham was dead, for writs were again issuing to him personally.[1] This case was exceptional only in its length. The justices were abnormally lax at this time. Earlier the Sussex sheriff was ordered to produce Philip de Hurst personally at the next Guildford gaol delivery when he failed to produce an indictment. On his non-attendance the *venire facias* was repeated, but it was again unsuccessful and the sheriff was then ordered to distrain him by all his lands to secure his attendance.[2] On another occasion this same coroner failed to come with the record of an abjuration to a Guildford gaol delivery; he was therefore amerced and distrained to appear at the next.[3] Finally, neither outlawries nor abjurations were legal if made in the coroner's absence, and therefore he was punished by imprisonment and fine if his absence was his own fault.[4]

The number of amercements imposed upon thirteenth-century coroners for omitting to perform necessary parts of their duties or for performing them inadequately were legion. Failure to attach 'first finders', neighbours and witnesses of deaths[5] or to attach them securely enough,[6] to appraise or attach forfeitable chattels[7] and to

[1] J.I.3/163, m. 2; 216A/4, mm. 50, 85, 86, 121, 154d, 176, 186, 200, 218; 217/3, mm. 38, 129, 139.
[2] J.I.3/111, mm. 6, 7; 112, m. 1.   [3] J.I.3/111, m. 10d.
[4] *Britton*, i.14.6; 17.7. This refutes *Britton's* other statement that coroners were not obliged to go to sanctuary seekers even if they wished to abjure (i.17.1). For an example of outlawries being delayed by the absence of all coroners from the county court, see *Sx. Arch. Colls.* XCVI, 21–2.
[5] E.g. J.I.1/912A, mm. 37, 44d, 45d; 921, m. 19; 930, m. 18.
[6] E.g. Beds. Hist. Rec. Soc. III, 150. One Sussex coroner was amerced at the 1279 eyre because a neighbour whom he had attached did not appear before the justices, and when a 'first finder' failed to attend that of 1288 both her sureties and the coroner were amerced (J.I.1/921, m. 18d; 926, m. 10d). These are unusual cases: the sureties alone were normally punished.
[7] E.g. Selden Soc. vol. 56, nos. 444, 463, 563, 856. Robert de Locwode, a

give correct orders for the arrest of suspected homicides[1] were only a few of the many traps.[2] When judgment was passed against a coroner for any such offence, the result was an amercement. In 1201 judgment was passed against the sheriff of Somerset and three coroners for not attaching appellees. One coroner was amerced at a hundred marks and the other two at one mark each.[3] Despite the fact that the amount of an amercement should have depended upon the guilty party's resources and that amercements were heavier at this time than later, the penalty imposed upon the first coroner is still unnaturally harsh in view of both the offence itself and the punishment of his colleagues, who must have been equally guilty. Thereafter amercements were much more moderate. In 1221, for example, a Gloucestershire coroner compounded with forty shillings for both his amercement and his removal from office,[4] and in the later thirteenth century amercements for single offences settled down in the neighbourhood of half a mark.[5] Few coroners can have escaped amercement during the course of a general eyre, and when, as frequently happened, they were amerced on several scores, they settled for a certain sum to cover them all.[6]

It was not only the coroners themselves who suffered from their defaults. Their offences, like their rolls, were inherited until atoned for or pardoned. Many of the general pardons of the fourteenth century included charges on the freehold of the heirs or holders of the lands of dead coroners.[7] Similarly, it was not only the coroners who were imprisoned and had their lands seized into the king's hand and their wives and children driven out by the sheriff for failing to attend general eyres or to bring their rolls on the appointed day; their

Staffordshire coroner, persistently omitted to appraise chattels (*Select Coroners' Rolls*, p. 100).

[1] See above, p. 22, n. 8.

[2] For their failure to supervise abjurations, appeals and outlawries adequately and to report cases to the eyre justices as they had enrolled them, see above, pp. 44, 59, 62, 105–7.

[3] Somerset Rec. Soc. XI, 84, 101.

[4] *Pleas of the Crown for Gloucester, 1221*, no. 465.

[5] Thus in 1279 the Arundel coroner was amerced at half a mark for allowing an abjuror to choose his own port and for officiating without a county coroner contrary to the local rule, and the two Chichester coroners at ten shillings, of which one paid forty pence and the other the rest, for holding an inquest which only twelve men had attended instead of the whole city (J.I.1/917, mm. 32, 40; 921, mm. 21d, 26).

[6] E.g. J.I.1/926, mm. 34, 36. The amount is only rarely stated.

[7] E.g. 36 Edw. III, stat. 2; 50 Edw. III, c. 3; 21 Ric. II, c. 15.

clerks suffered the same fate for similar defaults,[1] as did the heirs, executors and holders of the lands of dead coroners,[2] while the county or borough was responsible for all the misdeeds of those coroners who had left neither heirs nor lands.[3]

[1] E.g. Selden Soc. vol. 53, no. 1231.
[2] E.g. *Year Books 30 & 31 Edward I*, p. 76; Selden Soc. vol. 24, pp. 5–6, 14, 23–4, 47–8, 54–5. Even if an heir alleged that some other representatives had the rolls, he was imprisoned until they brought them (e.g. *ibid.* pp. 23–4). At the Northamptonshire eyre of 1330 one of the coroners had not his rolls with him and said that they were in the town, whereupon he was allowed to go and fetch them under the guard of the marshal (H. M. Cam, 'The Marshalsy of the Eyre', *Cambridge Hist. Journ.* I, 136), but the justices showed abnormal leniency in this case.
[3] See below, p. 176.

CHAPTER VIII

CORONERS' DISTRICTS

ARTICLE twenty of the 1194 eyre, which provided that there should be four coroners for every county,[1] may never have been universally executed. While many counties retained four throughout and beyond the Middle Ages, others had fewer from at least the early thirteenth century. Hampshire had only two as early as 1204 and by 1228 so had Sussex.[2] In October 1246 there was only one county coroner in Sussex and the election of a second was consequently ordered. Between 1255 and 1262 there were two, but from 1275 until 1279 there appear to have been three. In 1279, however, the number was reduced to two, at which it remained throughout the Middle Ages.[3] In many other counties the number oscillated during the thirteenth century[4] before ultimately becoming stabilised—at two or four in most cases. The decision as to which number was most suitable may well have been made by the justices in eyre and based on past experience. At the end of each eyre a new team of coroners was elected, and it was at the 1279 Sussex eyre, for example, that the number there was reduced from three to two. Between eyres, however, the sheriff had considerable discretion in the early thirteenth century: in 1232 the king removed a Leicestershire coroner from office, but the consequent writ merely ordered the election of another 'if it should be necessary'.[5]

It did not necessarily follow that counties which shared a sheriff had fewer coroners than the others. Surrey and Sussex shared a sheriff and had only two coroners each,[6] but Shropshire and Staffordshire had four each when they formed a single shrievalty as did Warwickshire which had a common sheriff with Leicestershire.[7] Hampshire, on the other hand, had its own sheriff but eventually only two coroners.[8] Yorkshire, on account of its size, and Kent, on

[1] *Select Charters*, p. 254.
[2] *Curia Regis Rolls*, III, 164; *Sx. Arch. Colls.* XCVIII, 44.   [3] *Ibid.*
[4] E.g. *Victoria County History: Wiltshire*, V, 15.
[5] *Close Rolls, 1231–1234*, p. 172.
[6] J.I.1/883, m. 1; *Sx. Arch. Colls.* XCVIII, 44.
[7] J.I.1/741, m. 1; 806, m. 17d; 961, m. 1.
[8] E.g. J.I.1/780, m. 1.

account of its division into five lathes, had five.[1] Most counties retained throughout the Middle Ages the number of coroners they had at the end of Edward I's reign, when the thirty-nine English counties had approximately 115 between them.[2] In 1366, however, the sheriffs of Northamptonshire and Shropshire and in 1367 the sheriff of Herefordshire received writs ordering them to increase by election the number of county coroners to four, if that was the customary number and if the allegations in the petitions of the commons of those counties that there were then only two in the first two counties and three in Herefordshire were true.[3]

In the first few years of the office every county coroner may have attended every inquest and abjuration within the county, as seems to have been intended by the provision of three knights and one clerk in 1194. But it rapidly became obvious that it was physically impossible for every county coroner to attend every inquest and abjuration and therefore, except in rare cases as when Richard de Oxendon and John de Tuwe, Northamptonshire coroners, jointly held an inquest in 1334 upon the body of Tuwe's slain son,[4] only one coroner was summoned. Thus for inquests and abjurations all counties came to be divided into coroners' districts. Some counties already had convenient administrative divisions. Thus Kent soon had five county coroners, one for each lathe; the North and West Ridings of Yorkshire had one each and the East Riding three; and each of the Lincolnshire coroners acted in only one of the parts of that county.[5] In Northumberland there were usually four coroners, two to the south and two to the north of the Coquet; in Westmorland the wards of Kendal and Westmorland had one each; and in the fourteenth century it came to be recognised that the four hundreds of

---

[1] J.I.1/1109, m. 2; 376, m. 61d.   [2] Calculated mainly from the eyre rolls.
[3] Cal. Close Rolls, 1364–1368, pp. 225, 335.
[4] J.I.2/111, m. 13. For another inquest, held jointly by two Cumberland coroners in 1386, see C.47/53/2, no. 51. In the county court, of course, the full complement of county coroners normally heard appeals, exactions and outlawries, and two or more often heard appeals of approvers, although in all these cases one could sit alone (Staundford, *Les Plees del Corone*, f. 53; above, p. 126). According to strict legal theory all inquisitions held on writs of redisseisin had to be held in the presence of at least two coroners or they were void, because the writs contained the phrase *assumptis tecum custodibus placitorum corone* (Staundford, *loc. cit.*; Selden Soc. vol. 71, p. 53). After 1256, however, writs *de odio et atia* also contained this phrase, but the returns confirm *Fleta's* implication that the presence of one coroner was sufficient (*Fleta*, i. 26: Selden Soc. vol. 72, p. 67. E.g. C.144/35, no. 6).
[5] E.g. J.I.1/376, m. 61d; 1109, m. 2; J.I.2/64, *passim*.

Warwickshire should each have its own coroner.[1] There was never a
coroner for every Sussex rape, but it was normal for one of the
county coroners to confine his activities to the three eastern rapes
and the other to act in the three western ones; the coroners' districts
thus coincided with what are now the administrative counties of
East and West Sussex.[2]

Few counties had so small a number of hundreds as Warwickshire
or intermediate divisions between county and hundred or natural
geographical sub-divisions, although some had out-lying parts,
such as the Scilly Isles and the Isle of Wight, which naturally had
their own coroners.[3] The result was that in no other county were
coroners' districts so rigid. They were not imposed upon the county
from above, but grew up gradually as a local convenience. The townships naturally summoned the nearest coroner to officiate at an inquest or abjuration. Thus the boundaries of coroners' districts were
very indistinct; the districts overlapped and might change with the
election of a new coroner.[4] But it was obviously desirable to have
contemporary coroners who lived in different parts of the county
and for the county to elect a coroner who lived in roughly the same
area as his predecessor. Although only one writ *de coronatore
eligendo*, for a Norfolk coroner in 1237, specifically stated that the
new coroner was to be 'of the same parts' as his predecessor,[5] this
must always have been understood, especially when the writs removed coroners for living in remote parts of the county.[6] The shift-
ing and formless nature of many coroners' districts is well illustrated
by two writs. The abbot of Peterborough complained that whereas
his liberty comprised a quarter of Northamptonshire and one of the
four county coroners had customarily been resident within it, recently all four had lived at least twenty miles from Peterborough
gaol and had failed to do their duty there on account of the distance.
The sheriff was ordered in 1355, if this were so, to have a coroner
elected from among any sufficient men within the liberty or from the
geldable near the gaol in place of the least sufficient of the existing
coroners.[7] Secondly, when Baldwin Malet, a Somerset coroner,

---

[1] E.g. J.I.1/642, m. 13; 648, mm. 15, 22; 653, m. 1; 979, m. 10; J.I.2/183;
185, m. 2; 186; 187.
[2] *Sx. Arch. Colls.* XCVIII, 44–5.   [3] E.g. J.I.1/112, m. 1; J.I.2/156.
[4] See the comments on Wiltshire coroners' districts in *Victoria County
History: Wiltshire*, V, 15, 27–8.
[5] *Close Rolls, 1234–1237*, p. 420.   [6] See below, p. 176.
[7] *Cal. Close Rolls, 1354–1360*, p. 131.

died, the writ for the election of his successor, issued in 1369, stated
that he was to be of the parts of Mendip, Brent Marsh, Wrington
Marsh, Dundry and Whitestone, since the other county coroners
dwelt over thirty leagues away.[1] It is clear from this that neither
Northamptonshire nor Somerset was divided into water-tight coroners' districts. Nor probably was Devon, where under Edward I
there were two coroners allotted to the northern part, one to the
south and one to the east.[2]

In 1343 the men of Nottingham living south of the Trent complained that contrary to custom both county coroners were living
north of the Trent and could not perform their duties south of it because of the frequent floods. A writ therefore issued for the election
of a coroner for the southern part of the county in place of one of the
existing coroners.[3] The only other county coroners' districts ever
specifically mentioned in writs *de coronatore eligendo* were the ridings and parts of Yorkshire and Lincolnshire, and the Isle of Wight,
and these were mentioned only occasionally.[4] All the other writs
ordered the new coroner to be elected by and for the whole county
without mentioning the district of the outgoing coroner. The reason
for this was that officially very few coroners' districts existed.
Coroners were elected to serve the whole county, and were never
amerced because they had failed to hold inquests in what the justices knew to be their districts but because they had failed to do so
after being summoned. Despite the theory, there were coroners' districts in all counties in practice.[5] Indeed, the Statute of Exeter
recognised that this was so,[6] and in 1284, when Wales was given
coroners, it was provided that there should be at least one in each
commote.[7]

In most counties some boroughs and liberties had coroners of
their own.[8] Strictly, the right to have a special coroner should
always have been specifically granted by the king,[9] but only about

---

[1] *Cal. Close Rolls, 1369–1374*, p. 57.

[2] J.I.1/186, m. 47d. Cf. J. G. Jenkins, 'An Early Coroner's Roll for Buckinghamshire', *Records of Buckinghamshire*, XIII, 164.

[3] *Cal. Close Rolls, 1343–1346*, p. 3.

[4] E.g. *Cal. Close Rolls, 1364–1368*, p. 362; *1389–1392*, pp. 36, 223; *1454–1461*,
p. 11.

[5] *The English Government at Work*, III, 158–9.

[6] *Statutes of the Realm*, I, 210–12.   [7] 12 Edw. I, c. 5. Cf. E.101/507/29.

[8] Boroughs and liberties cannot be sharply distinguished, since boroughs such
as Reading and St Albans were parts of large ecclesiastical liberties.

[9] *Placita de Quo Warranto*, p. 18.

twenty such grants are known to have been made to boroughs before
1300,[1] by which date there were approximately a hundred coroners
in some fifty-seven towns.[2] The number of franchisal coroners can
be less easily estimated, but there were well over fifty by 1300, whereas very few grants are known. During the *quo warranto* proceedings,
a specific grant of the right was rarely insisted upon; it was sufficient
if the jurors said that the right had not been usurped and that it had
been in long and continuous use. Thus in Sussex both Chichester
and Arundel were allowed to retain their coroners although they
could not produce charters to support their claims, while the abbot
of Battle, who succeeded in retaining the right to appoint coroners
within his liberty, had no specific grant but merely a charter from
William the Conqueror granting his liberty exemption in general
terms from all royal officials.[3] Similar stories can be related of other
counties. For example, of the four Wiltshire boroughs which had
coroners of their own only one had the privilege granted by royal
charter.[4] In 1254 the burgesses of Colchester justified their election
of their own coroners by citing a royal charter of 1189, which was
confirmed in 1252, granting them the right to elect their own justiciar.[5] They were probably allowed to continue to have coroners of
their own because many of the coroner's duties had previously belonged to the justiciar. The citizens of Norwich and the liberty of
Beverley were much less ethical; the former could only cite a grant
by Stephen which can never have been made, while the latter had to
forge a charter.[6] In 1353 and 1393 the abbots and convents of Bury
St Edmunds and Byland, as a result of their petitions, were granted
the right to have their own coroners—a right which they had for long
exercised but which they feared they might lose because they had
previously had no specific grant of it; its previous use in Bury St
Edmunds was also specifically condoned.[7] Similarly, the grant to the
church of St Mary, Ashridge, of the right to have its own coroners,
originally made by Edmund son of Richard earl of Cornwall, was
later confirmed by the king, as was that of the bishop of Durham to

---

[1] Ballard and Tait, *British Borough Charters, 1216–1307*, p. lx. Such grants
were occasionally made by letters patent, but usually by charter (*ibid.* p. xix).
[2] Calculated from the eyre rolls.
[3] *Sx. Arch. Colls.* XCVIII, 45–6. When Edward II confirmed this charter he gave
the abbot permission to continue to appoint coroners despite its general terms.
[4] *Victoria County History: Wiltshire*, v, 24.
[5] *Trans. R. Hist. Soc.* 5th ser. VIII, 90–1.
[6] *Ibid.* pp. 85–6.   [7] *Cal. Charter Rolls*, v, 138, 335.

the hospital of Greatham, within his county palatine, of exemption from his coroners.[1]

Although a specific grant by the king was theoretically necessary, in practice the important thing was therefore that the town or franchise should have long, continuously and properly used the privilege. If it had, a confirmation of the privilege could easily be obtained if required. If, however, the right was found not to have been exercised continuously or properly, or if its usurpation had been recent, it was normally withdrawn, at least temporarily. When, for example, the coroners' rolls revealed during the eyres of 1329–30 that the officials, including the coroners, of the towns of Bedford and Northampton had exceeded their liberty of *infangenetheof*, the coronerships and other local offices were taken into the king's hand and the king appointed coroners to act within the towns.[2] More frequently, when franchisal coroners failed to perform their duties adequately or abused their office, the right to have coroners was withdrawn and county coroners acted within the liberty.[3] When the prior of Dunstable omitted to replace one of the two coroners of his liberty who had died, the liberty was taken into the king's hand,[4] although Edward II confirmed the abbot of Battle's right to appoint his own coroners despite the fact that the exercise of this right had been discontinued for many years.[5] Finally, when the lord of Lifton hundred, Devon, was found at one general eyre not to have had his own coroners at the time of the previous eyre, his claim to have them failed and the county coroners were ordered to act in the hundred.[6]

Grants of coroners to boroughs and franchises were made throughout the Middle Ages, but there were three periods during which they were particularly numerous. In all three periods the kings who granted them were in need of support. The first was confined to the year 1200 when John, who wanted both stability and money, began the process with grants to five boroughs.[7] Secondly, in 1252 and 1256 Henry III granted the right to have coroners to

---

[1] *Cal. Charter Rolls*, II, 251, 384, 386, 464.
[2] *Placita de Quo Warranto*, p. 18; J.I.1/635, m. 78.
[3] E.g. A. E. Levett, *Studies in Manorial History*, ed. H. M. Cam, M. Coate and L. S. Sutherland (Oxford, 1938), p. 107.
[4] J.I.1/10, m. 27.
[5] *Placita de Quo Warranto*, pp. 333–4; J.I.1/384A, m. 8.
[6] *Placita de Quo Warranto*, p. 170.
[7] *Rotuli Chartarum*, pp. 46 (*bis*), 56, 57, 65.

eleven towns,[1] although the charter to Ipswich was largely a repetition of John's[2] and some of the others merely legalised existing practice.[3] Some of the grants of 1256 were probably due to the nation-wide general *quo warranto* proceedings of 1254–5,[4] but it is also significant that this was a time when Henry III wanted all the support he could get against the barons. Two towns were granted coroners, again significantly, in 1267 and four more, in the north, received them between 1299 and 1302 when Edward I needed support against the Scots,[5] but the third main period was the troublesome middle of the fifteenth century, when Lancastrians and Yorkists were alternately lavish with regalian rights as bribes. Between 1441 and 1448 Henry VI granted about ten boroughs and liberties the right to have their own coroners, while Edward IV made almost as many grants in 1462 alone and several more between 1462 and 1468.[6] The prodigality of these two kings did not stop here. Between 1445 and 1460 Henry VI granted many other towns and liberties exemption from county coroners and Edward IV again continued this policy in the 1460's.[7] Such grants resulted in the boroughs and liberties either securing coroners of their own or giving the coroner's duties to some existing official, and Edward IV specifically granted to two towns the right to have existing officials acting as coroners.[8]

The number of coroners in particular boroughs, as in counties, tended to decline during the thirteenth century. In 1208 the justices in eyre appointed twelve burgesses to act as coroners in Stamford.[9] They recall the 'twelve sworn coroners' established by John in the Channel Islands 'to keep the pleas and rights pertaining to the crown', who, whether or not they were the forerunners of the later jurats, almost certainly acted as coroners until the coroners' duties

[1] Ballard and Tait, *op. cit.* pp. 358–9.

[2] *Rotuli Chartarum*, p. 65.

[3] For example, those to Bristol and Dunwich: cf. *Pleas of the Crown for Gloucester, 1221*, no. 507; J.I.1/818, m. 44.

[4] See H. M. Cam, 'The Evolution of the Mediaeval English Franchise', *Speculum*, XXXII, 439.

[5] Ballard and Tait, *op. cit.* pp. 359–60.

[6] *Rotuli Parliamentorum*, V, 85, 100; *Cal. Charter Rolls*, VI, 13, 32, 54, 64, 66–7, 104–5, 153–4, 158, 166, 173–4, 177, 180, 201, 213, 224, 231; *Victoria County History: Sussex*, IX, 3.

[7] *Cal. Charter Rolls*, VI, 45, 80, 81, 86, 88, 89, 100–1, 103, 107, 120, 123, 137, 150, 193, 207, 217–18, 234.

[8] *Ibid.* pp. 182, 219–20.

[9] Selden Soc. vol. 53, no. 864. Cf. p. xxxvi.

were taken over by the bailiffs.[1] Among boroughs, however, Stamford was unique. John's charters of 1200 granted four coroners to all the towns concerned,[2] but thereafter it was normal to grant only one or two. John's second charter to Shrewsbury, issued in 1205, reduced the four coroners allowed in 1200 to two.[3] Later charters rarely state the number of coroners the town might have, and most towns elected either one or two. By Edward I's reign only Gloucester, Lincoln, Northampton and Berwick still had four,[4] but Berwick lost two of its four by a charter of 1317[5] and Gloucester also lost two during the fourteenth century.[6] During the 1329–30 eyre, Northampton still claimed to have four on the grounds that, although one coroner was adequate, the majority of the burgesses were merchants who had to travel widely; hence the retention of four coroners, two acting at a time while the other two were away on business.[7] After the eyre justices had taken the Northampton coronerships into the king's hand because of the abuse of the liberty of *infangenetheof*, the number of coroners was temporarily reduced to two, but there were four again from long before the end of the century until Charles II's reign.[8] The only other towns to have more than two coroners after 1300 were York and Lincoln, which both had three.[9]

The changes in number were probably more often made by the towns themselves than by the central government. This was certainly true of Oxford, where there were sometimes both coroners for the town and others for Northgate hundred in the suburbs and sometimes only town coroners who acted in both areas.[10] The Northgate hundred coroners' roll for most of Richard II's reign shows that between 1377 and 1382 there were two coroners who acted together except at a few inquests, one of which Thomas Houkyn held alone

---

[1] J. H. Le Patourel, *The Medieval Administration of the Channel Islands, 1199–1399* (Oxford, 1937), pp. 43–4, 90, 114–15. It is perhaps significant that in the fourteenth century the jurats co-operated with the bailiff in his work as coroner.

[2] *Rotuli Chartarum*, pp. 46 (*bis*), 56, 57, 65.   [3] *Ibid.* p. 142.

[4] J.I.1/284, m. 30; 497, m. 48; 635, m. 78; *Cal. Charter Rolls*, III, 344.

[5] *Ibid.*

[6] J.I.2/34, mm. 15–17; 35, mm. 7–8; 36, m. 5; 38, mm. 7–11; 40; 45, m. 1.

[7] J.I.1/635, m. 78.

[8] *Ibid.*; J.I.2/118; *Ass. Arch. Socs.* XXXII, 191, n. 13.

[9] J.I.2/64, m. 10; 67, mm. 41–50; 209, mm. 1–2; 215, mm. 1–10.

[10] *Records of Mediaeval Oxford*, pp. 1–50; Oxon. Hist. Soc. XVIII, 150–75, 223. Cf. H. M. Cam, 'The Hundred Outside the North Gate of Oxford', *Oxoniensia*, I, 123–4.

because it was upon the body of a child who had been accidentally drowned by falling into a well owned by his fellow coroner, Richard de Adynton, and he had to order Adynton to fill it up. In 1382, however, Adynton died of a burst tumour while walking behind his plough. Houkyn held an inquest upon him and thereafter continued to act alone as no coroner was elected to replace Adynton.[1]

Boroughs were too small to have coroners' districts and therefore in those which had more than one coroner, although one sometimes acted alone, they more often acted together. The two Chichester coroners normally acted together,[2] while in Leicester both coroners even held the inquest on the daughter of one of them after her death by misadventure.[3] All four Northampton coroners sometimes jointly held inquests and abjurations,[4] and at the 1285 Oxfordshire eyre all four coroners of Northgate hundred were amerced for not attaching those present in a house in which a homicide had been committed.[5] Large liberties naturally had a number of coroners, each with his own district. There was one for each ward in the county palatine of Durham and at least one for each hundred in the palatinate of Chester,[6] while in the liberty of the abbot of Battle, which lay in several parts in various counties, there was a coroner for each part.[7]

As a result of grants and usurpations, most counties by 1500 contained many special enclaves either with their own coroners or exempt from those of the county. In Sussex, for example, there were at least ten county, borough and franchisal coroners, as well as four other officials who performed the duties of coroner, among others, within the liberty of the Cinque Ports,[8] but this number is small compared with some counties. Many of the Sussex coroners were not established until the fifteenth century, whereas Wiltshire had twelve, Gloucestershire and Lincolnshire at least fourteen each and Yorkshire more still by 1300.[9]

The inevitable result of these complications was intermittent border disputes. In the thirteenth century the Sussex county

[1] *Records of Mediaeval Oxford*, pp. 41–7.
[2] E.g. *Sx. Arch. Colls.* xcv, 53, 55; xcvi, 26; xcviii, 46, 65–8.
[3] J.I.2/53, m. 4.   [4] E.g. J.I.2/118, m. 2.
[5] Oxon. Hist. Soc. XVIII, 219.
[6] Lapsley, *The County Palatine of Durham*, p. 86; Chester 17/13, m. 19.
[7] E.g. *Placita de Quo Warranto*, pp. 333–4; *Sx. Arch. Colls.* xcviii, 69.
[8] *Ibid.* pp. 44–8.
[9] J.I.1/284, mm. 2, 19, 29, 30, 35, 38; 497, mm. 1, 39, 40, 46, 47d, 48; 1011, mm. 59d, 62d, 63d, 64, 64d; 1078, mm. 1, 72d, 73, 83, 85; E.137/216/3.

coroners and those of the city of Chichester clashed over the receiving of abjurations from a church which was near the boundary of
their jurisdictions, while a little later the abbot of Battle and the
archbishop of Canterbury differed over the area of jurisdiction of the
abbot's coroner in his liberty of Wye in Kent.[1] In Canterbury the
steward of the prior of Christ Church refused to admit the city
coroner to hold an inquest within the priory and sent for the county
coroners instead, although the city coroners had customarily acted
there.[2] Similarly, there were differences of opinion as to whether the
city or county coroners should hold inquests on prisoners dying in
Canterbury castle and once a city and county coroner held separate
inquests upon the same body. The justices ordered that in future
either the city coroner should act alone or the two should act together, as the castle was indisputably within the city.[3] One unusual
approver's appeal was heard in Winchester gaol partly by the sheriff
of Hampshire and one of the city coroners and partly by one of the
county coroners,[4] but normally, when a gaol was situated in a city
or town which had its own coroners, and many were, those coroners
were responsible for holding inquests on dead prisoners and hearing
approvers' appeals there, whatever the provenance of the prisoners.[5]
There was rarely any objection to this, but in 1315 the men of Berkshire complained that the county gaol was at Windsor within the
liberty of Windsor forest, which meant that the coroner of the
liberty, over whom they had no control, heard the confessions of all
Berkshire approvers.[6]

Appeals of approvers best illustrate the rule that, just as county,
borough and franchisal coroners could not normally operate within
each others' areas except to produce their rolls in superior courts, so
any action by a county coroner in another county was invalid. At a
Guildford gaol delivery in 1310 a large number of men who had
been appealed by two approvers pleaded that they were not bound to

[1] *Sx. Arch. Colls.* XCVIII, 46–7; *Placita de Quo Warranto*, p. 335.
[2] Selden Soc. vol. 24, lvii–lviii.
[3] *Ibid.* p. lvi.   [4] J.I.1/797, *passim.*
[5] E.g. J.I.2/9, m. 1; 108A, m. 1.
[6] *Cal. Pat. Rolls, 1313–1317*, p. 329. For other disputes concerning the areas
of coroners' jurisdiction, see E. Miller, *The Abbey and Bishopric of Ely* (Cambridge, 1951), p. 238; W. Dugdale, *Monasticon Anglicanum*, ed. J. Caley, H.
Ellis and B. Bandinel (1846), II, 447; Surtees Soc. LXXXVIII, 355; *Calendar of
Ancient Records of Dublin*, I (1889), ed. J. T. Gilbert, pp. 155–6; *Cal. Pat. Rolls,
1266–1272*, pp. 212, 278–9; J.I.1/247, m. 36; *Mediaeval Archives of the University
of Oxford*, ed. H. E. Salter, I (Oxon. Hist. Soc. LXX), 199.

answer because the appeals had been made before Ralph Paynel, a Sussex coroner, who had no authority to act outside his county. It was found that Sussex coroners had not customarily acted outside their county and all the appellees were therefore acquitted.[1] Surrey and Sussex shared Guildford castle as their county gaol and the Surrey coroners had to hold inquests on the bodies of all Sussex prisoners who died there as well as to hear the appeals of those who turned approver.[2] The Sussex coroners were only required at Guildford when the gaol was delivered, and it was only when Sussex prisoners there turned approver during gaol deliveries that they officiated.[3]

This was practically the limit of the Sussex county coroners' duties in connection with deaths and appeals in gaol. Felons from the archbishop of Canterbury's Sussex lands were imprisoned at Maidstone, where the Kent coroners dealt with such matters.[4] The only gaols in Sussex in which prisoners might legitimately be kept for more than a day and a night were those at Chichester and Battle, and even at gaol deliveries the city and franchisal coroners were assigned to approvers there.[5] It would probably be untrue to say that Sussex county coroners never had occasion to hold inquests on dead prisoners. Anybody under arrest was a prisoner, and felons could be kept in local prisons for a night and a day pending their transfer to a royal gaol.[6] In 1395, for example, an inquest had to be held on the death of a man in the custody of the mayor and bailiffs of Oxford, although he had died in the house of one of the bailiffs.[7] But the Sussex coroner who was called upon to hold many such inquests might legitimately feel that the fates were against him. By contrast, the Surrey coroners were very hard worked in this respect. As well as dealing with their own and Sussex prisoners in Guildford gaol, they also had often to hold inquests and hear appeals of approvers in the King's Bench Marshalsea.[8] Some compensation was, however, provided by the fact that whereas the Sussex coroners had to travel regularly to Guildford and sometimes to Maidstone gaol deliveries, as well as to those at Chichester and Battle, the Surrey coroners had no comparable travelling.

Between those areas which were unreservedly under the juris-

[1] J.I.3/111, m. 7d.   [2] E.g. *ibid*. mm. 6, 8.
[3] E.g. *Sx. Arch. Colls*. xcvi, 29–32.   [4] E.g. J.I.3/129, m. 44.
[5] E.g. J.I.3/163, m. 12.   [6] *Britton*, i.21.5.
[7] *Records of Mediaeval Oxford*, p. 50.
[8] E.g. K.B.9/210, m. 39; 265, m. 33.

diction of the county coroners and those which had coroners of their own and complete exemption from the county coroners, there were others with varying degrees of privilege as far as coroners were concerned. Boroughs usually received an outright grant of the right to have their own coroners. This was suitable both to the crown, which gained both a fee and support, and to the boroughs, which always desired independence of the county officials. In the thirteenth century, however, there was a rule that a county coroner had to be summoned to officiate with the borough coroner at abjurations in Arundel and in the fourteenth century the Wilton coroner acted in the suburbs jointly with a Wiltshire county coroner.[1] A few smaller boroughs without coroners of their own established the right of their bailiffs to sit with the county coroners at borough inquests.[2] A few other small towns had to be satisfied with the privilege of attending upon county coroners only within the town and without representatives of neighbouring townships.[3]

Most lords of large liberties had early obtained grants of deodands, *murdrum* fines and the chattels of felons and fugitives forfeited in their lands. Their desire to have their own coroners was therefore the more willingly granted by the crown, which would have received no financial advantage if county coroners had acted there. Such lords probably sought coroners of their own to have the profits of crown pleas safeguarded by their own officials and also because they liked to make their administrations independent and a complete reflection of the king's. Other liberties, especially the smaller ones, often did not have their own coroners. Gross thought that this was because kings were less willing to grant coroners to liberties than to towns,[4] but the lords of liberties may often have been less anxious to have them because, although they might appoint them, the coroners were still theoretically 'the king's coroners'.[5] Franchisal powers were as much a duty as a privilege and could be withdrawn if abused or not used.[6] This may well have been why some lords did not secure coroners of their own, but contented themselves with gaining exemption from the county coroners for their fairs[7] or with the privilege of having one of their officials, usually the steward,

---

[1] *Sx. Arch. Colls.* xcviii, 46; J.I.2/196, m. 5.
[2] E.g. J.I.2/151, m. 1d; Chester 18/1, m. 5.
[3] E.g. *Placita de Quo Warranto*, pp. 138 (*bis*), 629.
[4] *Select Coroners' Rolls*, pp. xxix–xxx.
[5] E.g. K.B.9/332, m. 12.   [6] See above, p. 139.
[7] E.g. *Cal. Charter Rolls*, VI, 81, 207, 225.

L

sitting with the county or borough coroners when they acted within their liberties.[1] Others were satisfied to receive the profits of crown pleas. The normal procedure then was for the county or borough coroner to appraise all homicides' chattels and deodands and commit them to safe keeping, the lords of the liberties claiming them at the eyre.[2] Normally, such escheats were only allowed to the lord before the eyre by special writ. The writ was usually addressed to the coroners,[3] but in Oxford one abjuror's chattels were delivered to the master and brethren of the hospital of St John of Jerusalem on a writ to the town bailiffs.[4] On two other occasions, when Oxford coroners delivered a fugitive homicide's goods to the same master and brethren and those of an abjuror to the prior of St Frideswide's, no writ is cited,[5] while one Yorkshire coroner enrolled the fact that, after he had held an inquisition into an abjuror's chattels, the escheator put Queen Philippa in possession of them.[6] Finally, many lords of liberties illegally took possession of forfeited chattels without warrant after their appraisal by the coroner but before the eyre, while others wished for more extensive liberties in connection with coroners than they had, usurping the right to appoint coroners of their own, claiming exemption from county coroners or refusing to allow their tenants to attend inquests outside their liberties or to sit within their liberties with men from outside.[7]

As well as boroughs and franchises, many counties had another privileged enclave—the royal forest. At least some areas so designated were for a time exempt from the county coroner's jurisdiction. At the 1221 Gloucestershire eyre the county stated that the custom of the Forest of Dean was that 'verderers present the pleas of the forest in place of coroners'.[8] In 1248 six 'coroners of the forest' were presented along with six county coroners as having held office since the previous eyre, and the jurors of the Forest of Dean presented that there were 'no coroners in that hundred other than the verderers of the forest'.[9] Very few Gloucestershire eyre rolls survive and no later mention of verderers taking the place of coroners is known. In the first half of the thirteenth century, however, they certainly exercised

[1] E.g. Hist. MSS. Comm., 6th Report, App. p. 508; Cal. Charter Rolls I, 121.
[2] E.g. J.I.1/929, m. 41.   [3] E.g. J.I.2/57, m. 13 schedule.
[4] Oxon. Hist. Soc. XVIII, 174-5.   [5] Ibid. pp. 153-4, 171-2.
[6] J.I.2/222, m. 6d.   [7] Sx. Arch. Colls. XCVIII, 47.
[8] Pleas of the Crown for Gloucester, 1221, no. 182.
[9] J.I.1/274, mm. 1, 11d, 16.

the coroner's functions, but only in the covert.[1] Similarly, the county coroners acted throughout Huntingdonshire, the whole of which was royal forest, except that the verderers held inquests upon dead bodies found within the king's demesne wood.[2] In 1334 a petition in Parliament, stating that foresters were not allowing county coroners to hold inquests within the forest, received the reply that coroners should act as well within as without the forest.[3] No further trouble is known, and the verderers presumably confined themselves to holding inquests on dead beasts of the forest,[4] although in Shropshire at least the practice for long seems to have been for one county coroner and one verderer to officiate jointly at inquests on dead humans found in the forest[5] and Macclesfield forest, in the county palatine of Chester, had its own coroner throughout the Middle Ages.[6]

The 'Seven Hundreds of Cookham and Bray' or the 'Seven Hundreds of Windsor Forest' had a coroner of their own.[7] They were part of the ancient demesne of the crown,[8] and some other hundreds which either were ancient demesne or had come into the king's hand after 1086, such as Lifton in Devon, Rochford in Essex, Milton in Kent, Kingston in Surrey and Lothingland in Suffolk, also had their own coroners.[9] Lothingland paid 110 shillings for the privilege[10] and presumably the other hundreds also bought theirs. It would be interesting to know the circumstances of these transactions. These

---

[1] E. C. Wright, 'Common Law in the Thirteenth-Century English Royal Forest', *Speculum*, III, 189–90. Townships were amerced there, for example, for burying men who died by misadventure *sine visu servientis vel viridarii* (e.g. *Pleas of the Crown for Gloucester, 1221*, no. 392).

[2] *Speculum*, III, 175, 179, 183; *Select Pleas of the Forest*, ed. G. J. Turner (Selden Soc. vol. 13), p. 19.

[3] *Rotuli Parliamentorum*, II, 376; Camden 3rd ser. LI, 236.

[4] Inquests on beasts, whether slain feloniously or by misadventure, paralleled those on men. They were held by the four neighbouring townships, who, with the four neighbours, 'first finders' and owners of the land on which they were found, had to find sureties for their appearance at the next forest eyre (Selden Soc. vol. 13, xxxviii-xxxix).

[5] E.g. J.I.2/146, m. 2.   [6] E.g. Chester 17/13, m. 19.

[7] J.I.1/40, m. 25d; 48, m. 39.   [8] *Victoria County History: Berkshire*, III, 117.

[9] *Placita de Quo Warranto*, p. 170; J.I.1/232 m. 12; 359, m. 25; 369, m. 1; 874A, m. 28; 877, m. 62; *Pipe Roll 26 Henry III*, ed. H. L. Cannon (New Haven, 1918), p. 205. For the connection of these hundreds with the crown see *The Book of Fees*, p. 1371; P. Morant, *The History and Antiquities of the County of Essex*, I (1816), 268; E. Hasted, *The History . . . of Kent* (Canterbury, 1797–1801), VI, 2; *Victoria County History: Surrey*, III, 481; W. A. Copinger, *The Manors of Suffolk* (Privately printed, 1905–11), V, 3.

[10] *Pipe Roll 26 Henry III*, p. 205.

hundreds may have been specially favoured, since no others are known to have purchased the right to have coroners; on the other hand, medieval kings regarded the royal demesne as a profitable source of revenue and the purchase of these grants may well have been enforced. Thirdly, or additionally, the crown may have wished to increase the administrative distinctiveness of these areas, just as in the fourteenth century the Chamber lands became virtually royal franchises with officials, including coroners, of their own.[1] Mines also had a very special relationship to the crown, for which reason the community of lead miners at Alston in Cumberland had the right of electing one of themselves, called the king's serjeant, to act as their coroner and bailiff.[2]

Another privileged area was peripatetic. This was the verge, which extended for twelve miles around the king's court. It had its own coroner, called the coroner of the king's household, coroner of the Marshalsea or coroner of the verge, who was normally also clerk of the market until Henry V's reign.[3] As coroner he not only had the duties of a normal coroner within the verge but also acted as the king's attorney in cases heard in the Marshalsea court.[4] During the thirteenth century, no other coroner was allowed to act within the verge, with the result that many felonies were not presented to the justices in eyre after the king's court had moved on. This was remedied in 1300 by the *Articuli Super Cartas*, which provided that the county coroner should sit with the coroner of the household at all inquests held within the verge and enrol them.[5] This provision was confirmed by the Ordinances of 1311 and again by the Statute of York in 1322,[6] although there is a note in the Year Books of the 1313–14 Kent eyre that the coroner of the verge should hold his inquest on misadventures occurring within the verge after the county coroner had held one.[7] The king's court did not visit all counties, but there are many examples of inquests held jointly by the county or borough coroner and the coroner of the household in those which it did, including some enrolled upon county and borough coroners' rolls.[8]

---

[1] Tout, *Chapters in the Administrative History of Mediaeval England*, IV, 253, 271–2.

[2] *Cal. Inqs. Misc.* III, 222.   [3] *Britton*, i.i.6.

[4] E.g. E.37/1–2, mm. 4, 7d.   [5] 28 Edw. I, c. 3.

[6] 5 Edw. II, c. 27; *Rotuli Parliamentorum*, I, 456.

[7] Selden Soc. vol. 24, p. 132.

[8] E.g. J.I.1/689, m. 2d; J.I.2/131, m. 1; *Records of Mediaeval Oxford*, pp. 15, 24–5, 28. For the prosecution of a Yorkshire coroner in the Marshalsea court for

The coroner of King's Bench was mainly employed as the king's attorney in cases heard in the court, but also held a few inquests.[1] Thus sewn to the side of a Coventry coroner's roll is a single inquest held in Coventry by Edmund Brudenell, coroner of King's Bench, when that court was sitting there in 1397.[2] Coroners of King's Bench also heard appeals of prisoners who turned approver in the King's Bench Marshalsea and held inquests on some who died,[3] although Surrey coroners held others.[4] The justices of King's Bench were regarded as 'sovereign coroners of the realm' and therefore able to hear appeals.[5]

Nothing is known of coroners of the Admiralty in the Middle Ages. Perhaps they did not exist; certainly they did not encroach upon the county coroner's jurisdiction. It was found at the 1313–14 Kent eyre, for example, that the Kent coroners had never held inquests upon men drowned in the tidal part of the Medway. The justices ordered that the coroners should in future hold inquests into deaths in ordinary rivers and in 'arms of the sea' where the deaths were or could have been witnessed from the opposite shore.[6] The ordinary coroners had also to hold inquests upon men who were drowned and found on the seashore, although boats were not adjudged deodand if they caused death on the sea or salt water.[7] In 1391, in reply to a petition concerning the extension of the Admiral's jurisdiction, it was provided by statute that all pleas arising 'within the bodies of counties, as well by land as by water', were outside the Admiral's jurisdiction, except for deaths and mayhems occurring in 'great ships' below the bridges of 'great rivers'.[8] It has been thought that this statute implies the existence of Admiralty coroners,[9] but this inference is not necessary.

holding an inquest in the verge without the coroner of the household, and his imprisonment until he paid a fine of 100s., see E.37/1–2, m. 4.

[1] The dual nature of his activities is always shown in the patents of appointment (e.g. *Cal. Pat. Rolls, 1385–1389*, p. 25, where, as in many similar *Calendar* entries, he is erroneously called coroner of the Common Bench).

[2] J.I.2/189, m. 3d schedule. It was estreated with the Warwickshire coroners' rolls (K.B. 27/546, Fines and Forfeitures, m. 7d).

[3] E.g. K.B.29/31, m. 17 (inquest); 40, m. 35 (appeal of approver).

[4] See above, p. 144.

[5] *Year Books 17 Edward III*, ed. L. O. Pike (Rolls Series, 1901), p. 214.

[6] Selden Soc. vol. 24, p. 133.   [7] *Britton*, i.2.12, 14; Bracton, II, 344.

[8] 15 Ric. II, c. 3.

[9] R. Henslowe Wellington, *The King's Coroner* (1905), p. 29.

CHAPTER IX

ELECTIONS AND QUALIFICATIONS

FOR fifty years the Northumberland county coronerships were hereditary, being attached to serjeanty tenures, until in 1246 these ser-
jeanties were taken into the king's hand and the county coronerships became elective. The only avowedly hereditary coronerships
elsewhere were in parts of the liberties of the bishops of Ely and
Durham.[1] All other coroners were either appointed or elected.

The coroners of King's Bench and of the verge were appointed
by the crown,[2] as were the king's butler, who was *ex officio* coroner
of the city of London although he rarely performed the duties of
coroner there, and the deputy coroner who usually acted for him.[3]
Nearly all grants of coroners to liberties gave the lords the right to
appoint them,[4] although this was sometimes disguised by the use of
the term 'elect and create' and by the appointment being made in
the *libera curia* of the franchise.[5] The abbot of St Albans, and probably others, sometimes granted the reversion of the office.[6] When
borough coronerships were taken into the king's hand the coroners
were appointed, as in Bedford and Northampton in 1329–30, and so
they were in some at least of the escheated estates which became
Chamber lands under Edward III.[7] Other coroners were only occasionally appointed, and only during two periods. Henry III appointed a number of county coroners, when informed of deaths or
disqualifications, and usually ordered the sheriff to take their oaths
in the county court,[8] and on one occasion he similarly appointed a
coroner for Milton hundred.[9] The other period was the 1380's when

---

[1] *Trans. R. Hist. Soc.* 5th ser. VIII, 99–100; R. L. Storey, *Thomas Langley and the Bishopric of Durham* (1961), p. 62.

[2] E.g. above, p. 149, n. 1; *Cal. Pat. Rolls, 1377–1381*, p. 19.

[3] *Cal. Coroners Rolls of London*, pp. viii–x, xii–xiii; *Cal. Pat. Rolls, 1381–1385*, p. 176.

[4] For good examples of appointments see Lapsley, *The County Palatine of Durham*, p. 87, n. 1; Miller, *The Abbey and Bishopric of Ely*, p. 238, n. 1.

[5] E.g. Levett, *Studies in Manorial History*, pp. 107–8.

[6] *Ibid.* p. 108.   [7] Above, p. 139; Tout, *op. cit.* IV, 272.

[8] E.g. *Rotuli Litterarum Clausarum*, I, 366, 560; *Close Rolls, 1231–1234*, p. 510; *1234–1237*, p. 3; *1237–1242*, p. 395; *1242–1247*, p. 309; *1256–1259*, p. 40.

[9] *Close Rolls, 1254–1256*, p. 365.

two crown appointments were made—one to a coronership in fourteen Norfolk hundreds and the other in Carmarthenshire—but the
first never took effect.[1] Some late fourteenth-century coroners are
described in their rolls as *factus* or *assignatus*,[2] but this does not
necessarily mean that they had been appointed.[3] It may merely
represent their attitude towards their election, for, apart from the
exceptions just noted, the essence of the office of coroner outside
franchises was that it was elective.

County coroners were elected in one of two ways: either before
royal justices or in the county court on writs *de coronatore eligendo*.
The 1194 eyre article concerning the election of county coroners was
almost certainly executed in the presence of the eyre justices. No
similar article is known for subsequent eyres, but the thirteenth-
century eyre rolls prove that a new team of coroners was elected before the justices at most, if not all, general eyres. Such elections were
made by all the knights and freeholders of the shire,[4] and most of the
coroners elected during eyres were assuming the office for the first
time, although there were notable exceptions such as Richard de
Bydeford, who was elected at two successive Hertfordshire eyres.[5]
It is impossible to discover in most cases whether the change was
desired by the men of the county, possibly in the hope that extortions would cease, or the justices for some reason opposed the
nomination of the outgoing coroners, but it seems certain that the
justices sometimes took advantage of these elections to change the
number of county coroners.[6] The action of the Hertfordshire eyre
justices, who removed the two existing county coroners without
seeing to the election of new ones, thereby necessitating the issue of
a writ *de coronatoribus eligendis*, was probably unique, although in
1246 the sheriff of Northumberland was ordered to see to the election of new county coroners in place of the two hereditary coroners
whose lands had been taken into the king's hand by the eyre justices.[7]

With the end of the general eyre came the virtual end of the election of coroners before justices. One Somerset coroner had been
elected and sworn in before the Ilchester gaol delivery justices in
1225, while an exceptional writ *de coronatore eligendo* of 1237 order-

---

[1] *Cal. Pat. Rolls, 1381–1385*, p. 385; *1385–1389*, p. 296.
[2] E.g. *Select Coroners' Rolls*, pp. 91–6.
[3] As thought by Gross (*ibid.* p. 91, n. 2).   [4] *Sx. Arch. Colls.* XCVIII, 48.
[5] J.I.1/324A, m. 42; 328, m. 9d.   [6] Above, p. 134.
[7] *Close Rolls, 1237–1242*, p. 260; *1242–1247*, p. 468.

ed the election of a county coroner in full county court by the assent
of the whole county and before the Salisbury gaol delivery justices,[1]
but these practices are not known to have been repeated. There were
also very occasional elections in the *Curia Regis* in the early thirteenth century,[2] although on one occasion the sheriff was ordered to
receive the oath of office in the county court.[3] There is one instance,
in 1296, of justices of oyer and terminer removing a Rutland coroner
from office, but the replacement was made by election on a writ *de
coronatore eligendo*.[4] Similar writs issued in 1306 and 1337 for the
replacement of coroners who had been imprisoned for trespasses,
but not removed from office, by justices of oyer and terminer.[5] The
roll of Peter Breton of Beelsby, coroner of the North Riding of Lincolnshire, has as its heading a note that in 1375 Breton entered upon
his office and took his oath before the justices of King's Bench at
Lincoln,[6] but this is the only known case later than 1330 of a county
coroner being elected otherwise than as a result of a writ *de coronatore
eligendo*.

These writs issued from Chancery to the sheriff. They normally
named the coroner or coroners to be replaced and the reason for their
replacement, and ordered the sheriff to cause another coroner or
coroners to be elected in their place in full county court with the assent of the county; that is to say, the elections were made by the
suitors—the knights and freemen of the shire. The writs always
warned the sheriff to see that men who knew how and were able to
perform the duties of coroner were elected. The elected coroners
had then to swear that they would perform and preserve those things
that pertained to their office without reward, and the sheriff had to
return their names to Chancery.[7] The only other local officials to be
similarly elected in the county court were verderers, for whom there
were almost identical writs *de viridario eligendo*.[8] Unfortunately, no

---

[1] Somerset Rec. Soc. XI, 381; *Close Rolls, 1234–1237*, p. 473.

[2] E.g. *Curia Regis Rolls*, XIV, 1905.   [3] *Ibid.* x, 69.

[4] *Cal. Close Rolls, 1288–1296*, p. 472.

[5] *Cal. Close Rolls, 1302–1307*, p. 385; *1337–1339*, p. 2.   [6] J.I.2/81, m. 1.

[7] For specimen writs see *Registrum Omnium Brevium: Originalium*, ff. 177–
177v.

[8] E.g. *ibid.* ff. 177v–178. Verderers were remarkably similar to coroners. They
were elected for life unless removed, and were removed for the same reasons as
coroners. They had to have land in the forest and were generally either knights or
possessed of considerable landed property. They had no salary or perquisites,
but were exempt from assizes, juries and recognitions. They held inquests upon
dead beasts and sometimes acted as or with coroners, while their main function
was to attend forest courts (Selden Soc. vol. 13, xix–xx; above, pp. 146–7).

account of a coroner's election exists, but it probably bore a close resemblance to the election of knights of the shire to Parliament.[1] The procedure for the election of coroners occasionally varied slightly. In 1228, when one of Stephen de Segrave's retainers was removed from office, the writ ordered that his successor be elected in the Leicestershire county court in Segrave's presence, while in 1231 the sheriff of Herefordshire was ordered to receive the oath of a county coroner who had not taken it after his election in Segrave's presence.[2] A third unusual case occurred in 1391 when a Huntingdonshire coroner, who had presumably been elected locally, took his oath in Chancery; the sheriff was then ordered to allow him to pursue his duties.[3]

When the first writ *de coronatore eligendo* issued it is impossible to say, because their enrolment upon the Close Rolls was erratic and very few returned writs now survive upon the Chancery files.[4] Perhaps they were often not returned, for a Nottinghamshire coroner's roll notes an election pursuant to a writ and adds: *J. de Vaus vicecomes habet breve penes se.*[5] Certainly a large number of writs were never enrolled on the Close Rolls; the total number of enrolled writs for all counties fluctuates considerably from decade to decade. Thus of the sixty-six men who are known to have been county coroners in Sussex in the Middle Ages writs are enrolled for the replacement of only forty-five, of whom nineteen are only known to have held office from the writs replacing them while the only additional information known of two others is the date of their election derived from the returned writs.[6] Since well over a half of the medieval Sussex coroners are not even known by name, only a small percentage of the writs issued can have been enrolled. The first writ replacing a particular Sussex coroner was not enrolled until 1253 and the last was in 1453, while the only writs *de coronatore eligendo* for any county enrolled after 1471 were those issued at the beginning of new reigns.[7]

---

[1] See H. G. Richardson, 'The Commons and Medieval Politics', *Trans. R. Hist. Soc.* 4th ser. XXVIII, 39–43. Gross sought the germ of the Parliamentary knights of the shire in the county coroners, since both were elected in the county court, and even called them prototypes of the knights of the shire (*Select Coroners' Rolls*, pp. xxxiv–xxxv). For a criticism of this, see D. J. Medley's review in *Eng. Hist. Rev.* XIII, 156–7.

[2] *Close Rolls, 1227–1231*, pp. 140–1, 476–7.

[3] *Cal. Close Rolls, 1389–1392*, p. 418.

[4] There are only four for Sussex for the whole of the Middle Ages (*Sx. Arch. Colls.* XCVIII, 57, 62). One of the four is not upon the Close Roll.

[5] J.I.1/692, m. 3.

[6] For details see *Sx. Arch. Colls.* XCVIII, 53–65.   [7] See below, p. 166.

It is obviously unwise to generalise overmuch on the basis of the enrolled writs, but it is perhaps significant that the first one does not appear until 1218[1] and that there are comparatively few before the middle of Edward I's reign. Probably few issued earlier, for eyres were fairly frequent, especially early in the century.[2] Sick or aged coroners would not have been elected in the presence of the justices, with the result that few coroners died in office. Of the nine Sussex county coroners whom the extant eyre rolls describe as having been in office since the previous eyres, four had been in office during the whole period and only two had died before the second eyre.[3] There are also signs that in many cases before 1300 writs for new coroners did not issue until the situation had become desperate. On four occasions four coroners were simultaneously replaced in a single county,[4] three were replaced on five occasions,[5] and some of the writs for the election of two coroners were for counties which had only two. On several occasions writs issued to bring the number of county coroners up from one to two,[6] from three to four[7] or from an uncertain number to four;[8] they ordered no specific coroner to be replaced, which suggests that at least one office had been vacant for a considerable time. There was no county coroner in Berkshire or Hertfordshire in 1263 or in Essex in 1276, individuals being specially commissioned to hold inquests on particular bodies.[9] Similarly, Middlesex had no county coroner in part of 1253 and 1254, and special orders had to be given to the sheriff to take knights and receive one abjuration and view seven bodies;[10] one of these orders was combined with a writ *de coronatore eligendo*.[11] Middlesex got into this position because an earlier writ *de coronatore eligendo* had not been executed,[12] but contact between Chancery and the counties was clearly not very close at this time. All three Buckinghamshire coroners elected on the same writ in 1265, for example, replaced

---

[1] *Rotuli Litterarum Clausarum*, I, 368.
[2] *Oxon. Studies in Soc. & Leg. Hist.* VI, 104–13.
[3] *Sx. Arch. Colls.* XCVIII, 53–6.
[4] *Close Rolls, 1237–1242*, p. 170; *1247–1251*, pp. 165–6, 512; *1256–1259*, p. 362.
[5] *Close Rolls, 1227–1231*, p. 371; *1231–1234*, p. 67; *1237–1242*, p. 105; *1256–1259*, p. 183; *1264–1268*, p. 15.
[6] E.g. *Close Rolls, 1242–1247*, pp. 298, 481; *1247–1251*, p. 197.
[7] E.g. *Close Rolls, 1264–1268*, p. 114.
[8] E.g. *Rotuli Litterarum Clausarum*, I, 402.
[9] *Cal. Pat. Rolls, 1258–1266*, pp. 251, 305; *1272–1281*, p. 157.
[10] *Close Rolls, 1253–1254*, pp. 10, 11, 25, 29, 48, 49, 58.
[11] *Ibid.* p. 48.   [12] *Ibid.*

dead ones, who can hardly have died at exactly the same time.[1] Writs
for the replacement of single coroners increased in number as the
century wore on, but it is probable that before the 1280's over half
of the county coroners were elected before justices. In the fourteenth
and fifteenth centuries, however, they were nearly all elected in the
county court on writs *de coronatore eligendo*.

Borough coroners were elected in the same two ways as county
coroners. A Bristol man 'was presented as coroner by the burgesses
of Bristol' in the *Curia Regis* in 1229 to replace one who had died,
and in 1243 a King's Lynn coroner was elected and sworn in in the
Curia Regis,[2] but such cases were unusual. A few boroughs were
granted the right to elect their coroners annually and a few others to
elect them as often as was necessary;[3] the first type of grant certainly
and the second possibly implied that the burgesses could proceed to
election without a writ. Most boroughs, however, had their coroners
elected and sworn in before the eyre justices in the thirteenth century,[4] and when a new coroner was needed between eyres or at any
time in the fourteenth and fifteenth centuries, the theory seems to
have been that the election should be held on a writ *de coronatore
eligendo*, but practice was far different. In the early thirteenth century many elections, as of county coroners, were delayed as long as
possible: the election of four Lincoln coroners was ordered in 1218,
of two Worcester ones in 1232 and of three more for Lincoln in 1243
to replace three who were dead.[5] Later many boroughs must have
proceeded to election without a writ.

Excluding those issued at the beginning of reigns, only sixty-six
writs among the large number enrolled upon the medieval Close
Rolls specifically state that they are for the election of borough
coroners, fifty-one of which belong to the period 1374–1461. They
relate to twenty-six boroughs, Oxford with ten and York and Lincoln with eight each having the most; there is one for each of twelve
towns. These figures are even more remarkable than they seem at
first sight. Thus all the York writs are confined to the forty years
beginning in 1416 and the Oxford ones to the period after 1375.

The paucity of enrolled writs for boroughs is more apparent than

---

[1] *Close Rolls, 1264–1268*, p. 15.
[2] *Curia Regis Rolls*, XIII, 1873; K.B.26/126, m. 2d.
[3] E.g. Ballard and Tait, *op. cit.* pp. 358–60.
[4] E.g. J.I.1/789, m. 37.
[5] *Rotuli Litterarum Clausarum*, I, 364; *Close Rolls, 1231–1234*, p. 177; *1242–
1247*, p. 82.

real, since many writs did not distinguish between county and borough coroners. All the Sussex writs *de coronatore eligendo*, whether for county or borough coroners, issued to the sheriff; they never described the area of jurisdiction of the outgoing coroner, but merely ordered the election of another coroner 'for the county'. It therefore appears at first sight that all the Sussex writs were for county coroners, but of the fifty-six different coroners whom they were to replace nine were Chichester and two Arundel officials.[1] The proportion of borough to county writs on the Close Rolls is undoubtedly small, but bigger than the writs themselves suggest.

The enrolment of writs for the election of county coroners fluctuated from decade to decade, but the paucity of borough writs on the Close Rolls and their erratic chronological distribution are much more extreme and need a more satisfactory explanation than nonenrolment because of pressure of work upon the Chancery clerks. The Chichester and Arundel writs, like those for York, Oxford and other places, are confined to a short period. Both places had coroners by prescriptive right only and were unwilling to draw attention to this by applying for writs in Chancery. They both seem to have elected their coroners without writs until 1288, when the justices discovered that on the recent death of one of the city coroners Chichester had elected another without a writ. Presumably as a result of this, the next seven Chichester coroners were all replaced by writs *de coronatore eligendo*, but only three other writs, all from the 1420's, were enrolled for Chichester coroners. When the same justices asked the burgesses of Arundel by what right they elected borough coroners, they replied that they had elected a coroner from among themselves and taken his oath in full borough court from time immemorial without the king's writ. It was presumably because of this disclosure that the next two Arundel coroners were replaced by writ, but no other Arundel writ is on the Close Rolls.[2] It seems clear that these two places were inspired by guilt and fear to apply for writs for a time, but ceased to do so after these feelings had subsided. They ceased with impunity because Chancery, perplexed by the multiplicity of borough privileges, can rarely have had time to enforce the law. There are many signs, however, that efforts were made to bring practice into line with theory in the late thirteenth century. In 1299 the charters granting coroners to Hull and Raven-

[1] *Sx. Arch. Colls.* xcviii, 49, 56–68.   [2] *Ibid.* pp. 45, 49.

ser stated that they should be elected on Chancery writs, and in 1302 Berwick-upon-Tweed had a similar grant except that the writs were to issue from the Scottish Chancery.[1] It is significant that the only enrolled writs *de coronatore eligendo* for Hull and Ravenser are of the year 1299, immediately after the grants.[2]

The burgesses of these two Yorkshire boroughs were granted the right to elect coroners from among themselves and to present them to the keepers of the towns, before whom they were to take their oath. The natural interpretation of this is that the elections should have been held in the borough courts, but the writs of 1299 issued to the sheriff of Yorkshire and ordered him to cause the burgesses of the two towns to elect their coroners in the county court. The writs agree with the pronouncement of the Essex eyre justices, when the burgesses of Colchester were found to have appointed coroners from among the borough bailiffs: that it was contrary to the custom of the realm for anyone to act as coroner who had not taken his oath of office before the justices or before the sheriff in the full county court at the king's command.[3] The charter of 1256 to Derby stated that the newly granted town coroner, when elected by the burgesses, should be presented by them to the sheriff who should receive his oath in full county court before he entered on his office; and the Devizes coroner, whom the burgesses in 1381 were granted the right to elect on the receipt of a writ, was also required to take his oath before the Wiltshire sheriff in full county court.[4] These are the only charters to contain such provisions, but of the sixty-six writs *de coronatore eligendo* on the Close Rolls which say that they are for borough coroners, twenty-three are addressed to sheriffs of counties and order elections in the county court. Also, in 1218, although the mayor and citizens of Lincoln were ordered to elect four city coroners, another writ issued to the sheriff of Lincolnshire ordering him to take their oath and return their names to William Marshal.[5] These manifestly borough writs, together with those which ordered the election of a new coroner 'for the county' in place of a man known to have been a borough coroner, produce a majority of borough writs on the Close Rolls, and probably a majority of those issued, addressed to the sheriff and ordering an election in the county court.

---

[1] Ballard and Tait, *op. cit.* p. 360.   [2] *Cal. Close Rolls, 1296–1302*, pp. 240–1.
[3] *Select Coroners' Rolls*, p. xxxvii.   [4] *Cal. Charter Rolls*, IV, 50; V, 274.
[5] *Rotuli Litterarum Clausarum*, I, 364.

Most burgesses were exempt from attendance at the county court and what happened in most cases must have been similar to the Sussex practice. In 1329 a writ issued to the sheriff for the election of a coroner 'for that county' in place of Peter de Brommore who had no lands in the county. Brommore, however, had for long been not a county but a Chichester city coroner. The sheriff therefore sent the writ to the city officials, who found by inquisition that Brommore held no lands in the city and then held an election in the full city court.[1] If writs addressed to the sheriff of the county and ordering elections in the county court could result in elections in borough courts, there can be no doubt that all other borough coroners were elected there. When boroughs proceeded to election without a writ, they must have done so, like Arundel,[2] in the borough court. This was the obvious interpretation of most borough charters, which merely authorised the burgesses to elect coroners 'from among themselves' or 'by common counsel of the town'.[3] Thus in 1200, a month after Ipswich had been granted the right to elect four coroners 'by common counsel of the burgesses', the whole town assembled in a churchyard and, among other business, unanimously elected four coroners, who then took their oath.[4] Some town coroners were required by charter to take their oath of office before one or more borough officials[5] or before the burgesses as a whole,[6] while the 1252 letters patent to Newcastle-upon-Tyne specifically stated that they should take it before the mayor and bailiffs in full court.[7] For Hull and Ravenser, it is true, although the oath was taken before the keepers of the towns, it was intended that the coroners should be elected in the county court,[8] but this practice must have been exceptional and forty-three of the borough writs *de coronatore eligendo* on the Close Rolls either ordered or implied that the elections were

[1] *Sx. Arch. Colls.* XCVIII, 49. The result of this was an indenture, one part, called 'the king's part', sealed with the city seal and presumably returned to Chancery with the writ, and the city's part sealed with the new coroner's seal and preserved in the common chest of the city. The king's part is no longer on the Chancery files, but the other is still among the Chichester archives ('Chichester City Deeds', ed. W. D. Peckham, *Sx. Arch. Colls.* LXXXIX, 122).

[2] Above, p. 156.   [3] Ballard and Tait, *op. cit.* pp. 357–60.

[4] Gross, *The Gild Merchant*, II, 116–17. They swore, in accordance with the charter, to keep the pleas of the crown and to do other things pertaining to the crown in the town and to see that the bailiffs justly and lawfully treated both poor and rich.

[5] E.g. *Cal. Charter Rolls*, v, 48 (mayor and bailiffs); Ballard and Tait, *op. cit.* p. 360 (mayor).

[6] E.g. *ibid.* p. 358.   [7] *Ibid.*   [8] Above, p. 157.

to be held in the borough courts. The most unusual of these issued
to the sheriff of Gloucestershire in 1254, ordering him to go to
Bristol and command the mayor and bailiffs to see to the election and
swearing in of a new Bristol coroner in the full hundred court before
the mayor, bailiffs and sheriff.[1]

The other forty-two writs issued to borough officials. The majority were addressed to the mayor and bailiffs, three to bailiffs alone,
one to the mayor and good men, one to the bailiffs and freemen, and
one to the mayor and jurats; one issued to the mayor and sheriffs of
Lincoln, while after 1412 all writs for York, Lincoln and Norwich
issued to the sheriffs of those cities; the only Stamford writ issued to
the keeper of the markets there in 1245, while a Worcester one of
1461 issued to the guardians of the peace in the city; and three others
issued to lords or officials of liberties. There was rarely any consis-
tent form of address to the writs issued for coroners for any particular town. Eight of the Oxford writs issued to the mayor and
bailiffs and the other two to the sheriff of the county; the second of
these two issued in May 1415, probably because the writ addressed
to the mayor and bailiffs in February for the replacement of the same
town coroner had not been executed.[2] In 1393 it was the mayor and
bailiffs of Leicester but in 1414 the mayor and jurats who received
writs for that town.[3] The Lincoln writs were the most varied. That
of 1218 issued to the mayor and citizens, while a supplementary one
issued to the sheriff of the county ordering him to take the oaths and
make the return.[4] There followed four writs addressed to the mayor
and bailiffs, ordering elections in the full city court in 1243, in full
hustings in 1253 and in the Guildhall in 1392. The fourth issued in
1406, followed in 1411 by one addressed to the mayor and sheriffs
and another in 1412 to the city sheriffs alone, which form seems to
have persisted.[5] Two main reasons account for these variations.
Firstly, borough constitutions changed during the Middle Ages.
Secondly, both the charters granting coroners and, even more, local
practice were so varied that the Chancery clerks must often have
been confused; not having the time or patience to discover to whom
the borough writs should have been addressed, they sometimes

[1] Close Rolls, 1253–1254, p. 39.
[2] Cal. Close Rolls, 1413–1419, pp. 174, 210.
[3] Cal. Close Rolls, 1392–1396, p. 56; 1413–1419, p. 123.
[4] Above, p. 157.
[5] Close Rolls, 1242–1247, p. 82; 1251–1253, p. 315; Cal. Close Rolls, 1389–1392,
p. 471; 1405–1409, p. 157; 1409–1413, pp. 140, 372; 1429–1435, p. 154.

guessed. Hence the alternate addressing of writs to the mayor and bailiffs of the town and the sheriff of the county, as for Oxford, Bedford and Carlisle coroners.

In the later Middle Ages towns were granted increasing autonomy, a less 'democratic' form of government and a concentration of offices upon a few burgesses. The increasing autonomy is witnessed by the fact that whereas Shaftesbury was the only town to be given the privilege of electing its coroners annually, and therefore without writs, in the thirteenth century,[1] such grants became fairly common later.[2] Secondly, while the thirteenth- and fourteenth-century charters invariably granted the burgesses the right to elect their own coroners, many later ones allowed only a restricted or indirect election. In 1446, for example, the citizens of Rochester were granted the privilege of electing a bailiff annually, who was then to choose a coroner with the assent of the citizens;[3] this was a slight restriction of the free election of coroners, for the wording of the charter implies that the bailiff would play a leading part in electing the coroner. Similarly, the Colchester and Wenlock charters of 1462 and 1468 respectively, which granted the bailiffs and burgesses the power to elect coroners, implied that the bailiffs would exercise considerable influence.[4] Far more restrictive were the charters of 1462 and 1463 by which the aldermen and burgesses of Stamford and Grantham were empowered to choose thirteen comburgesses annually, from whom they were then to choose one to be the borough coroner, while the charter granted to Great Yarmouth in 1494 empowered the bailiffs to choose two coroners from the burgesses, to be removable at the will of the bailiffs and burgesses and to take their oaths before the burgesses.[5]

These developments were generally desired by at least the leading burgesses, as is proved by the agreement made at Shrewsbury in 1389 between the bailiffs and burgesses and confirmed ten years later, whereby the bailiffs and coroners were to be elected annually by twenty-five sworn 'cessors', who were themselves nominated by the outgoing bailiffs.[6] Under Henry VI the Shrewsbury elections

---

[1] Ballard and Tait, *op. cit.* p. 358.
[2] E.g. *Cal. Charter Rolls*, v, 87, 303, 338–9, 352; vi, 64, 158, 166, 177, 201, 231.
[3] *Ibid.* p. 64. By another charter in 1462 it was the mayor of Rochester who was to be elected annually and to choose a coroner with the citizens immediately afterwards (*ibid.* p. 177).
[4] *Ibid.* pp. 150, 231.   [5] *Ibid.* pp. 165–6, 199–201, 272.
[6] Owen and Blakeway, *A History of Shrewsbury*, I, 172–3.

became even more indirect, although the closeness of the town administration was slightly mitigated by the provision that no officer
could be re-elected until after three years.[1] One grant which cannot
have been generally desired was that of 1395 giving the burgesses of
Cardigan the right to have their own coroner by annual choice of the
chamberlain of South Wales or his lieutenant, before whom he had
also to be sworn in.[2]

Thirdly, the fifteenth century saw the gathering together of borough offices into a few hands officially recognised. A charter to Don-
caster in 1467 made the annually elected mayor borough coroner as
well as a J.P. for his term of office, in 1484 the mayor and burgesses
of Pontefract were authorised to execute the duties of coroner there,
in 1486 the mayor of Hereford was allowed to be the city coroner,
and in 1485 the annually chosen bailiff of Llandovery was also made
both escheator and coroner in the borough.[3] Similarly, in 1451 the
Coventry coroner was made clerk for taking recognizances of debts
and after 1462 the four jurats of Romney Marsh, who were chosen
annually to be keepers of the peace, were also coroners.[4]

This third tendency, like the other two, although intensified and
legalised in the fifteenth century, had originated much earlier. The
towns of the Cinque Ports, for example, had always combined the
office of coroner with that of mayor or bailiff, the bailiffs of Bury St
Edmunds were often coroners there and before 1254 the burgesses
of Colchester appointed coroners from among the borough bailiffs.[5]
In fourteenth-century Dunwich the same two men were both
coroners and bailiffs and one mayor of Northampton was simultaneously a town coroner.[6] The most interesting example, however,
comes from the year 1200, when the burgesses of Ipswich met in a
churchyard to hold elections under their new charter. They first
elected two bailiffs and then four coroners, who took the oath which
included the promise to see that the bailiffs justly and lawfully treated both poor and rich. But of these four coroners, two had just been
elected bailiffs also. A few days later the burgesses met again to elect
twelve 'chief portmen' to govern the town. The bailiffs and coroners

---

[1] *Rotuli Parliamentorum*, IV, 476; V, 121–3.
[2] *Cal. Charter Rolls*, V, 352.
[3] *Ibid.* VI, 219–20, 261, 263; *Cal. Pat. Rolls, 1485–1494*, p. 67.
[4] *Cal. Charter Rolls*, VI, 116–17, 181–2.
[5] *Sx. Arch. Colls.* XCVIII, 45; M. D. Lobel, *The Borough of Bury St Edmunds*
(Oxford, 1935), pp. 63–4; *Select Coroners' Rolls*, p. xxxvii.
[6] J.I.2/178, m. 2; *Victoria County History: Northamptonshire*, III, 8.

M

chose four men from each parish who elected the twelve 'portmen'. All four coroners were among the twelve elected. On the same day it was decided that the new charter should be consigned to the custody of two burgesses; the two appointed were both coroners, including a coroner-bailiff. Later, three burgesses were elected to keep the borough seal; all three were coroners. The fourth coroner was elected, on the same day, as one of the four burgesses to be associated with the alderman in the government of the Gild Merchant.[1] The Ipswich coroners were clearly no check on the other branches of the borough administration. This may have been an extreme case. There are a number of later examples of coroners elsewhere being replaced on becoming town bailiffs,[2] while the Shrewsbury coroners were forbidden to occupy the office of serjeant,[3] but the pluralist tendency existed in all towns because the number of possible candidates for local office was limited.

Pluralism was also a feature of franchises. In the Sussex part of the liberty of King's College, Cambridge, the offices of coroner and steward were combined, and in Holderness one man was both coroner and bailiff and another was later coroner and escheator, while the coroner of Beverley was also steward of the court of the liberty.[4] In St Albans the abbot's steward was coroner until 1278 and later the bailiff was sometimes coroner, a constable of Berkhamsted castle and later a steward of the liberty were coroners of the liberty of Berkhamsted, the constables of Carisbrooke and Cockermouth castles were for long coroners of the liberties of the Isle of Wight and Cockermouth, and so the list could be continued.[5]

Although most franchisal coroners were appointed, some were elected. The bishop of Salisbury had the right to appoint his own coroners in the city,[6] but he normally issued letters to the mayor to have them elected,[7] and in 1310 Edward II granted Piers Gaveston two coroners in his liberty of Knaresborough to be elected in the

[1] Gross, *The Gild Merchant,* II, 116–21.   [2] See below, p. 169.

[3] *Rotuli Parliamentorum,* V, 123.

[4] *Sx. Arch. Colls.* XCVIII, 70; J.I.2/215, mm. 43–4; *Cal. Fine Rolls,* XVII, 62; *Cal. Inqs. Misc.* IV, 396.

[5] Levett, *Studies in Manorial History,* pp. 106–8; J.I.1/320, m. 32; 324A, m. 44; N. Denholm-Young, *Seignorial Administration in England* (Oxford, 1937), pp. 104–8, 112. See also Miller, *The Abbey and Bishopric of Ely,* pp. 217–18.

[6] *Rotuli Parliamentorum,* V, 578.

[7] E.g. *Hist. MSS. Comm., Reports on MSS. in Various Collections,* IV, 211–12.

county court.[1] The only known thirteenth-century case of franchisal coroners being elected before justices in eyre was when the coroners of the bishop of Ely's liberty remained in office after the 1299 Cambridgeshire eyre 'by election of the whole county',[2] but whenever the eyre rolls mention that men 'remained' coroners of franchises after the eyre there had probably been an election or an appointment before the justices;[3] on one eyre roll a Berkhamsted coroner is called *de novo creatus*.[4]

Writs *de coronatore eligendo* are known to have issued for only a few liberties, although the duke of Lancaster issued such writs for his county palatine of Lancaster.[5] In 1337 the abbot of Furness was granted the right to have a coroner in his lands in Lancashire, who was to be elected in his court by his men and tenants on the receipt of a writ. This was because the grant was less of a privilege than an administrative convenience, since the county coroners had lived far away and neglected their duties in the liberty.[6] The first writ issued in 1337 to the sheriff, with instructions for him to send it on to the abbot.[7] During the next thirty-two years, five more issued directly to the abbot and at least one to Henry duke of Lancaster with instructions for him to send it on, and the duke then ordered the abbot to make his return to the king's Chancery *via* the duke's Chancery.[8] The four writs known to have issued to the abbot of Reading for the election of coroners in the borough and in other parts of his liberty are all of the year 1441.[9] Two of them cite the judgment of thirteenth-century justices in eyre upholding the abbot's claim to have coroners elected there by royal writ, and two were applied for by the abbot himself, who gave information of the insufficiency of the existing coroners. Only two other writs for franchisal coroners are enrolled on the Close Rolls. One issued to the Cambridgeshire sheriff for the election of a coroner for the isle of Ely in 1384 and the other to the prior of Dunstable's bailiffs in 1292 for the election in the prior's

[1] *Cal. Charter Rolls*, III, 140.
[2] J.I.1/96, m. 77; Miller, *op. cit.* p. 238. Some of the bishop of Ely's coroners were appointed, some elected and some held the office by serjeanty tenure (*ibid.*).
[3] E.g. J.I.1/328, m. 12d.   [4] J.I.1/318, m. 29d.
[5] R. Somerville, *History of the Duchy of Lancaster*, I (1953), 60.
[6] *Cal. Close Rolls, 1369–1374*, p. 4.
[7] *Cal. Close Rolls, 1337–1339*, pp. 21–2.
[8] *Ibid.* p. 321; *Cal. Close Rolls, 1341–1343*, p. 307; *1343–1346*, pp. 272, 628; *1369–1374*, p. 4; *The Coucher Book of Furness Abbey*, ed. J. C. Atkinson, I (Chetham Soc. N.S. IX), 166–8.
[9] *Cal. Close Rolls, 1435–1441*, p. 406; *1441–1447*, pp. 1–2, 4–5, 8.

court of a coroner for Dunstable town.[1] Whether elected or appointed, all franchisal coroners had to take an oath of office—usually to
the lord,[2] and in Durham before the bishop's chancellor in his Exchequer.[3] Both the coroners and the liberty were punished if the
coroners acted without being sworn in.[4]

The coroners of hundreds and other areas which were of the ancient demesne were normally elected in the same two ways as county
coroners. In the thirteenth century they were elected before the
eyre justices,[5] while enrolled on the Close Rolls are one writ for the
election of coroners for each of the hundreds of Rochford, Lothingland and Faringdon and two each for the seven hundreds of Cookham and Bray and Milton hundred.[6] These areas experienced the
same delays in holding elections in the thirteenth century as did the
counties and boroughs, and in 1258 and 1261 there was no coroner
in Cookham and Bray, individuals having to be specially commissioned to hold inquests on particular bodies.[7] When liberties came
into the king's hand they were sometimes treated in the same way as
ancient demesne land. Thus in 1380 one writ and in 1386 two more
issued to the sheriff of Hertfordshire for the election of coroners for
the king's honour of Berkhamsted.[8]

Writs *de coronatore eligendo* were of two main kinds: some ordered
the replacement of one or more particular coroners for a stated
reason and others required that all the coroners of a particular
county or town should be replaced. The second were much the
rarer and usually only issued at the beginning of a new reign. Coke,
repeating earlier writers and a fifteenth-century judgment, taught
that coroners, being elected and not appointed, remained in power
after the king's death.[9] It is true that coroners did not immediately
cease to act on the king's death, but from the accession of Edward II
onwards writs issued for the election of new coroners soon after the
beginning of each new reign.

---

[1] *Cal. Close Rolls, 1381–1385,* p. 364; *1288–1296,* p. 242.
[2] E.g. *Placita de Quo Warranto,* p. 222.   [3] Lapsley, *op. cit.* p. 87.
[4] E.g. J.I.1/568, m. 13.   [5] E.g. J.I.1/232, m. 12; 376, m. 61d.
[6] *Close Rolls, 1256–1259,* p. 34; *Cal. Close Rolls, 1302–1307,* p. 385; *1349–1354,* p. 42; *1381–1385,* p. 27; *1447–1454,* p. 295; *Close Rolls, 1237–1242,* p. 334; *1254–1256,* p. 365.
[7] *Close Rolls, 1256–1259,* p. 186; *1261–1264,* p. 4.
[8] *Cal. Close Rolls, 1377–1381,* p. 286; *1385–1389,* p. 189.
[9] Coke, *Second Institute,* p. 175; A. FitzHerbert, *The New Natura Brevium,* 9th ed. (1794), 163.

Edward II came to the throne on 8 July 1307 and on 1 December writs issued for the election of coroners in all counties both from those who had served under Edward I and from all other lawful men, with the exception that any who had been elected coroner in the new reign might remain in office without re-election.[1] In May 1327, when Edward III's reign was nearly four months old, all sheriffs were ordered to remove and to replace by election any unqualified coroners and to take the oath afresh from those who were qualified, including those elected in previous reigns.[2] In practice this probably meant the same as the previous order, but on the second day of Richard II's reign completely new elections were ordered in all counties.[3] Henry IV acceded at the end of September 1399 and on twenty-five separate days between 20 October 1399 and 12 March 1401 writs issued to the sheriffs of twenty-one counties and Bristol, and twice to four of them, ordering the election of other coroners in the place of those elected under Richard II, since their powers ceased with his death.[4] Yet another variation occurred in 1413. The writs were worded as in 1399, but they issued for thirty-three counties on the same day, the first of the new reign. In addition, on 20 August, five months later, a similar writ issued to the sheriff of Wiltshire for new Salisbury coroners and on 24 November 1414 another issued to the same sheriff for new Marlborough coroners.[5] Exactly a month after Henry VI's accession writs, again in the same terms, issued for elections in thirty-two counties. Just over a year later the order was repeated for Kent and given for the first time for Herefordshire. Midway between, the Wiltshire sheriff was ordered to replace both Salisbury coroners for the same reason, and at some uncertain date, but probably much later, the two Marlborough coroners also. Finally, in February 1424, practically eighteen months after Henry VI's accession, a similar writ issued to the mayor and bailiffs of Oxford in respect of the two town coroners.[6]

On 5 June 1461, three months into Edward IV's reign, writs for new coroners issued to thirty-four counties, 'as the king has learned that as yet no coroner has been elected therein by his command'. On

[1] Cal. Close Rolls, 1307–1313, p. 13.
[2] Cal. Close Rolls, 1327–1330, p. 126. For examples of the execution of this writ see The English Government at Work, III, 151.
[3] Cal. Close Rolls, 1377–1381, p. 5.
[4] Cal. Close Rolls, 1399–1402, pp. 13, 19–21, 83, 232.
[5] Cal. Close Rolls, 1413–1419, pp. 1, 34, 153.
[6] Cal. Close Rolls, 1422–1429, pp. 1, 35, 80, 86, 286.

nine dates between 30 May and 30 November these writs were duplicated for eight counties, three issued for Devon and one to the mayor and bailiffs of Hereford for city coroners.[1] Immediately after the restoration of Henry VI in 1470 writs issued, all on the same day, for the election of coroners in all thirty-six non-palatine counties, that to the sheriff of Oxfordshire being repeated five months later.[2] Edward IV regained the throne in mid-April 1471, the result being writs for new coroners in sixteen counties issued on thirteen different days from 29 May to 1 August.[3] On 23 April and 30 June 1483, shortly after the accessions of Edward V and Richard III, thirty-four counties were ordered to elect new coroners, while three months after Henry VII's accession writs were sent to all sheriffs in November 1485.[4]

Clearly there was considerable uncertainty in Chancery as to what should be done at the beginning of a reign. It is just possible that writs issued to every county every time and that not all were enrolled, but this does not explain why all the writs were not always issued on the same day and why there was often a gap of months between the accession and their issue. These facts alone would suggest that each county was expected to proceed to new elections without a writ as soon as the king died and that a writ only issued later if and when Chancery discovered that it had not done so; but this is refuted by those cases in which writs issued to all or many counties on the same day, especially when this was within a few days of the accession, and by the fact that no county is known to have elected a coroner except by writ.

As a result of the political troubles of 1340, Edward III and his council ordered that all sheriffs, escheators, coroners and other officials who were in office before his return to England should be removed and others substituted; writs for new coroners consequently issued to all sheriffs on 15 January 1341.[5] The only other occasion on which writs issued to all sheriffs was on 1 February 1392, when they were ordered to see that coroners were newly elected from the most lawful and wisest knights of the shire in place of those who had been elected contrary to the first Statute of Westminster. This occasion was unique in that the writs issued not only

[1] *Cal. Close Rolls, 1461–1468*, p. 42.
[2] *Cal. Close Rolls, 1468–1476*, pp. 148–9. [3] *Ibid.* p. 183.
[4] *Cal. Close Rolls, 1476–1485*, pp. 308–9; *1485–1500*, p. 2.
[5] *Cal. Close Rolls, 1339–1341*, p. 607.

to all sheriffs but also to John of Gaunt for the duchy of Lancaster.[1]
Occasionally, a general writ *de coronatore eligendo* issued to one
sheriff only. Thus in the thirteenth and, less frequently, in the fourteenth centuries, writs sometimes issued for the election of county
coroners to make up the accustomed number.[2] Writs issued to the
sheriff of Somerset and Dorset in 1259 for new coroners in those
counties to fill the gaps caused by death and sickness, and to the
sheriff of Gloucestershire in 1261 for two new coroners because
certain of the coroners were insufficient.[3] Again, in 1358 the Yorkshire sheriff was ordered to remove all insufficient coroners and have
others elected in their place.[4] In these three instances Chancery had
obtained information and acted upon it without waiting for or without disclosing details such as the names of the coroners to be replaced. Writs issued shortly after the grants of coroners to towns are
the only others which did not name the coroner or coroners to be
replaced.

Coroners were replaced for four main reasons: death, sickness
and/or old age, engagement upon other business, and unfitness or
insufficient qualification.[5] It is instructive to compare the incidence
of these reasons in the enrolled writs *de coronatore eligendo*. Possibly
only a minority of all writs are on the Close Rolls, but the number for
the reigns of Edward I and Richard II, between three and four hundred for each, are large enough to allow a few generalisations. Thus,
only a minority of coroners died in office and the proportion seems
to have decreased during the Middle Ages: in Edward I's reign
slightly over a third of the enrolled writs issued because a coroner
had died, but under Richard II these were under a fifth. This decrease coincided with a slight increase in the number of coroners
replaced because of old age and infirmity, which accounted for a
quarter of the writs of Edward I's reign and a third of those of
Richard II's.

An old man was naturally of little use in an office which entailed
so much travelling. The Commons presented two petitions on this
subject in 1377.[6] The first, that nobody over sixty should be bur-

---

[1] *Cal. Close Rolls, 1389–1392*, pp. 449–50. For a discussion of these writs, see
below, pp. 173–4.
[2] See above, p. 135.   [3] *Close Rolls, 1256–1259*, p. 451; *1259–1261*, p. 428.
[4] *Cal. Close Rolls, 1354–1360*, pp. 475–6.
[5] The nine different writs *de coronatore eligendo* in *Registrum Omnium Brevium:
Originalium*, ff. 177–177v, fall into these four groups.
[6] *Rotuli Parliamentorum*, II, 370; III, 22.

dened with the offices of sheriff, escheator, coroner or any other, was not granted. The second asked that both men over sixty and those who had served or should in future serve in wars might not be appointed to these offices against their will; the second part of this was refused, but the reply to the first was that the statute concerning the aged and impotent should be observed. No such statute is known, nor was one ever cited in the writs. It was merely a custom that sick and aged coroners should be replaced, but the increasing number of such writs shows that individual cases were sympathetically considered. The writs rarely mention any particular illness or infirmity apart from blindness and paralysis.[1] Similarly, a precise age is rarely given, but a newly elected Nottinghamshire coroner was replaced in 1290 because he was over seventy and insufficiently qualified.[2]

Only a very small proportion of the enrolled writs issued for the replacement of coroners who had been appointed to other offices or had other duties—well under 10 per cent of the total Sussex writs, of the Yorkshire writs between 1327 and 1399, and of those issued for all counties under Edward I and Richard II. The five Sussex writs were to replace two coroners who were on the king's business and one on the king's son's business in the county, one who was of the king's household and was required for the king's service in Scotland and one who had been appointed under-sheriff.[3] Of the eleven Yorkshire coroners so replaced nine were on the king's business, including six definitely in Yorkshire, one was overseas with John of Gaunt and the other was a collector of customs in Hull. Twenty-six such writs issued under Edward I and twenty-nine under Richard II, the majority of which either did not state the nature of the business which prevented the coroner from remaining in office or merely called it the king's business or service. Under Edward I four coroners were replaced because they were on or were required on the king's business in Scotland, one because he was a voyaging merchant and one because he was a professional soldier. Seven were replaced during the reign on entering upon other offices: two became sheriffs, two mayors, two verderers and one a regardor. An eighth was replaced shortly after his election because he had been sub-escheator for over three years and was also a verderer. There were eight similar

---

[1] E.g. *Close Rolls, 1253–1254*, pp. 65–6; *Cal. Close Rolls, 1302–1307*, p. 483.
[2] *Cal. Close Rolls, 1288–1296*, p. 107. There was a tradition that the oldest inhabitant of the town was invariably chosen as coroner of Lidford (C. Worthy, *Devonshire Parishes*, I (1887), 239).
[3] *Sx. Arch. Colls.* xcviii, 56–64.

replacements under Richard II because three coroners became town bailiffs, two escheators, one a J.P., one an under-sheriff and one marshal of the Marshalsea. A ninth was replaced in 1381 because he was appearing as attorney of the abbot of Dieulacres against the king in a case concerning felons' and fugitives' chattels then pending in the Exchequer of Pleas.

During the thirteenth century, a number of coroners were replaced because they were of the household or in the service of princes or magnates. Two, for example, were replaced in 1230 because they were retainers of Hubert de Burgh.[1] Just as around 1300 four were replaced because they were in the king's service in Scotland, so were two others in 1257, one because he was with Roger Mortimer's army in Wales and the other because he was with Prince Edward's army there.[2] A third was replaced in 1259 because he was going to Ireland with the countess of Lincoln and a fourth a few years earlier because he owed castle-guard at Dover and frequently had to stay there to perform it.[3] This type of reason for replacing coroners became very rare after 1307, although John Fermer was replaced as Essex coroner in 1339 because he was the earl of Oxford's steward and the earl had appointed him to take his place as keeper of the maritime land in Essex and to perform other services for him.[4] There are two known instances, in 1241 and 1253, of writs for the replacement of coroners who had entered monasteries, and in 1330 one was replaced in order that he might go overseas on pilgrimage.[5]

Surprisingly few coroners were replaced because they already had or were later appointed or elected to other offices. A few became sheriffs, under-sheriffs, escheators, verderers and town bailiffs, fewer still mayors, foresters, agistors, stewards of forests and J.P.'s. Only one is known to have been replaced because he was the constable of a castle, one because he was appointed a justice of the court of Common Pleas, one because he was an apprentice of that court and one because he was engaged on the king's business in the Exchequer.[6]

---

[1] *Close Rolls, 1227–1231*, p. 344.   [2] *Close Rolls, 1256–1259*, pp. 31, 35.
[3] *Ibid.* p. 382; *Close Rolls, 1253–1254*, pp. 57–8.
[4] *Cal. Close Rolls, 1339–1341*, p. 195.
[5] *Close Rolls, 1237–1242*, p. 266; *1253–1254*, p. 6; *Cal. Close Rolls, 1330–1333*, p. 73.
[6] *Ibid.* p. 371; *Close Rolls, 1231–1234*, p. 24; *Cal. Close Rolls, 1360–1364*, p. 481; *1435–1441*, p. 147.

Although very few men seem to have been appointed to other offices while occupying that of coroner, even fewer are known to have moved immediately from another office to that of coroner. There are only two writs on the medieval Close Rolls for the election of verderers because the existing verderers had become coroners.[1] In Ipswich and other towns and liberties the office of coroner was sometimes held jointly with another,[2] but this can rarely have been practicable in counties where coroners' districts were large. There are, however, a few examples from counties. In the early thirteenth century a Northumberland coronership was held with a forestership, in 1254 an Essex coroner was replaced because he was escheator and weak in body, in 1258 Thomas Maunsel died and had to be replaced as both coroner and escheator in Buckinghamshire and in 1339 a Somerset coroner was replaced because he was also verderer of Selwood forest and was too broken by age to execute both offices.[3] Finally, it was specifically granted in 1250 that a Nottinghamshire coroner should not be made a regardor or verderer while he remained coroner.[4] These cases show that it was not regarded as illegal for a coroner to occupy another office, and the writs replacing those who received another appointment merely stated that they could not conveniently exercise, or had not the leisure to exercise, both offices. In 1317, however, the Council determined that no sheriff or coroner should be made a justice of assize, gaol delivery or oyer and terminer or perform any judicial duties, and this was confirmed in 1355.[5]

Although not usually occupying other offices during or immediately before or after their tenure of a coronership, coroners were nevertheless of that knightly or near-knightly class which has been called *buzones* and which undertook all the tasks of local administration. Of the sixty-six Sussex county coroners who are known, thirty-seven definitely had at least one other office before or after their coronerships. One was a member of the royal household and five represented Sussex or one of its boroughs in Parliament. The

---

[1] *Rotuli Litterarum Clausarum*, I, 366; *Cal. Close Rolls, 1330–1333*, p. 268.

[2] See above, pp. 161–2.

[3] *Close Rolls, 1237–1242*, p. 164; *1254–1256*, p. 4; *1256–1259*, p. 257; *Cal. Close Rolls, 1339–1341*, p. 169.

[4] *Close Rolls, 1247–1251*, p. 289.

[5] *Cal. Close Rolls, 1313–1318*, p. 463; *Rotuli Parliamentorum*, II, 265. This rule was not strictly applied to the activities of borough coroners in local courts (see above, pp. 93–4).

activities of the rest were confined to Sussex and the three neigh-bouring counties. One was an escheator, two sub-escheators, one a J.P., one an under-sheriff, one constable of a castle, one bailiff of a rape and one a village constable. Eleven were assessors and collectors of taxes, some on many separate occasions, one surveyor of the array of arms and thirteen acted at least once on various commissions of inquiry, gaol delivery, assize, oyer and terminer and *de walliis et fossatis*. Others were active in liberties, eight being stewards or bailiffs, one an under-bailiff, two feodaries and two keepers of gaols. Two were keepers of manors and one a keeper of the temporalities of the bishopric of Chichester.[1] These figures produce a picture which is true for the whole country.[2] In the fourteenth and fifteenth centuries grants of exemption were usually obtained not from the office of coroner alone but from a large number of local offices.[3] But the *buzones*, although a small class, had their hierarchy. Those at the top became sheriffs, escheators and J.P.'s. Coroners were generally of a slightly lower social stratum, although often from rising families. Thus, although comparatively few coroners either had been or became sheriffs, escheators or J.P.'s, their descendants often did. Many of the medieval Sussex coroners helped to found families which were pre-eminent in the county for centuries, and the two Pelhams were ancestors of peers of the realm and Prime Ministers.

By contrast, the most eminent families provided the coroners as well as the mayors and other officials of cities and towns. Thus of the ten medieval Chichester coroners who are known to have held other offices, one was mayor, six were bailiffs or reeves, two were M.P.'s for the city and four had duties in connection with taxation and cus-toms there. Similarly, five of the seven known Arundel coroners at some time held other offices in or in connection with the borough: one was mayor and four were M.P.'s.[4] Once again these Sussex ex-amples are typical of the whole country, for borough offices were of necessity continually redistributed among the same few people.[5] The same is true of franchisal offices, and of the three known coron-

---

[1] *Sx. Arch. Colls.* xcviii, 53–65.

[2] For Wiltshire examples see *Victoria County History: Wiltshire*, v, 15, 25–6, 28–9. See also Yorks. Arch. Soc., Rec. Ser. c, xlii; *Rolls of the Gloucestershire Sessions of the Peace 1361–1398*, ed. E. G. Kimball (Bristol & Glos. Arch. Soc. LXII), p. 31.

[3] See below, p. 187, n. 7.

[4] *Sx. Arch. Colls.* xcviii, 65–9.   [5] See above, pp. 161–2

ers of the abbot of Battle's Sussex liberty one had been the abbot's steward and another was for long his beadle.[1]

Under Edward I a third of the coroners known to have been replaced by writ were replaced because they were insufficiently qualified, almost as many as had died in office. Under Richard II nearly half the replacements were for insufficient qualification, as were well over a half of the Yorkshire writs enrolled between 1327 and 1399 and of the medieval Sussex writs. The vast majority of the writs give no details of the insufficiency. Of the Sussex coroners so replaced, however, four were said to have no lands in the county, one not to be living there, one to be living in the remotest parts of the county, another to be living within the liberty of the Cinque Ports and four to be unfit persons, including one who had for long been an outlaw.[2] The Yorkshire writs replaced twelve coroners who had no lands or none in fee in the county, two who lived in the remotest parts of it, one who dwelt more in the bishopric of Durham than in Yorkshire, one who lived in Grimsby, one North Riding coroner who did not live in that riding, and two who were unsuitable, including one who was appealed of felonies. Edward I's writs for all counties replaced one coroner who had land and rent worth only ten marks yearly, one who did not have land and rent in his county worth fifty shillings yearly, one who had sold all his land in the county, one whose lands were all ancient demesne, one whose lands had been destroyed by the Scots, one who was resident only intermittently because of the smallness of his lands in the county, one who was ill-behaved, one who was imprisoned for alleged trespasses in Wychwood forest, one who had been convicted of trespasses before justices of oyer and terminer and was in gaol, and one who had been removed from office by justices of oyer and terminer. Richard II's reign saw the replacement of one coroner who lived overseas, four who were not knights, one because of his quarrels and irregular election and three for their oppressions. In both reigns the possession of no lands in the county and non-residence there were specifically mentioned in a number of writs.

---

[1] *Sx. Arch. Colls.* xcviii, 69. The other Sussex liberties obtained their own coroners much later, but the known coroners of the liberty of King's College and of the Eagle were both M.P.'s and one was also a distributor of a tax allowance in Sussex (*ibid.* p. 70). The fact that their other activities were not confined to the liberties of which they were coroners is probably due to the fact that these were small outlying portions of much larger liberties. For other examples, see above, p. 162.

[2] *Sx. Arch. Colls.* xcviii, 56–68.

One lesson of these writs is that for most of the Middle Ages there was no insistence upon knighthood. In 1194 it was provided that the four coroners to be elected in each county should consist of three knights and a clerk. The clerk was replaced by a fourth knight in Cambridgeshire, and probably in all other counties, by 1198, and only two medieval coroners are definitely known to have been clerks.[1] In the early thirteenth century the county coroners were almost invariably knights,[2] but the percentage of knights gradually declined as the century wore on. Two reasons account for this. The office of coroner was unpaid and therefore unpopular with many. The first recorded purchase of a grant of exemption from the office is under the year 1202, and such grants became very numerous later.[3] Secondly, while the number of eligible knights thus declined, there was a steadily increasing number of offices for them to fill and duties for them to perform. They had to be sheriffs, escheators, collectors and assessors of subsidies, commissioners of array, keepers of the peace and M.P.'s, to name but a few, and by the late thirteenth century it was clear that there were not enough knights to go round.[4] The first Statute of Westminster noted the tendency to elect 'mean persons, and undiscreet' as coroners, whereas they should be 'honest, lawful and wise', and tried to arrest it by ordering that in future coroners should be chosen 'of the most wise and discreet knights'.[5] Despite this, a laxer rule obtained in practice, especially after 1300, and this was given statutory recognition in 1340 and 1354, when statutes concerning the qualifications of coroners did not mention knighthood.[6]

After 1300 it was the exception rather than the rule for coroners to be knights,[7] but the Statute of Westminster remained unrepealed and in 1392 an attempt was made to enforce it, a general order issuing to all sheriffs for the election of knights in all counties where elections had not been held in accordance with it.[8] One result of this was that in the next two years four coroners, three of whom were

---

[1] See above, p. 116.

[2] E.g. *Curia Regis Rolls*, IV, 163, 282; Linc. Rec. Soc. XXII, xlv.

[3] See below, p. 187.

[4] Thus under Edward III by no means all county M.P.'s were knights, although knights were always summoned (K. L. Wood-Legh, 'Sheriffs, Lawyers and Belted Knights in the Parliaments of Edward III', *Eng. Hist. Rev.* XLVI, 381–5).

[5] 3 Edw. I, c. 10.   [6] 14 Edw. III, stat. I, c. 8; 28 Edw. III, c. 6.

[7] Cf. *Sx. Arch. Colls.* XCVIII, 56–65; *Victoria County History: Wiltshire*, V, 28

[8] *Cal. Close Rolls, 1389–1392*, pp. 449–50.

Cornish, petitioned that they had been elected although they were
not knights and that this was contrary to the Statute of Westminster;
writs accordingly issued for the election of fresh coroners from
among the trustworthy and lawful knights of the shire in their
stead.[1] For several years the proportion of knights among the county
coroners was unusually high,[2] but the statute was then conveniently
forgotten once more. Previously, even in the early thirteenth century when nearly all writs ordered the elections to be made from
among knights, there was no known writ which survives ordering a
replacement for lack of knighthood, except for one replacing an
Essex coroner in 1254, and he had the additional disqualifications
of being in the service of another than the king and being young,
insufficient and not discreet.[3] The writ by which a Northampton
town coroner was replaced in 1306 because he intended to dwell
outside the town mentioned incidentally that he had recently
been elected before he had received knighthood,[4] but this point
was quite irrelevant unless it was emphasising his youth: knighthood
is nowhere mentioned as a necessary qualification for borough
coroners, even John's charters requiring only 'lawful and discreet
men'.[5]

Although most medieval coroners were below the knightly class,
they were usually only slightly below, since they had to be substantial landowners. The 1340 statute decreed 'that no coroner be
chosen unless he have land in fee sufficient in the same county,
whereof he may answer to all manner of people'.[6] This was merely
declaratory of existing custom, for writs had issued earlier to replace
coroners who had no lands in fee,[7] while in 1339 a Wiltshire coroner
was replaced because he had no lands there except for life and a term
of years.[8] The statute temporarily increased the number of writs of
this type and for a few years it was cited in them,[9] while in 1349 and
1354 a Leicestershire coroner was replaced because his only lands in
the county were in fee-tail.[10] Very few writs mentioned either the

---

[1] *Cal. Close Rolls, 1392–1396*, pp. 10, 315, 327.
[2] E.g. J.I.2/43; 138–140.   [3] *Close Rolls, 1253–1254*, p. 25.
[4] *Cal. Close Rolls, 1302–1307*, p. 388.
[5] *Rotuli Chartarum*, pp. 46 (*bis*), 56, 57, 65, 142.
[6] 14 Edw. III, stat. 1, c. 8.   [7] E.g. *Cal. Close Rolls, 1330–1333*, p. 345.
[8] *Cal. Close Rolls, 1339–1341*, p. 2.
[9] E.g. *Cal. Close Rolls, 1341–1343*, p. 603. The statute was misquoted in 1341
when a Northamptonshire coroner, who had 'no lands in the county in fee or for
life, in accordance with the statute', was replaced (*ibid.* p. 311).
[10] *Cal. Close Rolls, 1349–1354*, p. 50; *1354–1360*, p. 9.

type or the amount of land required to qualify a man for the office of coroner. Most writs merely called the outgoing coroner 'insufficient' or 'insufficiently qualified'. That these phrases, when used by themselves as they are in the great majority of writs, usually mean that the coroner did not hold enough land in the county is illustrated by the fact that, as a result of a petition stating that John de Hothale, a Sussex coroner, did not hold lands worth a hundred shillings a year in the county, a writ issued ordering his replacement on the score of insufficient qualification.[1] Similarly, the exceptional writ of 1358 for the replacement of all unfit and insufficient Yorkshire coroners required the sheriff to make a return of the amount of land held by the new ones as well as their names.[2]

The reasons given for the need of a coroner to hold lands in the county vary. While the 1340 statute said that it was to ensure that he could 'answer to all manner of people',[3] the corresponding writ in the Register orders a coroner's replacement because 'he has no lands and tenements in the same county on which he can live according to his estate for the exercise of his office'.[4] There seems to have been a change in emphasis in the mid-fourteenth century. In the earlier period coroners without any or sufficient land in the county were replaced mainly because they could not exercise the office without great inconvenience and expense to themselves: because, as the writs stated, they had no lands in the county sufficient for their support throughout the year or by which they could be 'suitably maintained'.[5] After about 1340, however, they were required to have lands in order to be able to account to the king and the people from them, if necessary.[6] Nevertheless, there were always these two distinct reasons for which coroners were required to have a substantial amount of land: to support them in an office which was unpaid and which lent itself to extortions and oppressions, and to guarantee

[1] S.C.1/32, no. 34; *Cal. Close Rolls, 1313–1318*, p. 533.
[2] *Cal. Close Rolls, 1354–1360*, pp. 475–6.
[3] See above, p. 174.
[4] *Registrum Omnium Brevium: Originalium*, f. 177v. T. F. T. Plucknett, *Statutes and their Interpretation in the First Half of the Fourteenth Century* (Cambridge, 1922), p. 55, is wrong in connecting this writ not with the statute of 14 Edw. III but with 4 Edw. III, c. 9, since the latter referred only to the qualifications of sheriffs, bailiffs and sub-escheators.
[5] E.g. *Close Rolls, 1256–1259*, p. 241; *Cal. Close Rolls, 1302–1307*, p. 373. For writs replacing such coroners to save them great inconvenience and expense, see *Close Rolls, 1242–1247*, pp. 264–5; *1253–1254*, p. 25; *1256–1259*, p. 270.
[6] E.g. *Cal. Close Rolls, 1354–1360*, pp. 475–6.

that they were distrainable and able to pay any amercements incurred to the king or damages inflicted upon his people.[1]

The electors of coroners who held no lands were responsible for the payment of their amercements. Judgment was thus passed against the county of Kent at the 1313–14 eyre for electing a man, dead by then, who was heirless and had held no land in the county except in right of his wife; he could not have been made answerable by this and the county court suitors were therefore made answerable for his acts and rolls.[2] Burgesses were similarly responsible when they elected coroners who had no possessions.[3] But, provided that a coroner had enough lands or chattels with which to pay his amercements, he must normally have been considered to be 'sufficient'. John de Hothale was replaced because he did not have lands worth a hundred shillings a year,[4] and this seems to have been the yearly value most frequently required, as against land in fee of a yearly value of £20 which was the qualification for both knighthood and the office of escheator,[5] but under Edward I one coroner was replaced because he had land and rent worth only ten marks, or 133s. 4d., yearly and another because he did not have land and rent in the county worth forty shillings yearly.[6] These cases were very exceptional. Normally, no amount of land was mentioned either as held by the coroner or as the desideratum, and the sheriff must have been allowed to decide what was sufficient.[7]

It was not enough that a coroner had sufficient lands in the county; they had also to be in or near his district. In almost every case those of the Sussex coroners were.[8] Men who lived in parts remote from their district were removed from office, either because of the inconvenience to which it put them[9] or because of the inconvenience which the king and his people experienced through their defaults.[10] 'Uttermost parts' therefore did not necessarily mean the borders of the county; it might mean far from the district in which the coroner was supposed to act, far from a gaol, or, as in the case of a coroner of

---

[1] Both reasons were also given in numerous fourteenth-century statutes for the necessity of sheriffs and escheators to have lands in their bailiwicks.

[2] Selden Soc. vol. 24, pp. 5, 14, 24–5, 47–8, 55. Cf. *The English Government at Work*, III, 152.

[3] E.g. J.I.1/26, m. 51; 635, m. 78.   [4] Above, p. 175.

[5] 42 Edw. III, c. 5. The amount required by sheriffs was never stated.

[6] *Cal. Close Rolls, 1288–1296*, pp. 159, 222.   [7] See below, pp. 182, 192.

[8] *Sx. Arch. Colls.* XCVIII, 53–70.

[9] E.g. *Registrum Omnium Brevium: Originalium*, f. 177v.

[10] See above, pp. 136–7.

the North Riding of Yorkshire in 1441, far from the county court.[1]

A county coroner had to have lands in the geldable. A Berkshire coroner was replaced in 1300, for example, because all his lands were in the manors of Cookham and Bray which were ancient demesne of the crown.[2] Conversely, in 1306 a Northampton coroner was replaced because he intended to live on his lands outside the town, as was a Salisbury coroner in 1395 who neither lived nor had lands in the city.[3] Residence had to be continuous, and castle-guard and other duties which entailed spending part of the year away from his bailiwick naturally led to a coroner's replacement.[4] The eyre justices accordingly disapproved of the relay system adopted by the Northampton town coroners, two performing the duties while the other two travelled as merchants.[5]

The statute of 1354 stipulated that coroners should be elected 'of the most meet and most lawful people',[6] but 'unfitness' or 'unsuitability' was a much less frequent cause of replacement than lack of landed qualification. The usual writ gave no details, merely saying that the outgoing coroner was unfit to support or exercise his office.[7] One of the reasons given for the replacement of a fifteenth-century Derbyshire coroner, however, was that he was illiterate.[8] Youth was one of the many disqualifications of an Essex coroner in 1254 and a Yorkshire coroner was replaced in 1260 for being a minor and insufficient, while an unusual writ for the election of a Herefordshire coroner in 1229 stated that he must be of age.[9] Another unusual writ was that of 1405, which removed John Lynne from a Middlesex coronership partly because he was 'a common baker and victualler' and therefore had no leisure for the office and partly because he was otherwise insufficiently qualified: a social disqualification is implicit here.[10] Naturally, unlike his modern counterpart, the medieval coroner was required to have neither legal nor medical qualifications, and William de Hastyngge, a Sussex coroner, was probably unique in that he was considered to be a surgeon.[11]

---

[1] *Ibid.; Cal. Close Rolls, 1435–1441*, p. 416.

[2] *Cal. Close Rolls, 1296–1302*, p. 346.

[3] *Cal. Close Rolls, 1302–1307*, p. 388; *1392–1396*, p. 333.

[4] See above, p. 169.   [5] *Ibid.* p. 141.   [6] 28 Edw. III, c. 6.

[7] E.g. *Registrum Omnium Brevium: Originalium*, ff. 177–177v; *Close Rolls, 1251–1253*, p. 410.

[8] *Cal. Close Rolls, 1441–1447*, p. 97.

[9] *Close Rolls, 1253–1254*, p. 25; *1259–1261*, p. 48; *1227–1231*, p. 143.

[10] *Cal. Close Rolls, 1402–1405*, p. 407.

[11] *Sx. Arch. Colls.* XCVIII, 51–2.

N

In Edward II's reign a petition to Parliament alleged that a man, who had been coroner in Suffolk for over six years, had previously been attainted of breaking his oath as a juror, thereby disqualifying himself from office. The petitioner was told to sue in Chancery.[1] Another kind of unfitness was the reason for a unique writ issued in 1422 for the replacement of all the Cornish coroners. In a case brought by a writ of entry and heard at *nisi prius* the defendants challenged the jury on the grounds of the sheriff's partiality to the plaintiff. A writ for a new array therefore issued to the coroners, but, since they were 'near the plaintiff in consanguinity and affinity', the king removed them.[2] This was a most unusual step in the circumstances: the coroners' unfitness was for this one case only, which did not entail an *ex officio* duty, while the writ implies that the defendants were deliberately prolonging the case. What normally happened when first the sheriff and then the coroners neglected or disobeyed a writ, or were suspected of partiality, was that the writ then issued to two clerks of the court or of the county or to some other local official.[3] Thus in 1204, after the sheriff of Hampshire had failed to produce a defendant in the *Curia Regis* and had omitted to return the writs addressed to him, the two county coroners were ordered to produce the defendant, and when they also failed the writ issued to the constable of Winchester castle, who was also ordered to produce the sheriff and coroners to show why they had failed.[4] Most frequently, however, the coroners were only by-passed after ignoring a *sicut alias* and at least one *sicut pluries*.[5]

By contrast with the fairly rigid insistence upon a landed qualification, a coroner's personal unfitness normally had to be excessive before he was replaced. John Tauke, who was imprisoned in the Fleet on account of debt, was replaced as Hampshire coroner in 1400 merely because he had not the freedom to exercise his office; and it was because he was in Oxford gaol, rather than because of the alleged trespasses in Wychwood forest which caused his imprisonment, that an Oxfordshire coroner was replaced in 1303.[6] Two coroners were replaced because they were imprisoned by justices of oyer and terminer, before whom they had been convicted of tres-

---

[1] *Rotuli Parliamentorum*, I, 428.   [2] *Cal. Close Rolls, 1419–1422*, p. 186.
[3] Hastings, *The Court of Common Pleas in Fifteenth Century England*, p. 203; *Select Cases in the Court of King's Bench under Edward I*, ed. G. O. Sayles, II (Selden Soc. vol. 57), p. xcii.
[4] *Curia Regis Rolls*, III, 164.   [5] E.g. K.B.27/228, m. 123.
[6] *Cal. Close Rolls, 1399–1402*, p. 214; *1302–1307*, p. 54.

passes, and one because he had been removed by justices of oyer and terminer.[1] In 1393 a Norfolk coroner was replaced not only because he was involved in disputes with a knight of the king's Chamber, but also because he had been elected illegally.[2] There are very few writs on the Close Rolls for the replacement of coroners who had used their office for purposes of oppression and extortion, and four of these are of the period 1374–89.[3] These four writs all emphasise that the coroners concerned had used oppression and extortion regularly, excessively and over a long period. The more moderate illegalities of others led at times to their amercement,[4] but rarely to their replacement, while no coroner is known to have been replaced for failing, through negligence or ignorance, to perform a necessary part of his duties or for ignorantly exceeding the bounds of his jurisdiction.

The eighty-seven known Sussex writs *de coronatore eligendo* which replaced specific county and borough coroners replaced only fifty-seven different ones: forty were replaced once, eleven twice, three three times, one four times, one five times and one seven times.[5] This was not a Sussex peculiarity, as forty-six of the Yorkshire coroners known to have been replaced by writ between 1327 and 1399 were replaced once, sixteen twice, fourteen three times, three four times, one five times, one six times and one seven times.[6] These figures are even more remarkable than they appear at first sight, since a number of the coroners for whom only one writ issued were either called 'lately elected' in the writ[7] or must be assumed to have been because they are not known ever to have carried out coroners' duties. It was therefore exceptional for the active coroners to have a single unbroken spell of office, and many were constantly being elected and removed. It must have been because of this that the chancellor was requested in 1279 not to remove by writ the Kent coroners who had just been elected.[8]

It was rare for a writ to issue because an earlier writ had not been executed, although this may be assumed to have been the reason for

[1] See above, p. 152.   [2] *Cal. Close Rolls, 1392–1396*, p. 157.
[3] *Cal. Close Rolls, 1374–1377*, p. 6; *1381–1385*, p. 360; *1385–1389*, p. 536; *1389–1392*, p. 36.
[4] See above, pp. 120–4, 131–2.   [5] *Sx. Arch. Colls.* XCVIII, 50.
[6] For the Wiltshire figures see *Victoria County History: Wiltshire*, v, 24–5.
[7] E.g. *Close Rolls, 1259–1261*, p. 382; *Cal. Close Rolls, 1381–1385*, p. 27.
[8] *Cal. Close Rolls, 1272–1279*, p. 533.

the issue of a second writ in identical terms within a month or two
and occasionally a sheriff was issued with a *sicut alias* or even a *sicut
pluries* after defaulting.[1] One writ of 10 September 1252 warned the
sheriff of Nottinghamshire that the new coroner was to be elected
before Michaelmas,[2] but in all other cases it was implicit that the
election should be held at the first county court after the receipt of
the writ.

Writs *de coronatore eligendo* were of two kinds. Some ordered a
new election because the king had removed a coroner from office or
had ordered the sheriff to do so, while the others ordered the sheriff
to remove one coroner and have another elected if information received by the king was true. The degree of trustworthiness or influence of those who provided the information often determined
which kind issued. The king would normally have reliable information about the appointment of coroners to other offices or their employment upon his business, and so writs for their replacement on
these grounds generally announced that the king had removed
them.[3] When the coroner was serving with a magnate, the magnate
often provided the information and requested the king to remove
him from office.[4] The king removed a Staffordshire coroner when
the barons of the Exchequer attested in Chancery that he was appearing as attorney of the abbot of Dieulacres against the king in the
Exchequer,[5] a forest justice testified that a Huntingdonshire coroner had for long been and still was an agistor,[6] and information was
more frequently given by local officials with special knowledge.[7]
Again, especially in the thirteenth century, the king frequently removed from office men who had been elected despite their possession of charters of exemption,[8] while in 1384 he ordered the
sheriff of Wiltshire to remove a Salisbury coroner who had such a
charter.[9] In the last case, and probably in many of the others, the

[1] E.g. *Cal. Close Rolls, 1377–1381*, p. 184.
[2] *Close Rolls, 1251–1253*, p. 246.
[3] E.g. *Registrum Omnium Brevium: Originalium*, f. 177.
[4] E.g. *Close Rolls, 1256–1259*, p. 31.
[5] *Cal. Close Rolls, 1377–1381*, p. 436.
[6] *Close Rolls, 1251–1253*, p. 421.
[7] For example, a Sussex coroner was removed by the king after the keeper of
Berwick-upon-Tweed had informed him that he was of the household and required in Scotland (*Sx. Arch. Colls.* xcviii, 56–7). Naturally sheriffs most frequently provided the information (e.g. *Cal. Close Rolls, 1296–1302*, p. 470).
[8] E.g. *Close Rolls, 1254–1256*, pp. 139–40, 370–1; *1256–1259*, pp. 34, 85–6,
180, 195–6.
[9] *Cal. Close Rolls, 1381–1385*, p. 372.

removal was upon the coroner's petition, but Chancery clerks would undoubtedly have verified from the Patent Rolls that the grants had been made. One Sussex man received his charter of exemption while serving as coroner and the writ announcing that the king had removed him from office issued on the same day.[1]

When coroners were replaced for reasons other than pressure of other business or exemption it was less usual for the king to remove them on the original information alone. He naturally removed a Hampshire coroner when informed by the warden of the Fleet that he was his prisoner, a Sussex coroner when the sheriff personally testified that he was physically incapacitated and others for various reasons when lay or ecclesiastical magnates bore witness to them.[2] The writs to the abbot of Reading ordering the election of new coroners in place of those to whose insufficiency the abbot himself testified did not say that the king had removed the old ones, but in the circumstances that was unnecessary.[3] By contrast, the Northamptonshire sheriff was allowed to decide whether or not the abbot of Peterborough's request to have a coroner in or near his liberty was justified.[4] In 1305 a Somerset coroner was removed when the escheator attested that he was insufficiently qualified.[5] Information was also sometimes provided by the mayor and bailiffs of towns, or by the burgesses by letters under their common seal,[6] but most writs merely say that it was given by credible or trustworthy witnesses.[7] It was usually given in Chancery, but occasionally before the Council or before the treasurer and barons of the Exchequer.[8]

When the king removed a coroner from office it was usually on the receipt of oral testimony, although he removed John de Hothale on the receipt of a letter.[9] Occasionally the coroner concerned made a personal appearance in Chancery, as did one in 1330 to assert that he was going overseas on pilgrimage, and another in 1395 when a personal view of him confirmed that he was too sick and aged for the office; the first was removed by the king, while the replacement of

---

[1] *Cal. Pat. Rolls, 1247–1258*, p. 177; *Close Rolls, 1251–1253*, p. 319.

[2] *Cal. Close Rolls, 1399–1402*, p. 214; *1296–1302*, p. 235; and, for example, *Cal. Close Rolls, 1288–1296*, p. 89; *1374–1377*, pp. 139–40.

[3] See above, p. 163.   [4] *Ibid.* p. 136.

[5] *Cal. Close Rolls, 1302–1307*, p. 247.

[6] E.g. *Close Rolls, 1253–1254*, p. 39; *Cal. Close Rolls, 1296–1302*, p. 237.

[7] E.g. *Cal. Close Rolls, 1360–1364*, p. 481; *1381–1385*, p. 360.

[8] E.g. *Close Rolls, 1253–1254*, p. 25; *Cal. Close Rolls, 1392–1396*, p. 443; *1296–1302*, p. 367.

[9] See above, p. 175.

the second was clearly imperative.[1] But when information was provided in writing, whether by the coroner or someone else, the writ
normally contained the 'saving clause': *si ita est*.[2] The practice of
holding an inquisition locally to discover whether or not the statement in the writ concerning the existing coroner was true was probably not general; only one is known to have been held, in Chichester
in 1329.[3] The clause *si ita est* allowed the sheriff and electors some
discretion,[4] but it was included only as a safety-valve in case false
information had been given to Chancery and there are signs that
Chancery normally expected such writs to be obeyed. Thus one
writ issued on 22 May 1318 for the replacement of a Sussex coroner,
alleging that he was ill and infirm and presumably containing the
discretionary clause, but on 15 June it was repeated without it and
with the statement that the king had removed him.[5] In 1346 writs
issued for the replacement of Robert Savage, a Derbyshire coroner:
on 10 March because he was insufficiently qualified, on 17 May because he had no lands in the county and on 25 July for both reasons.
On 26 October a fourth writ repeated the order under pain of ex-
emplary punishment of the sheriff for his disobedience and contempt in merely removing Savage by virtue of the previous writ and
then securing his re-election by collusion with him and his friends.[6]
Savage's roll confirms this story. The first two writs were apparently
disregarded. On the third he was removed in August, but no successor was elected and he was re-elected next month, before he was
finally removed and replaced on the October writ in January 1347.[7]
Writs must have been ignored elsewhere on other occasions, but
these instances prove that coroners were expected to be removed
when a writ issued, and probably they normally were. When several
writs issued for the replacement of one coroner, they usually issued
at intervals and not in rapid succession as they would have done if
they had not been executed.[8]

Some coroners were replaced several times for the same reason,
usually insufficient qualification.[9] It is very difficult to interpret this

---

[1] *Cal. Close Rolls, 1330–1333*, p. 73; *1392–1396*, p. 333.
[2] E.g. *Registrum Omnium Brevium: Originalium*, ff. 177–177v.
[3] See above, p. 158.   [4] *The English Government at Work*, III, 151.
[5] *Sx. Arch. Colls.* XCVIII, 58.
[6] *Cal. Close Rolls, 1346–1349*, pp. 18, 31, 100, 119. He is erroneously called a
Devon coroner in the second writ.
[7] J.I.2/25, mm. 2, 3, 3d.
[8] See, for example, the many writs replacing the two Thomas de Pelhams,
Sussex coroners (*Sx. Arch. Colls.* XCVIII, 58, 60).   [9] E.g. *ibid.*

in most cases. Were they continually elected against their will, with the result that their lives were a constant struggle to free themselves from office, or did they like the office and make efforts to get themselves re-elected each time their opponents removed them? Even the occasional allegations that they had disqualified themselves by alienating their lands in the county after their election[1] may have been false, and the attractive theory that such coroners made over their property to trustees on their election in order to avoid its seizure for their defaults has not been proved.[2] Moreover, it cannot account for the more frequent case of writs issuing for the replacement of the same coroner for different reasons.

A writ issued for the replacement of one Sussex coroner merely because he lived within the liberty of the Cinque Ports, although fifteen months before another had called him 'aged and infirm'. Another was replaced because he was insufficiently qualified, only to be replaced again in the following year on his appointment as under-sheriff. Yet another was replaced for living in the remotest part of Sussex nearly seven years after his replacement on the score of sickness and age. The most extraordinary writs, however, were those replacing Thomas atte Bergh. The first four called him insufficiently qualified, a fifth said that he was dead, and then two more issued on the grounds of his insufficient qualification.[3] These examples, which could be paralleled by many others from other counties,[4] prove only one thing, which can sometimes be confirmed from other sources:[5] that many of the reasons given in the writs for the replacement of coroners were untrue. There is generally no indication whether it was the coroner, or someone acting for him, or another who provided the information, and therefore it is usually impossible to tell whether the coroner was escaping from an unwanted office or being forced from one he liked.

Occasionally, Chancery issued writs of *supersedeas*, ordering the sheriff not to execute a recent writ *de coronatore eligendo* or to restore the former coroner to office if he had already been replaced, further

---

[1] E.g. *Sx. Arch. Colls.* xcviii, 58.

[2] L. F. Salzman, 'The Persistent Coroner', *Sx. Notes & Queries*, xiii, 55.

[3] *Sx. Arch. Colls.* xcviii, 50.

[4] E.g. *The English Government at Work*, iii, 150–1; *Victoria County History: Wiltshire*, v, 25.

[5] E.g. *Kent Keepers of the Peace, 1316–1317*, ed. B. H. Putnam (Kent Arch. Soc., Rec. Branch, xiii), p. xxxi; *Some Sessions of the Peace in Lincolnshire, 1360–1375*, ed. R. Sillem (Linc. Rec. Soc. xxx), p. lxxxvi.

information having been received in Chancery, before the Council or in Parliament proving that the original information was false. In most of these cases the original information was that the coroner was not sufficiently qualified, while it was later established that he was,[1] but John Grym was first replaced because he stayed in Derbyshire and elsewhere, as well as in Staffordshire where he was coroner, and then restored to office when it was learned that he was staying in Staffordshire and that he was sufficient.[2] A writ issued for the replacement of William Leverik, a Lincolnshire coroner, for insufficient qualification in 1381 and a *supersedeas* followed three days later when 'credible witnesses' informed the king that he was sufficiently qualified; the first writ was repeated five years later, followed by another *supersedeas* within three months.[3] Another Lincolnshire coroner, John de Tothill, was replaced by a writ of February 1339 because he was insufficiently qualified, but the writ was reversed in October after it had been witnessed in Parliament that he was a fit person and had behaved well as coroner, only for another to issue in the following May alleging that he had insufficient lands and tenements in fee in the county.[4] In May 1382 John Holthorp, a Yorkshire coroner, was replaced because he was insufficiently qualified, but he was restored in February 1384 after it had been attested in Chancery that he was sufficiently qualified. In June, however, another writ issued for his replacement because he was a North Riding coroner but did not live in that riding. He was replaced on four subsequent occasions: in January 1385 because he was engaged upon other business in the county, in March for having no lands there, in May for insufficient qualification and in May 1388 again for having no lands in the county.[5] An earlier Yorkshire coroner, Nicholas de Metham, had a similar career, being replaced because he was insufficiently qualified in May 1329, restored in July and replaced three more times in the next three years, twice for the same reason and once because of old age and infirmity.[6]

These cases give rise to yet greater doubts. Did the coroner or his enemies provide the original information? And, whoever provided

[1] E.g. *Cal. Close Rolls, 1369–1374*, p. 526; *1374–1377*, p. 511; *1381–1385*, p. 359.
[2] *Cal. Close Rolls, 1346–1349*, p. 481.
[3] *Cal. Close Rolls, 1381–1385*, pp. 20, 96; *1385–1389*, pp. 177, 201.
[4] *Cal. Close Rolls, 1339–1341*, pp. 14, 212, 395.
[5] *Cal. Close Rolls, 1381–1385*, pp. 67, 359, 464, 520, 547; *1385–1389*, p. 406.
[6] *Cal. Close Rolls, 1327–1330*, pp. 459, 477–8; *1330–1333*, pp. 59, 444, 468.

it, was it this information or that upon which the *supersedeas* was based that was false? Or did coroners sometimes become qualified shortly after their removal from office? Even the case of Hamo de Barsham, a Norfolk coroner, is hard to explain. A writ ordered his replacement in October 1346 because he had no lands in fee in the county. A month later it was ordered that he be restored, if the county would agree, since the men of the county had shown that the sheriff had removed him by virtue of the first writ, although he had always performed his duties faithfully and held sufficient land in the county, and had substituted for him Thomas Colyn, who was also coroner of the bishop of Ely's Norfolk liberty of Marshland; but if the county would not agree to Hamo's restoration, another coroner was to be elected for the body of the county in place of Colyn. Hamo was apparently restored, because in April 1348 his replacement was again ordered for the same reason. Again it was subsequently testified in Chancery that he had sufficient lands and that the sheriff had caused an unqualified man to be elected in his place; therefore in July the sheriff was ordered to allow Hamo to continue to act as coroner. In 1356 and again in May 1360 writs issued for his replacement on the grounds of insufficient qualification. In June 1360 the election of another Norfolk coroner was ordered as the sheriff had replaced Hamo by another unqualified man without the assent of the county. It seems that Hamo was yet again elected, for in October he was finally removed by the king as insufficiently qualified.[1] There was clearly intense local rivalry in Norfolk. The sheriffs were opposed to Hamo as coroner, but whether or not this suited Hamo it is impossible to tell.

Some reasons for the replacement of coroners had short periods of extreme popularity. The Cornish coroners became suddenly aware in the 1390's that they could gain their freedom by pleading that they were not knights.[2] Similarly, replacements for oppression, although not confined to one county, had only a short period of comparative popularity.[3] In 1375 Henry Percy testified in Chancery that three Northumberland coroners were insufficiently qualified,[4] and there are other writs for the simultaneous replacement of four, and in one case five, coroners of other counties for the same reason.[5]

---

[1] *Cal. Close Rolls, 1346–1349*, pp. 115, 129–30, 445, 476; *1354–1360*, p. 290; *1360–1364*, pp. 29, 39, 70.   [2] See above, pp. 173–4.

[3] *Ibid.* p. 179.   [4] *Cal. Close Rolls, 1374–1377*, pp. 139–40.

[5] E.g. *Cal. Close Rolls, 1346–1349*, p. 119; *1354–1360*, p. 339; *1381–1385*, p. 541; *1349–1354*, p. 456.

Within less than a month of 1385 writs issued for the replacement of four Yorkshire coroners because they were engaged on other business, and on 8 November 1416 two York city coroners were replaced because they were sick and aged.[1] These are more than coincidences. They represent either concerted attempts by the coroners to rid themselves of office or by others to get rid of them. The replacement of four or five coroners of the same county on the same day for varying reasons shows equal determination but more originality.[2]

It is sometimes possible to tell whether a coroner wished to escape from office or to retain it, and occasionally where the truth of the matter lay. Those coroners who petitioned for removal for lack of knighthood clearly wished to escape, as did those who pleaded age and infirmity by proxy or in writing and those who appeared personally in Chancery or before the Council to put their case, which was presumably a good one, especially if they were pleading age and infirmity.[3] In 1290 John Gentil maintained that, although he had been sub-escheator for over three years and was also a verderer, his enemies, 'to aggrieve him further', had recently procured his election as a Lancashire coroner. His statements could easily be checked and he was probably telling the truth, but, because he might have quoted the other offices as a bluff, hoping that no check would be made and that he would be removed forthwith, Chancery took no chances, ordering his replacement only if his allegations were true.[4] Another coroner who desperately wished to escape from office, but whose services seem to have been in urgent demand, was Michael Salesbury. In February 1415 the mayor and bailiffs of Oxford were ordered to replace him as town coroner because he was non-resident, and in May a similar writ issued to the sheriff of the county because Salesbury dwelt continually in Gloucestershire. In 1431 a writ for his replacement as a Gloucestershire coroner issued on the grounds that he lived at Oxford.[5] He seems to have escaped from the burdens of office by flight, real or alleged.

Other men had other feelings. The law-books assumed that

---

[1] *Cal. Close Rolls, 1381–1385*, p. 520; *1413–1419*, p. 313.

[2] E.g. *Cal. Close Rolls, 1364–1368*, pp. 100–1; *1441–1447*, p. 17.

[3] E.g. above, pp. 173–4, 181.

[4] *Cal. Close Rolls, 1288–1296*, p. 83. Cf. the letter to the Chancellor which stated, rightly or wrongly, that John de Hothale had been elected by his enemies (S.C. 1/32, no. 34).

[5] *Cal. Close Rolls, 1413–1419*, pp. 174, 210; *1429–1435*, p. 86.

coroners were frequently removed on the false suggestions of others
—*Britton* particularly mentioned sheriffs[1]—in which case they
could sue for an inquiry and, if it was successful, a *supersedeas*.[2]
There are several known instances of replaced coroners petitioning
to be restored,[3] and in 1308 an inquiry was ordered into Thomas de
Meynil's petition that, although he had served as a Leicestershire
coroner for over twenty years under Edward I and had been duly
re-elected by writ at the beginning of the new reign, the sheriff, who
was a bachelor of the earl of Warwick, wished to replace him by another without the assent of the county; he urged that the sheriff be
ordered not to remove him from office.[4] Robert Savage of Derbyshire also liked the office and retained it for longer than he should
have done by collusion with the sheriff, while, despite a writ to replace him for insufficient qualification and the election of Thomas de
Byntre as his successor, Hugh Trussebut, a Norfolk knight, would
not vacate the office of county coroner and refused to let Byntre
exercise it until he was personally ordered to do so by a writ.[5]
Finally, when coroners were removed as a result of petitions alleging
extortion and oppression,[6] they presumably wished to remain in
office.

The conclusion to be drawn from the writs *de coronatore eligendo*
is therefore that some coroners liked and others disliked the office.
This is supported by other evidence. From 1202 onwards many men
were willing to pay for exemption from the office. Charters of exemption were granted throughout the Middle Ages, but particularly
profusely in the 1250's when Henry III wanted support.[7] Occasionally, serving coroners bought their removal from office,[8] and others,
after their election, had to be distrained by the sheriff before they
would undertake their duties.[9] Thomas Torel noted in his roll that
he was forced into the office in Cambridgeshire under pain of for-

---

[1] i.22.7.   [2] E.g. Staundford, *op. cit.* ff. 48v–49.
[3] E.g. Camden 3rd ser. LI, 57.   [4] *Cal. Chancery Warrants*, I, 271.
[5] Above, p. 182; *Cal. Close Rolls, 1339–1341*, pp. 350, 407.
[6] E.g. *Cal. Close Rolls, 1374–1377*, p. 6.
[7] E.g. *Rôles Gascons*, I (Paris, 1885), ed. F. Michel, *passim*. The later charters
included exemptions from an increasing number of local offices (*Cal. Pat. Rolls*,
passim). For the first grant see *Pipe Roll 4 John*, p. 157. The recipients were often
elected in spite of their charters, but were always removed on their petition
(see above, pp. 180–1).
[8] E.g. *Pleas of the Crown for Gloucester, 1221*, no. 465.
[9] That this was not abnormal is shown by *Close Rolls, 1253–1254*, p. 39;
1259–1261, p. 349.

feiture, in 1258 the newly elected Herefordshire coroner had to be specifically ordered by writ to perform his duties, and the sheriff's return to a writ of 1331 was that the newly elected Cumberland coroner 'did not care to take the oath of office'.[1] There was thus always a large number of eligible men who would go to some expense and trouble to avoid this onerous and unpaid office, in which defaults of one kind or another, leading to amercement, distraint or even imprisonment, were unavoidable and which sometimes involved physical dangers.[2]

On the other side of the picture, the office carried with it certain privileges from its earliest years. Coroners were exempt from performing suit to hundred and county courts outside the county in which they were serving[3] and there was a general rule that no serving coroner should be compelled to serve on juries, assizes and recognitions,[4] although this privilege had often to be specially claimed.[5] A few coronerships had perquisites attached to them, but more important were the chances of extortion, which, although strictly illegal, was universally practised with comparative or complete impunity.[6] This must have rendered the office extremely attractive to some men. There was undoubtedly a real cause for the complaint in 1354 that some men procured the office of coroner by making large gifts and then used it for their own profit by constant extortion.[7] Thus against those who bought exemptions or escaped from office as soon as they were elected must be placed those who bought the office, those like William Hurst of Sussex, who served for thirty or more years without a break and without, as far as is known, making any effort to get himself removed, and those who seem to have regarded the office as a family perquisite.[8]

The evidence seems to suggest that more men disliked than welcomed the prospect of being elected coroner in the thirteenth century, when most coroners were knights and many knights probably regarded the office as socially inferior to that of sheriff and less digni-

---

[1] J.I.2/21, m. 9; *Close Rolls, 1256–1259*, p. 203; *The English Government at Work*, III, 152.

[2] See above, pp. 118–32.   [3] E.g. *Rotuli Litterarum Clausarum*, I, 423.

[4] *Ibid.* II, 191.

[5] E.g. ibid.; *Close Rolls, 1247–1251*, pp. 289, 334, 342, 440; *1251–1253*, pp. 12, 73, 91. Sometimes the coroners did not bother to claim it (e.g. Kent Arch. Soc., Rec. Branch, XIII, xxxi).

[6] See above, pp. 118–26.   [7] *Rotuli Parliamentorum*, II, 260.

[8] *Sx. Arch. Colls.* XCVIII, 60; *The English Government at Work*, III, 156, n. 78; *Victoria County History: Wiltshire*, V, 15.

fied than military or other service with the king. Moreover, extortion had not yet reached its full maturity and was still regularly punished by the eyre justices. In the fourteenth and fifteenth centuries the office was still unpopular with many, but, with the waiving of the knighthood qualification, it was open to more, on some of whom it undoubtedly conferred a status to which they aspired and might otherwise not have attained. Also, by this time extortion had become firmly established, was consistently practised and only rarely punished. The office therefore appealed increasingly to families which were struggling to rise and to the unscrupulous.

CHAPTER X

THE DECLINING YEARS

THE office of coroner was at its zenith in the second half of the thirteenth century. It had finally emerged from the lengthy transitional period, during which inquests, abjurations and confessions were divided, apparently arbitrarily, among coroners and hundred serjeants or dealt with jointly by both,[1] with the sheriff, the hundred serjeant's master, occasionally intervening and acting alone.[2] The memory of this period was kept alive by Bracton, who stated that sheriffs, coroners or serjeants might hear confessions and that justices might receive abjurations.[3] In fact, sheriffs and justices are not known ever to have performed a coroner's duty alone and unordered after about 1225, while serjeants were amerced for doing so,[4] as were all others, officials or private individuals.[5] And just as it was thereafter an offence for anyone to assume any of the coroner's *ex officio* duties without a special warrant, so, with the exception of the king's butler, who was coroner of London and normally had a deputy to perform all the duties of coroner, the coroner of the

[1] *Trans. R. Hist. Soc.* 5th ser. VIII, 93–5.

[2] E.g. Selden Soc. vol. 59, no. 1241. This was an abjuration made before the Gloucestershire sheriff *in comitatu Glouc'*. This cannot mean 'in the Gloucestershire county court', which the county coroners would naturally have attended, because an abjuration from a law court was illegal; there is no doubt that it occurred in a sanctuary 'in the county of Gloucester'. In another case two serjeants of the abbot of Cirencester and five townships were amerced for an abjuration made *sine coronatoribus et sine vicecomite* (*Pleas of the Crown for Gloucester, 1221*, no. 150). Langbein was therefore incorrect to maintain that after 1194 only the coroner might officiate at abjurations, any other official being amerced for doing so (*Columbia Law Rev.* XXXIII, 1355).

[3] II, 383, 425.

[4] E.g. *Trans. R. Hist. Soc.* 5th ser. VIII, 93, n. 2, 94.

[5] E.g. J.I.1/455, m. 2d (inquest held by a parson, who appointed himself coroner for this case; I am indebted to Mr C. A. F. Meekings for this reference); 909A, m. 27d (abjuration before a bailiff's catchpole); Somerset Rec. Soc. XI, 827 (abjuration before a man acting as deputy coroner without warrant); *Bristol & Glos. Arch. Soc.* XXII, 163 (abjuration before the constable, mayor and bailiffs of Bristol in the borough court; the constable and mayor died before the eyre, but judgment was passed against the bailiffs and whole borough because the bailiffs had assumed the office of coroner); J.I.1/921 m. 15d (steward of a liberty receiving an approver's appeal). The illegal execution of coroners' functions by franchisal officials was regarded as serious even when it was of long standing (e.g. *Placita de Quo Warranto*, p. 309).

Tower of London and the Durham coroners,[1] coroners could not appoint deputies and were amerced for sending anyone, even their clerks, to act for them.[2] *Britton* was not exaggerating when it categorically stated that any abjuration taken without warrant by another than the coroner was null and void and could be disavowed,[3] nor the author of *The Mirror of Justices* when he said that nobody could act in place of the coroner for appeals of approvers.[4] Finally, outlawries could not be promulgated in the coroners' absence.[5]

Thus by 1250 the identity of the office of coroner was firmly established. Usually filled by men of some eminence locally,[6] for the next half-century it was second in importance to that of sheriff alone in the hierarchy of county offices. It was, however, definitely second and not equal to the shrievalty. Gross maintained that during the thirteenth century the coroners gained power at the sheriff's expense, quoting in support the fact that they could enter liberties from which he was excluded.[7] This is true, and in the thirteenth century the county coroners, and not the sheriff, even held tourns within the abbot of Furness's liberty,[8] but county coroners could no more enter liberties which had their own coroners than the sheriff could enter those which had the return of writs. Moreover, only very occasionally did franchisal coroners default to such an extent that the lord's right to have them was withdrawn and county coroners acted in their stead,[9] while it was a common occurrence for sheriffs to be empowered to act in liberties by the writ *non omittas propter libertatem*.[10]

Coroners were originally established to act as a check on the sheriff,[11] but the check soon began to work both ways. Whereas

[1] Above, pp. 36, 150; Lapsley, *The County Palatine of Durham*, p. 87.

[2] Thus Robert de Pappeworth, a Surrey coroner, was amerced in 1263 for sending another man under his letters patent to view a body, as was this man and the four townships (J.I.1/874A, m. 26d: I am indebted to Mr C. A. F. Meekings for this reference), but it was normally their clerks whom coroners sent (e.g. J.I.1/909A, m. 20; 921, m. 5d). In Oxford, when the town coroners were summoned before Parliament at Westminster in 1305, an inquest was held by another man on a body which they had viewed before leaving on the previous day, while six days later two men, who had been specially chosen before the mayor and bailiffs, held another inquest in place of the absent coroners (*Records of Mediaeval Oxford*, pp. 12–13).

[3] i.17.7.   [4] v.1.18.   [5] Above, p. 131.   [6] *Ibid.* pp. 173–6.

[7] *Select Coroners' Rolls*, pp. xxvi–xxvii, xxx.

[8] *Placita de Quo Warranto*, p. 371.   [9] See above, p. 139.

[10] *The English Government at Work*, III, 156.

[11] *Trans. R. Hist. Soc.* 5th ser. VIII, 103–4.

coroners occasionally had to attach or distrain sheriffs to appear in one of the central courts, the sheriff received orders to summon the coroners to every eyre, gaol delivery and quarter sessions and to distrain them if they defaulted.[1] Again, only for two years and in very few counties did coroners supervise the election of sheriffs, whereas writs *de coronatore eligendo* always issued to the sheriff, who supervised the elections, received the oaths and could distrain any coroner who had been elected in order to force him to serve; he was also frequently empowered to decide whether or not a coroner should be replaced.[2] Sheriffs therefore had considerable influence in the election of coroners, which they, not unnaturally, sometimes abused. Some kept coroners in office or had them re-elected shortly after their replacement out of favour for them,[3] while a Derbyshire sheriff removed one coroner on the receipt of a writ but replaced him 'secretly and unlawfully' by Robert Shawe, whose replacement was therefore ordered in June 1443 because he was illiterate, unqualified and not duly elected. If Shawe was ever replaced, the sheriff soon allowed him to be re-elected or perhaps re-appointed him, for in February 1444 another writ issued for his replacement because he was insufficiently qualified.[4] In 1375 writs issued for the replacement of three Northumberland coroners who had been elected by the sheriff alone and not by the whole county.[5] Another Northumberland sheriff was accused in 1304 of securing or allowing the election of William de Tynemuth as coroner, although he had no lands, sparing the rich men who had lands; strangely in the circumstances, the writ ordered the sheriff to remove Tynemuth only if he had no lands.[6] Finally, in the 1440's it was said of Thomas Parr, the lawless under-sheriff of Westmorland, that 'the coroners of the same Shire bene his meynyall men', and in 1308 the Leicestershire sheriff was accused of wishing to replace a faithful coroner by another on his own authority.[7]

Not only must sheriffs have often played a decisive part in the election of coroners; they could also act jointly with them in the performance of their duties. Stewards of liberties sometimes sat with county or borough coroners within their liberties, coroners and

---

[1] See above, pp. 89–91, 97, 100, 112, 131.   [2] *Ibid.* pp. 86–7, 152, 182, 187.
[3] *Ibid.* pp. 182, 185.   [4] *Cal. Close Rolls, 1441–1447*, pp. 97, 172.
[5] *Cal. Close Rolls, 1374–1377*, p. 127.
[6] *Cal. Close Rolls, 1302–1307*, p. 226.
[7] R. L. Storey, 'Disorders in Lancastrian Westmorland', *Cumberland & Westmorland Antiq. & Arch. Soc.* N.S. LIII, 77; above, p. 187.

verderers occasionally held inquests within the forest jointly and
the keeper of Scarborough castle and the town coroners together
held inquests in the castle,[1] but these other officials only sat with the
coroners of grace. The sheriff, however, seems to have had the right
to act with the county coroners at any time. He naturally heard all
appeals, exactions and outlawries with them in the county court, and
he attended many approvers' appeals, although not all as, according
to *Britton*, he should have done.[2] There is only one example of a
sheriff and coroner jointly receiving an abjuration and that is an
early one,[3] but sheriffs were more often concerned with inquests.
The *Modus Tenendi Curias* stated that the sheriff and coroners
should jointly hold inquests in cases of homicide,[4] *Fleta* maintained
that both the sheriff and the nearest coroner should be informed of
unnatural deaths and attend the inquests,[5] and the Statute of Wales
assumed that the sheriff might attend them.[6] As late as the 1240's
both sheriff and coroners were sometimes amerced for not holding
inquests or for not performing duties connected with them,[7] and
in 1252 the sheriff and coroners of Worcestershire were summoned
to King's Bench, the coroners to show why they had refused to view
a body and the sheriff to show why he had not sent them to do so.[8]
In 1248 a former sheriff of Hertfordshire was punished for not holding an inquest into a death by misadventure, which had occurred
during a period of almost a year when there had been no county
coroner.[9] After the 1250's no sheriff was punished for neglecting the
coroners' duties, but there were some fourteenth-century inquests
held jointly by sheriff and coroner(s).[10] The strict legal position of
this time was probably that expounded by the *Officium Justiciario-
rum*: either the sheriff or his bailiff should attend every coroner's
inquest.[11] This probably held good for inquests into treasure trove
and wreck of the sea in those counties in which coroners held them,

[1] Above, pp. 145–7; J.I.2/249, m. 2.   [2] See above, p. 126.
[3] Selden Soc. vol. 53, no. 1255.
[4] *The Court Baron*, ed. F. W. Maitland and W. P. Baildon (Selden Soc. vol. 4),
p. 90.
[5] i.25 (Selden Soc. vol. 72, p. 64).   [6] See above, p. 22, n. 8.
[7] E.g. J.I.1/909A, mm. 27d, 28; Somerset Rec. Soc. XI, 832; Beds. Hist. Rec.
Soc. XXI, 657.
[8] *Close Rolls, 1251–1253*, pp. 433, 496.
[9] J.I.1/318, m. 24d. I am indebted to Mr C. A. F. Meekings for this reference.
[10] E.g. J.I.2/111, m. 17d; 120, m. 17(2)d.
[11] Cited by Langbein, *Columbia Law Rev.* XXXIII, 1355, n. 96.

since they are known sometimes to have acted with the sheriff.[1] Whereas the bailiff always attended inquests as a subordinate, the sheriff naturally sat as the coroner's equal. This was the remnant of the concurrent jurisdiction in coroners' cases which both sheriff and bailiff possessed in the early thirteenth century.

Sheriffs also intervened in coroners' affairs on special orders, although the majority of such orders were confined to the reign of Henry III. They might be ordered to hold an inquest without the coroners,[2] to go with them to receive an abjuration[3] or to send them to do so,[4] and on one occasion the sheriff of Berkshire was ordered to see that the coroners enrolled an abjuration made without warrant before the abbot of Faringdon's bailiff.[5] They were also frequently ordered to hold inquisitions with the coroners into homicides committed in self-defence and other similar occurrences before a pardon was issued, although a coroner had previously held an inquest on view of the body.[6] Again, at their tourns sheriffs received indictments of homicide as well as of felonies which were outside the coroner's sphere.[7]

From the early thirteenth century sheriffs kept rolls of crown pleas, which were duplicates of those of the contemporary coroners and which were often consulted by the eyre justices when the coroners' rolls were challenged,[8] while the first Statute of Westminster decreed, among other measures to check coroners' misdeeds, that 'sheriffs should have counter-rolls with the coroners' of all crown pleas.[9] Britton also regarded the sheriff as the 'counter-roller' or 'controller' of the coroners.[10] It is doubtful whether the sheriff kept his 'counter-roll' for long after 1300 and the justices had virtually ceased to refer to it earlier still.[11] The coroners' rolls had always been regarded as more authoritative both in theory and in practice, because they alone were 'of record';[12] and in practice, since many sheriffs' rolls were not arranged by county courts[13] and sheriffs rarely attended inquests and abjurations, they may often have been

---

[1] Bull. Inst. Hist. Research, XXXII, 131–3.
[2] E.g. Close Rolls, 1253–1254, p. 48; 1259–1261, p. 305.
[3] E.g. Rotuli Litterarum Clausarum, I, 432; Close Rolls, 1234–1237, p. 461; 1247–1251, p. 140.
[4] E.g. Close Rolls, 1231–1234, p. 99.
[5] Rotuli Litterarum Clausarum, I, 641–2.
[6] See above, pp. 77–81.   [7] E.g. J.I.3/111, m. 4.   [8] See above, pp. 104–6.
[9] 3 Edw. I, c. 10.   [10] i.2.16.   [11] See above, p. 106.
[12] Bracton, II, 395–6; above, p. 106.
[13] E.g. J.I.2/110; 111, mm. 18–26.

compiled from the coroners' rolls or files. Nevertheless, during the thirteenth century the sheriff's crown plea roll was a perennial manifestation of the sheriff's position of control.

According to later teaching, writs of *certiorari* for appeals had always to be addressed to the sheriff and coroners because appeals were made before both,[1] and practice accorded with this. When an appeal was discontinued in King's Bench or details were wanted for some other reason, the *certiorari* always ordered the sheriff and coroners to search their rolls and memoranda for any appeals or indictments of the appellee for the felony.[2] If the appeal was removed to King's Bench before the county court stage was completed, the writ was addressed to the sheriff alone.[3] By contrast, there was no consistency about the writs of *certiorari* when the record of outlawries was required. Some were addressed to the sheriff and coroners,[4] some to the coroners alone,[5] some to one particular coroner[6] and some, when other details of the original case were also required, to the J.P.'s or other justices who had initiated the exigent.[7] When inquests and abjurations were wanted, the *certiorari* normally issued to the sheriff and coroners until the middle of the fourteenth century.[8] Later it issued either to all the county coroners[9] or, when he was known, to the one who had officiated;[10] in either case the officiating coroner alone usually made the return. It is strange that the coroners alone were sometimes required to supply records of outlawries, with which the sheriff was always concerned, whereas the sheriff and coroners were for long jointly responsible for providing inquests and abjurations, which one coroner had normally held. Most surviving writs of *certiorari* for confessions and appeals of approvers issued to one coroner, but they are mainly from the later Middle Ages.[11]

These writs emphasise that there was no part of the coroner's duties from which the sheriff could be excluded. The sheriff was a

---

[1] Staundford, *Les Plees del Corone*, f. 64v.
[2] E.g. *Registrum Omnium Brevium: Judicialium*, f. 76v.
[3] E.g. *Select Coroners' Rolls*, pp. 85–6.
[4] E.g. C.47/81/5, no. 147; 6, nos. 198–9; 9, nos. 267, 285.
[5] E.g. K.B.29/43, m. 21. [6] E.g. C.47/132/5, no. 3.
[7] E.g. K.B.9/164, m. 106.
[8] E.g. *Select Coroners' Rolls*, p. 70; J.I.2/111, m. 20.
[9] E.g. J.I.2/86, m. 2 schedule.
[10] E.g. K.B.9/185, m. 41; 199, m. 22; 352, m. 16.
[11] E.g. *Registrum Omnium Brevium: Judicialium*, f. 77v; K.B.9/224, m. 188; 227, m. 72.

O*

permanent check upon the coroner, who, by contrast, could only act with or in place of the sheriff in financial and general administrative matters when specifically authorised.[1] The fact that a sheriff's county court roll of non-crown pleas was found among the muniments of the family of a contemporary coroner could be explained in one of a number of ways, such as descent by marriage or with lands. There is no evidence that coroners kept a 'counter-roll' of these pleas,[2] although their own rolls of crown pleas sometimes led to the sheriff's amercement.[3] It clearly is not true that even in the thirteenth century the coroner was the sheriff's equal. Nearly the whole range of the sheriff's activities was outside the coroner's ken, whereas even the lawfully elected coroner was continually supervised by the sheriff from the day of his election onwards.

The coroner's position *vis-à-vis* the sheriff did not decline during the Middle Ages; indeed, it may have been slightly strengthened by those fifteenth-century statutes which brought the sheriff a little more under his control.[4] It is true that the office of coroner was filled by slightly less eminent men after 1300 than before[5] and that in 1424 a writ issued for a new Leicestershire coroner in place of one who had been 'advanced' to be under-sheriff,[6] but no additional restrictions were placed on its tenure. The sheriff, on the other hand, grew rapidly weaker after 1300. He could no longer buy his shrievalty and make a large profit from it, but was appointed for one year only.[7] He must also have had his prestige seriously diminished and his activities curtailed by the escheators and J.P.'s, permanent shire officials of considerable status, and such temporary officials as collectors and assessors of taxes.

Borough coroners likewise maintained their position as against the other borough officials, which was practically one of equality. Borough offices were confined to and circulated among a small number of people, who were often pluralists[8] and who can have regarded the office of coroner as little if at all inferior to any other. In many boroughs the bailiffs or mayor nearly always sat with the

---

[1] See above, pp. 76–92.

[2] G. E. Woodbine, 'County Court Rolls and County Court Records', *Harvard Law Rev.* XLIII, 1089, n. 23. Cf. *Rolls from the Office of the Sheriff of Beds. and Bucks. 1332–1334*, ed. G. H. Fowler (Quarto Memoirs of the Beds. Hist. Rec. Soc. III), p. 47.

[3] See above, p. 110   [4] *Ibid.* pp. 86–7.   [5] *Ibid.* p. 173.

[6] *Cal. Close Rolls, 1422–1429*, p. 165.

[7] E.g. *The English Government at Work*, II, 42, 47.

[8] See above, pp. 161–2.

coroners for inquests, abjurations, appeals of approvers and confessions,[1] but to counter-balance this the coroners sat with the
bailiffs to administer and adjudicate in the borough court.[2] In
Ipswich the bailiffs heard and punished offences against the coroners and the coroners those against the bailiffs.[3] The mayor and
bailiffs usually organised the election of coroners,[4] but the coroners
often had similar duties. In 1378, for example, it was provided that
the mayors of Coventry should be sworn in before the town coroner
in the presence of the commonalty,[5] and in Northampton the
coroners and bailiffs organised the election of a mayor in the event of
one dying in office.[6]

Nevertheless, both county and borough coroners declined in
importance during the fourteenth and fifteenth centuries. There are
several reasons to account for this. Firstly, there was the very marked
decrease in the number of appeals during the thirteenth century,
followed in the later fifteenth century by a decrease in the number of
appeals of approvers.[7] Secondly, the abolition of the *murdrum* fine
decreased the amount of revenue resulting from coroners' inquests,
although this did not mean a considerable decline in the importance
of inquests as has recently been maintained.[8] Much more important
were the cessation of the general eyre, with which the coroner had
always been closely connected as a major link between the local and
central law courts and to which he largely owed his origin, and the
fact that it was not followed by the establishment of any regular
check upon the coroner. This led to the duplication of some of his
duties and their exercise by the two most rapidly rising local
officials, the escheator and the keeper, who became the justice, of the
peace.

[1] E.g. J.I.2/34, mm. 1–5; 178, mm. 13–15; *The Records of the City of Norwich*,
I, 207, 212. By contrast the coroners of Arundel and Chichester normally acted
alone (e.g. *Sx. Arch. Colls.* xcv, 47, 53, 55; xcvi, 26–7, 34). There is no evidence
that any borough official ever kept a duplicate copy of the coroners' rolls or was
expected to. In the thirteenth century when inquests or abjurations were required, the *certiorari* often issued to the coroner and either the mayor or bailiffs,
but later it issued to one or more borough coroners, as did writs of *certiorari* for
appeals of approvers (e.g. *Hist. MSS. Comm., 6th Report*, App. p. 505; C.47/81/6,
no. 188; K.B.29/12, m. 38d; K.B.9/168, m. 64). Borough coroners were naturally rarely troubled for appeals and outlawries.

[2] See above, pp. 93–4.

[3] N. Bacon, *The Annalls of Ipswche*, ed. W. H. Richardson (Ipswich, 1884),
p. 28.

[4] See above, pp. 158–61.   [5] *Cal. Charter Rolls*, v, 243.

[6] See above, p. 94   [7] *Ibid.* pp. 55, 73.

[8] Havard, *The Detection of Secret Homicide*, pp. 13, 28.

The escheator, unlike the coroner, had to render a regular account at the Exchequer, and therefore in the fourteenth century he began to hold inquisitions *ex officio* into, appraise and take possession of deodands and the lands and goods of outlaws, abjurors of the realm, suicides and fugitives for homicide,[1] as well as treasure trove and wreck of the sea.[2] In the later Middle Ages both the coroner and the escheator thus had the duty of making these appraisals *ex officio*,[3] but the escheator's appraisal was the more important in that he accounted. To emphasise their comparative importance in the shire generally, a statute of 1368 required escheators to have land in fee of an annual value of twenty pounds, far more than was ever demanded of coroners at this time.[4]

Yet more serious for the coroner was the challenge of the J.P.'s. Their rise probably prevented him from taking over preliminary inquiries into all felonies,[5] and by the late fourteenth century the vast scope of their jurisdiction made them very much more important than the coroner, for they could 'hold' nearly all crown pleas, while he only 'kept' a few. Not only that, but they took over two duties previously performed most frequently by the sheriff and coroners: receiving sureties for keeping the peace both from those who were about to receive charters of pardon and others,[6] and holding inquisitions *de gestu et fama*.[7] Also Richard III empowered them to inquire into escapes of men who were imprisoned for felony, a duty previously belonging in theory to the coroner.[8] J.P.'s could not hear appeals or record and legalise exactions and outlawries, but they occasionally heard appeals of approvers with the coroners,[9] often, although illegally, assigned coroners to approvers,[10] and issued writs of exigent whose execution involved the coroners,[11] while the *certiorari* for the record of outlawries which they had initiated sometimes even issued to them.[12] More important, they received

---

[1] E.g. E.153/1760, m. 11; 1783, mm. 9–13.
[2] *Bull. Inst. Hist. Research*, XXXII, 136.
[3] For an example of both acting in the same case, the escheator by virtue of a writ, see *Cal. Inqs. Misc.* IV, 307. Cf. J.I.2/240, m. 3, for the coroner enrolling the seizure of the goods by the escheator.
[4] 42 Edw. III, c. 5; above, pp. 172, 175.
[5] *Bull. Inst. Hist. Research*, XXXII, 125.
[6] E.g. above, pp. 75–80; C.47/81/9, no. 287; 3 Hen. VII, c.2.
[7] E.g. *Sx. Notes & Queries*, XIV, 119. Cf. above, p. 78.
[8] 1 Ric. III, c. 3; *Bull. Inst. Hist. Research*, XXXII, 118–20.
[9] E.g. J.I.1/690, mm. 10d, 11d.
[10] See above, p. 71.   [11] *Ibid.* p. 65, n. 2.   [12] *Ibid.* p. 195.

indictments of homicide even when they were only keepers of the peace.[1] It is true that indictments made upon view of the body remained the coroner's monopoly and that these, and sometimes even appeals, were made before the indictments of the same matters could be made before the J.P.'s;[2] but whereas previously King's Bench and Chancery had sent writs of *certiorari* only for the coroner's indictment of a homicide, although the sheriff had sometimes also heard it at his tourn, from the late fourteenth century the indictments taken by both coroner and J.P.'s were often required.[3] Similarly, when coroners failed to produce their indictments at gaol deliveries, those made before the J.P.'s might be sent for,[4] and in 1487 both coroners at their inquests and J.P.'s were ordered to inquire concerning day-time escapes of homicides.[5] Coroners were required to attend the sessions of the justices, and earlier those of the keepers, of the peace,[6] and serving coroners occasionally even sat on their juries;[7] it is hard to imagine J.P.'s on coroners' juries. Finally, whether legally or not, from the mid-fourteenth century J.P.'s heard indictments of coroners' misdeeds and even punished those coroners who were convicted before them; this position was legalised in 1380 and later enforced by statute.[8]

The coroner thus had no important duty taken from him in the later Middle Ages, but some of them came to exercise him far less frequently, and he, like the sheriff, became relatively less important with the rise of the escheator and the J.P. Nevertheless, the office still survives, vigorous if much criticised, deprived of most of its original functions but having successfully taken root in the New World.

---

[1] *Proceedings before the Justices of the Peace in the Fourteenth and Fifteenth Centuries*, pp. xxi–xxiii.

[2] E.g. *Some Sessions of the Peace in Cambridgeshire in the Fourteenth Century, 1340, 1380–83*, ed. M. M. Taylor (Camb. Antiq. Soc. LV), p. lxiv.

[3] E.g. *Sx. Arch. Colls.* XCV, 50–4, 56–7.   [4] E.g. J.I.3/216A/4, m. 154d.

[5] 3 Hen. VII, c. 2.   [6] See above, p. 97.

[7] E.g. Kent Arch. Soc., Rec. Branch, XIII, xxxi.

[8] See above, p. 120; 23 Hen. VI, c. 9; 1 Hen. VIII, c. 7.

SELECT GLOSSARY

agistor. An officer of the royal forest concerned primarily with agistment, i.e. the pasturing of livestock in the forest. For further details see Selden Soc. vol. 13, xxvi.

amercement. A financial penalty.

ancient demesne. Land which could be proved by Domesday Book to have belonged to the crown under either Edward the Confessor or William the Conqueror; such land was held by a peculiar tenure.

assize of darrein presentment. An action concerned, in the event of disturbance, with the last presentation to a benefice.

assize of mort d'ancestor. An action concerned with dispossession of freehold held by the heir's immediate ancestor.

assize of novel disseisin. An action concerned with recent dispossession of freehold.

attach. Either to arrest or, as usually in this work, to secure by means of sureties for future attendance in court.

attachies. A writ ordering that somebody be attached.

attaint jury. A jury of twenty-four, summoned to inquire whether a previous jury had returned a false verdict.

bachelor. A young knight, not old enough or having too few vassals to display his own banner and who therefore followed the banner of another; a novice in arms.

beaupleader fine. A fine for amending a defective plea.

capias. A writ ordering an arrest and appearance in a court.

capias utlagatum. A like writ for an outlaw.

catchpole. A petty official, usually serving under the sheriff and mainly concerned with making arrests.

certiorari. A writ calling for the record of some matter.

'cessors'. Assessors.

Chamber lands. Lands forfeited to the king which were administered by officials responsible and accounting to the Chamber.

Chancery fashion. The method of constructing a roll by sewing the parchment membranes together head to foot, thus forming one long skin which was then rolled up.

clerk of the market. The official of the king's household in charge of the king's measures, which were the standard measures for the whole kingdom.

commote. A Welsh territorial division for administrative purposes, originally containing fifty villages, usually subordinate to a cantred or hundred.

de gestu et fama. A writ or inquisition concerning a person's behaviour and reputation.

de walliis et fossatis. A commission of sewers, concerned with the repair of sea-banks and walls, maintenance of rivers, ditches, etc.

distringas. A writ ordering distraint, i.e. the seizure of a person's goods and sometimes also his lands in order to compel him to pay his rent, perform his services, appear in court, etc.

escheator. An official concerned primarily with escheats, i.e. lands and goods taken into the king's hands either as forfeitures or for feudal incidents. For his *ex officio* duties see *Statutes of the Realm*, I, 238–41, and for an account of the early history of the office see *The English Government at Work*, II, 109–67.

essoins. Excuses for non-appearance in a court of law at the appointed time. Essoins were permitted for pilgrimage, the king's service, illness, etc.

essoins *de malo lecti.* Essoins by reason of sickness in bed.

estreats. Extracts of those parts of original records relating to fines, amercements, etc., made to facilitate their levying.

Exchequer fashion. The method of constructing a roll by placing the parchment membranes on top of each other and sewing them together at one end, usually the head; they were then rolled up.

feodary. A franchisal official who had duties under the lord in some franchises similar to those of the escheator.

gaol delivery. The commission under which justices heard and determined pleas involving persons in gaol.

geldable. Land subject to normal taxation and administration.

general eyre. The periodical circuit of justices commissioned to hear and determine all manner of pleas (*ad omnia placita*).

hustings. A court of law known in only a few cities and towns.

infangenetheof. The right of a lord to jurisdiction over thieves caught within his liberty.

inquisition *ad quod damnum.* An inquisition held on a writ of like name to discover whether the granting of liberties, etc., would be prejudicial to others.

inquisition *post mortem.* An inquisition held on the death of a tenant-in-chief to establish who was the next heir and to ensure that the king obtained all feudal incidents due; or on a sub-tenant for the benefit of his immediate lord.

jurat. A municipal official holding a position similar to that of an alderman; a magistrate of the Channel Islands.

mainour. Stolen goods found in a thief's possession on his arrest.

mainpast. A lord's household in its legal aspect; virtually a private tithing, the lord being responsible for all his servants.

manucaption *or* mainprise. The finding of sureties or mainpernors to be

responsible for a man's appearance in court or for his future good
behaviour; hence the term manucaption is sometimes applied to the
written record of a mainprise.

Marshalsea. The court or seat of the marshal of the king's household.

Marshalsea of King's Bench. The prison in which were kept prisoners
awaiting trial in King's Bench, so called because such prisoners
were in the custody of the marshal of King's Bench.

nisi prius. A commission under which an issue was tried locally rather
than at Westminster.

oyer and terminer. A commission whereby justices 'heard and determined' certain defined pleas.

peine forte et dure. The physical punishment inflicted in prison upon those
accused of treason or felony who refused to plead.

pone. A writ whereby a cause was removed from an inferior court to
Westminster.

prisage. A custom levied on imported wine.

quare impedit. A writ obtainable by anyone disturbed in his right of ad-
vowson by the presentment of a clerk to the benefice by another.

quo warranto. A writ and/or inquiry to discover 'by what warrant' a
liberty or franchise was held.

recordari facias. A writ ordering a record of proceedings made in the
county court to be sent to Westminster.

regardor. An official concerned primarily with offences committed in the
royal forest. For details see Selden Soc. vol. 13, lxxv–lxxxvii.

serjeanty tenure. The holding of land in return for performing some
specified service or services.

sicut alias or *alias*. A second writ issued after failure to execute the first.

sicut pluries or *pluries*. A third or subsequent writ issued after failure to
execute the first and the *sicut alias*.

statute merchant. A bond.

supersedeas. A writ ordering that proceedings be stayed.

tithing. Originally an association of ten men mutually bound for the good
behaviour of each other; in some areas tithings came to be terri-
torialised.

tithingman. The head of a tithing; a petty constable.

tourn. The court held by the sheriff twice yearly in each hundred, whose
proceedings are usually known as the 'view of frankpledge'.

trailbaston. The name given to certain fourteenth-century commissions
for the hearing and determining of specified offences involving
violence and breaches of the peace.

venire facias. A writ ordering that some person or persons, usually jurors,
be caused to appear in a court.

verderer. A forest official, whose duties are fully described in Selden
Soc. vol. 13, xix–xx.

verge. The area extending for twelve miles around the king's court, wherever it might be.

view of frankpledge. Proceedings at the sheriff's tourn; offences were presented by the tithings, and the sheriff ascertained that every male over twelve was in a tithing or mainpast.

wage peace. To find sureties or be bound over to keep the peace, usually in respect of a certain person or persons previously threatened.

waive. To 'outlaw' a woman. Women could not technically be outlawed because they did not swear to keep the law as members of a tithing.

writs *de cursu*. Writs 'of course' which could be purchased without the king's special 'grace'.

INDEX

P

DATE DUE

GAYLORD   PRINTED IN U.S.A.